Celebrating SACRAMENTS

*To all the people
who have been sacraments
in my life—
especially Susan, Katie, Pat, and Tim*

Nihil Obstat: Rev. Msgr. William T. Magee
             Censor Deputatus
             11 August 1992
Imprimatur: † Most Rev. John G. Vlazny, DD
             Bishop of Winona
             14 August 1992

The publishing team included Julia Ahlers and Barbara Allaire, development editors; Stephan Nagel and Robert Smith, FSC, consulting editors; Charles Capek, copy editor; Barbara Bartelson, production editor and typesetter; Mary Duerson Kraemer, indexer; Penny Koehler, photo researcher; McCormick Creative and Evy Abrahamson, art, photo direction, and graphic design; and Evy Abrahamson, color illustrator.

The acknowledgments continue on page 303.

Printed in the United States of America

Printing: 6

Year: 1999 98

ISBN 0-88489-279-4

Saint Mary's Press

Christian Brothers Publications

Winona, Minnesota

 Genuine recycled paper with 10% post-consumer waste. Printed with soy-based ink.

*Have you noticed
    how clean and glistening
    the cobblestones in the street are
    after the rain? Real works of art!
And flowers?
No words can describe them.
One can only exclaim "Ah!"
    in admiration.
You must learn to understand
    the "Ah!" of things.*
                    (*A Zen master's comment*)

Celebrating SACRAMENTS

Joseph Stoutzenberger

Contents

The Sacraments of Healing

The Sacraments of Vocation

> Gracious God, we begin this course
>   seeking to know you better
>   and to continually discover
>   your loving presence in our life.
> As we talk, pray, create, and explore together,
>   may we experience wonder
>   at the marvels that surround us
>   and find cause to celebrate a world
>   alive with your glory and goodness.
> Amen.

1

Sacraments: Encountering the Sacred

Mice are very busy creatures. They gather seeds and grain and collect little bits of straw or sticks for their nests. Always keeping their nose and eyes to the ground, they scurry here and there looking for whatever food and bedding they can find. Normally, this is all they do and all they ever expect to do. A story from a Native American tradition, however, tells about one mouse who was different.

One day, a busy little mouse began to hear a faint thundering noise in the distance. She inquired of the other mice if they too heard it. No one else did, so she decided to forget the matter and busied herself all the more. Yet she continued to hear the thundering noise. Try as she would, she could not ignore it.

Determined to discover the source of the thunder, the mouse set out on a perilous journey across the open prairie. Along the way, she encountered predators, as well as numerous animal friends who assisted her in her quest. When she finally arrived at a river—the source of the thundering noise—a frog suggested that if the mouse wished to see the river beyond the cattail reeds, she should leap as high into the air as she could. In so doing, she not only saw the river but also caught sight of the sacred mountains—powerful and brilliant, though still far away. At the same time, she also received a nickname—"Jumping Mouse"—from the frog.

Jumping Mouse returned to the other mice and told them of her journey, of the thunderous river, and of the sacred mountains. Some merely ignored her, some feared her, and some laughed at her, mocking her new name. But they all preferred to remain busy about their work.

Jumping Mouse decided that she must see the mysterious mountains up close, even if it meant journeying there alone. Again she was assisted by other animals of the prairie who either admired her courage or pitied her silly curiosity. When at last she arrived at a lake near the mountains, she jumped once more into the air to get a better glimpse of them. Carried by the mountain wind, she ascended higher and higher and higher—up to the mountain peaks. In the process, she was changed and received another name, the name by which she has been known ever since—Eagle.

Sacramental Awareness

Listening for Thunder, Searching for Sacred Mountains

By and large, we modern people are very busy creatures—like the mice in the opening story. Lawn mowers, automobiles, televisions, radios, and all sorts of electronic games and appliances provide the soundtracks to our many activities. With so much busyness and noise going on, it is no wonder that we sometimes cannot hear any thunder in our life, much less take the time to think about its source. And with our nose so often close to the ground, or our eyes mesmerized by television, we fail to catch sight of the majestic mountains out on the horizon.

This course on the seven sacraments of the Catholic faith suggests that the sacred is right before our eyes. But to encounter the sacred, we must, like Jumping Mouse, be willing to open ourselves up to it and let it touch our life. This course, therefore, asks you to take a journey deep into the world around you, to listen and look without haste and with an essential openness. The practice of listening for thunder and searching for sacred mountains leads to a special appreciation of the sacred in the world, to an awareness known as **sacramental awareness**. Let's take a closer look at what sacramental awareness is all about.

God Is Everywhere

The view of the world that underlies the Catholic church's teachings on the sacraments challenges the belief held by some people that "nothing is sacred." The Catholic church's view about the presence of the sacred in the world can be summed up by paraphrasing the Baltimore Catechism (a question-and-answer booklet of Catholic teachings that was popular until the 1960s):

Question: "Where is God?"
Answer: "God is everywhere."

The Catholic belief about sacraments is that God communicates through the people, places, actions, events, and experiences that shape a person's life. Sacramental awareness reveals that God is present in and communicates with us through all of creation. An outlook shaped by sacramental awareness, then, declares that "all of creation is sacred," because God speaks and can be seen through all things. Sacramental awareness sees the marvels of God where other outlooks might see only dull routine and boring repetition.

1. Sacramental awareness begins with an attitude of wonder. What images does the word *wonder* evoke for you? Write about a time when you were filled with wonder at something in nature, in the news, or in the world around you.

2. Write four different endings to the following sentence:
- I believe all of creation is sacred because . . .

Christianity—especially Catholic Christianity—possesses a great and long tradition of sacramental awareness. The Christian view of reality sees God both as present in the very midst of creation and as transcending creation. Christianity shares this tradition of seeing God in creation with other religions, many of which suggest that the way to know God is to know about life and the world. The story of Jumping Mouse, for example, suggests the reverence that many Native Americans hold for the things of the earth—animals, plants, water, mountains, the land. So the message of the Catholic church today is this: If we cultivate a sacramental awareness, we will grow in love of both creation and the gift of life, as well as in faith in God.

All of creation is sacred, because God speaks and can be seen through all things.

Sacramental Blindness

If God can be found in the midst of life and creation, as well as beyond life and creation, why are we not always aware of God's presence? No one, simple response will fully answer this question, but people's lack of sacramental awareness can be thought of in this way: Those who cannot see the sacred in their life or in the world suffer from what could be termed *sacramental blindness.*

Many people are so preoccupied with the daily routines of living that they simply cannot perceive God's presence in their life.

Possible Causes of Sacramental Blindness

Sacramental blindness, the inability to see the sacred in life or in the world, can have several causes:

People are too busy. The story of Jumping Mouse suggests one possible cause of sacramental blindness. People are so preoccupied with the daily routines of living that they simply cannot see or hear the signs and signals of God's presence in their life.

A great deal of pain and suffering exists in the world. Another reason people might not see the sacred is that a great deal of pain and suffering exists in their own life and in the world. Many people become overwhelmed by all the problems facing themselves personally and the world as a whole—broken relationships, unsatisfying jobs, war, poverty, the destruction of the environment, and so forth. When this happens, their vision of life becomes dominated by gloom and pessimism.

People do not know where to look or what to look for. Perhaps another reason some people have a hard time seeing God in their midst is that they do not really know where to look or what to look for. How often have we looked for something and not recognized it, even though it was right there in front of us? We may have been expecting whatever we were searching for to look different, or to find it in a different place. The same can happen when people look for God in their life or in the world.

Taking a Second Look: A Cure for Sacramental Blindness

The antidote to sacramental blindness may be a lot like the antidote to prejudice. Prejudice toward a person or group usually melts away once we take a closer look, once we take some time to know more about the person or group. If taking a second look becomes the manner by which we approach other persons, we are soon able to shed our blind spots and prejudices about them. Similarly, seeing the sacred in our life and in the world requires taking a second, even closer look to see if there is something we might have missed the first time around. In the process, we are able to shed whatever it is that blinds us from the sacred.

Just as it can help in overcoming prejudice, a little assistance from another perspective can help in overcoming sacramental blindness. Christian faith teaches that God created us and the entire world out of love and that this makes all of creation sacred. This perspective, if we really take it on, can literally open up a whole new world for us. Sacramental awareness, which is central to this course and to appreciating all the sacraments, begins in taking a second, closer look at our life and our world.

For Review

- What does sacramental awareness reveal about God's presence to us in creation?
- Define the term *sacramental blindness* and list three possible causes of sacramental blindness.
- Briefly describe how sacramental blindness can be cured.

3. Write a one-page, fictional story about someone who suffered from sacramental blindness and how that person experienced a cure.

This Course and You

As you have probably noticed by now, this course does not begin by immediately going into the seven sacraments of the Catholic church. That kind of start would be like walking into the middle of a movie. You may already know quite a bit about the seven sacraments, and by this time you may have celebrated several of them. Before considering the seven sacraments themselves, however, this course will explore the rich vision that sees all of creation as sacramental, as communicating God's love to us.

So this course begins by recognizing God's presence in the world and by becoming familiar with the ways God and people communicate with one another, such as through symbols, rituals, and prayer. From there, the journey moves to Jesus, the center of life for Christians, and to his continuing presence in the world as witnessed by the history of the Christian church. Only after this foundation is laid does the course move on to the seven official sacraments of the Catholic church. The finale, however, is a sacrament called YOU.

This course begins with a focus on your world and life and ends with that same focus, in a kind of circular journey. And even though you may have studied the sacraments before, your high school years are an ideal time to consider sacramental awareness as it is presented in this course. You are at a time in your life when it is natural to look deeper into your world and seek new meaning, to weave dreams for your future and discover great visions. In this sense, your own story may come to resemble the story of Jumping Mouse, who responded to the inner call that led her to the sacred mountains.

Remember that along with her vision, Jumping Mouse also had friends who aided her on her journey. Friendship is a help to everyone. The spiritual awakenings that occur during or following our high school years often result directly from sharing new hopes and visions with our friends. These spiritual awakenings

may happen during a special experience, such as a school retreat, or in everyday conversations with close friends, parents, or counselors. They may accompany intense new friendships, or they may come about with "falling in love."

During the next few months, this course will offer you much to think about in terms of your faith journey and life with God. Along the way, there will be plenty of opportunities to speak your mind about the subject matter. Let this book be a springboard to discussion. If the material sparks personal insights, use the class activities and reflection opportunities to help you explore those insights. If something does not ring true to your experience of the world, your life, or the Catholic church's practices, use those differences as grounds for conversation with friends, other students, and your teacher.

It may be that you have had a number of religion courses during your schooling, and probably you have heard a number of the terms that will be mentioned in this course. If religion courses are something new to you, however, you should know that this course will deal with many concepts basic to all religions and many other concepts common to all Christians—Protestant, Orthodox, and Catholic. In any case, the aim is to introduce you to key concepts in light of current teachings of the Catholic church and in relation to your life as a growing young person in the world today.

Blessings for your journey.

Grace: God's Loving Presence in the World

Christians have a special way of describing God's presence in the world, a way that helps God's presence to be understood in a here-and-now, personal light. This central Christian belief is called **grace**.

God loves us and cares for us unconditionally, and no matter what happens, God is with us and for us. For Christians, the word *grace* expresses this reality, this loving presence of God in the world. In addition, God's love and concern extend not only to people but to all of creation. So to say that all of creation is sacred means that all of creation is graced.

You might be wondering at this point: How does God communicate this love and concern for us? How does God make this loving presence known to us? "Because God is everywhere," as an old teaching says, "God speaks to us in many ways."

Flesh-and-Blood Communication

To understand how God communicates with us, we need to appreciate something about how we humans communicate with one another—the fact that our body language and gestures often "speak" louder than our words.

Speaking with Our Body

The notion that we communicate with our body and our gestures has long been a part of human wisdom. Researchers who study what is called "body language" inform us that a person reveals what is going on "inside" by the way he or she acts on the "outside." If a person is fidgeting with her watch, for example, she might be communicating that she is anxious to make the time pass. Direct eye contact can signal self-confidence or interest in another person. A blush may indicate several feelings—embarrassment, pleasure, or even anger.

Body language is not an earthshaking concept, but it does reinforce something we already know: Consciously or unconsciously, our body communicates our feelings. We "speak" with one another through physical expressions, and our nonverbal, or body, messages often speak louder than our verbal messages.

Studies have also suggested that when a spoken (or verbal) message conflicts with a body (or nonverbal) message, people more often respond to the nonverbal message. In

4. List five examples of body language and the messages they communicate.

Our human flesh expresses our human spirit.

other words, if you told a friend, "I like your new haircut," but then started to snicker, your friend would "hear" the insincerity more clearly than the spoken compliment. Or if you said to someone, "I really want to hear more about last night," but then continually yawned during the story, that person would likely feel that you didn't really want to hear what he or she had to say.

So our smiles, tears, laughter, sighs, touches, looks, open hands of friendship, closed hands of rejection, hugs—all of our expressions and gestures—communicate who and what we are to one another. Our human flesh thus expresses our human spirit. Amplifying a message by using flesh-and-blood terms is the normal human way of communicating intensely.

God's Body Language

Because we are creatures of flesh, creatures of the earth, God chooses to speak to us using the human language of physical reality. Thus, God employs a kind of body language, examples of which abound.

Examples from the Bible: The Bible is filled with examples of God's body language. In the Hebrew Scriptures, for instance, we read that Moses recognized God in a burning bush. Samuel saw God in a dream; Elijah, in a gentle breeze; Abraham and Jacob, in passing strangers. The prophets were constantly observing the world around them and seeing God:

> "I [God] will be to the people of Israel
>   like rain in a dry land.
>
> . . . .
>
> Like an evergreen tree I will shelter them."
>
> (Hosea 14:5–8, GNB)

In the Gospels, Jesus described God's grace using images from nature—fish, birds, trees—and happenings from people's everyday lives—a father welcoming home his wayward son, a woman rejoicing at the finding of her lost coin, a landowner treating his workers generously. From the Scriptures, then, we can conclude that all of creation serves as God's body language.

Examples from today: The God of the Bible continues to communicate and be revealed today. The evergreen tree that gave shelter to the Israelites is still with us. Rain still brings new life to parched lands; strangers still cross our paths and become friends. And although we may not be aware of it, we are always bumping into God in the daily business of life. Even when we gather for worship with others who also experience God in their own unique circumstances, we celebrate these various precious encounters.

By recognizing the many hints of God's grace in our life, we experience **sacraments** in the broadest sense of the term: *God's loving presence made visible in our life here and now.* An appreciation of this meaning of the term *sacrament* can help us understand more deeply the meaning of the official sacraments of the Catholic church, which we will be looking at later in this course. Sacraments are not *about* God; rather, they are meant to provide an experience *of* God—an earthy, bodily experience that is also a spiritual experience.

God Speaks Through Our Friendships

The following comment by a modern Catholic theologian reveals another clue about how God communicates love and concern to people: "Perhaps the most basic sacrament of God's saving presence to human life is the sacrament of human love and friendship" (Cooke, *Sacraments and Sacramentality,* pages 81–82). In other words, we especially experience God's love and concern in many earthly and bodily ways through our relationships with other people, particularly in our friendships.

5. Look through a Bible and write down five descriptions that use images of nature. Choose one of those images and briefly describe how it can speak to us about God's presence.

God's grace is revealed to us in our friendships.

6. First, imagine that your closest friend goes away for four years and cannot communicate with you. In writing, do the following:
- Name five ways your friend continues to be present with you.
- Name five things your friend might like you to know.
- Name five things you could do to be reminded of your friend.

Second, imagine that your closest friend is Jesus. Complete the above three exercises as they might apply to Jesus.

Human friendships come and go; sometimes they are rekindled, and other times they die. Nonetheless, friendships—whether short-lived or long-lasting—sustain us, nourish us, keep us human, identify us as who we are. And in the Christian vision, our personal friendships reveal God's friendship with us as well. Friends who are open, honest, and caring toward each other not only let another person into their life, but they also make room for God. As the First Letter of John says, "God is love, and those who abide in love abide in God, and God abides in them" (4:16).

God's friendship as grace is revealed to us in the profound intricacy of our natural world, in the words and stories of the Scriptures, in the inspiring lives of church heroes past and present, and in the intimacy that exists between friends. And these are just some of the ways God "converses" with us.

For Review

- What do Christians mean by the word *grace?*
- What role does body language play in human communication?
- Describe three examples of God's "body language."
- Define *sacrament* in a broad sense.

Receiving God's Offer of Friendship

As you probably know from your experience, maintaining strong, healthy friendships depends on honest communication. The same is true for establishing and maintaining a friendship with God. Real communication happens when messages are both sent and received. Read the following story to see how two young teenagers experienced true communication not only with each other but also with God.

Evening was coming quickly to Camp LaCrosse. Already the calm that followed sunset had fallen over the patch of woods where two boys sat by a still lake. Pat, who had been quiet for most of the week, was now talking freely. Tony, usually loud, boisterous, and always the joker, now spoke in softer, thoughtful tones:

"Yeah, I don't see much of my dad at all," said Tony.

Tony couldn't believe that he was talking like this. Secrets that he had kept inside all his life he was now sharing with a near stranger.

"I have a real nice family," said Pat. "We're actually very close, but no one shows it. Everyone's just busy."

Surprising himself, Pat was discovering these truths as he said them. They came from deep inside—so deep that he had not known they existed.

The two boys sat staring at the lake. They both felt captivated—under the spell of the place, the moment, the company. At camp, Tony had worked hard at being "Mr. Good Times." And he was quite successful at it. He had developed his own following, a bunch of guys ready to join him in whatever practical jokes he suggested. Pat, on the other hand, had spent his week at camp doing what came naturally for him—lying low, keeping quiet, smiling a lot, and not causing any trouble.

Yet now, these two unlikely companions found themselves together really talking to each other, involved in a conversation that neither had ever experienced before—deep talk, personal talk, talk from the heart. Their conversation was the kind of talk that friendships are made of.

Of course, thirteen-year-olds don't talk about friendships much. Both boys knew, however, that they were on different terms this night. They were revealing themselves and listening to each other as neither had ever done before or had even thought possible. So they knew this moment was special.

Tony and Pat were not great conversationalists—at least not until that night. That night, Tony put aside his mask and revealed himself as he truly was. Pat also chanced speaking about his real feelings. That unlikely evening encounter between two seemingly different persons was very special indeed. For insofar as they said yes to some honest sharing and mutual giving, they made an act of friendship with each other. And whether they realized it or not, their yes to each other was a yes to God as well. Tony and Pat made God's presence real to each other in their open and honest communication, in their listening and responding to each other. By acting in friendship with each other, they were also acting in friendship with God.

Sacramental Skills

In their special moment together, Tony and Pat were learning for the first time two very important skills necessary for real communication: listening and responding. If we are to truly communicate with God, listening and responding must be a part of our understanding of sacraments. Listening and

Listening implies the ability to "hear" with our whole self.

responding are the skills necessary for sacramental awareness; they help us to fully experience the beauty, the excitement, and the deep meaning of our encounters with God.

The next three chapters will name other skills that enhance our experience of the sacraments. But for now, let's take a closer look at how listening and responding are essential to sacramental awareness.

Listening for God

Listening skills are important for our growth throughout life. Of course, applied to sacraments, listening is not confined to our ability to hear. The art of listening implies all kinds of receptivity—the ability to receive, to take in what has been sent our way. Insofar as it involves receptivity, listening can play a critical role in overcoming what was referred to as "sacramental blindness" earlier.

Listening is affirming and nonjudgmental. Listening means letting go of ourselves and opening up to the outpouring of experiences through which God constantly speaks to us. Indeed, listening can be uncomfortable and even painful. What we "hear" when we pause and listen may not always be pleasant. That is why it is important for us to hear again and again the story of Jesus, who addresses our pain and pleasures, sorrows and joys.

The seven official sacraments of the Catholic faith involve receiving—for example, receiving forgiveness and healing, or receiving Communion. By developing the skill of listening (receptivity), those who experience life sacramentally or participate in the seven sacraments are making themselves fertile ground in which grace can bear fruit.

7. Develop your ability to listen by spending fifteen minutes alone in each of the following three situations: (1) in silence, (2) listening to music, and (3) in a park or woods. Write a half-page reflection for each experience.

Responding to God

Sacramental awareness requires the skill of responding. Typically, listening occurs as part of the back-and-forth communication in a conversation. Responding to another person in conversation signals that we have been taking in what the other person has communicated to us. If true listening has occurred, genuine responses flow out of us almost naturally. Even responses as simple as a nod of the head or a smile of approval can move a conversation along to deeper levels. Responses are critical to continuing communication; they tell the other person that you heard what he or she said to you.

Similarly, sacramental experiences call for a response. Whenever we are given a gift, receive a hug, or hear our name called with genuine affection, we are drawn to respond. As we will see later in this course, the official sacraments are seven key ways that Christians receive positive,

When we are really listening, genuine responses flow from us naturally.

affirming strokes from their friend and savior, Jesus. Sacraments are meant to be experiences of real conversion leading to a positive response in the way people treat themselves and others. Therefore, the skill of responding involves developing ways to improve our continuing conversation with God in our life.

Sacramental Moments in Daily Life

Once we begin to learn the skills of sacramental awareness, we start to recognize many events in our daily life as experiences of God's loving presence, experiences that can be called "sacramental moments." Consider the following examples:

• Juanita stayed in bed as long as she could. Starting at a new school in the middle of the year just had to be the most dreadful situation she had ever faced. How was she going to make it through the day? Everyone would be staring at her all day and probably laughing at her accent.

God's Many Precious Gems

God places in our grasp many precious gems whose beauty we can easily overlook—unless we have the skills to see them for what they are.

A young man presented himself to the local expert on gems and said he wanted to become a gemologist. The expert brushed him off because he feared that the youth would not have the patience to learn. The young man pleaded for a chance. Finally the expert consented and told the youth, "Be here tomorrow."

The next morning the expert put a jade stone in the boy's hand and told him to hold it. The expert then went about his work, cutting, weighing, and setting gems. The boy sat quietly and waited.

The following morning the expert again placed the jade stone in the youth's hand and told him to hold it. On the third, fourth, and fifth day the expert repeated the exercise and the instructions.

On the sixth day the youth held the jade stone, but could no longer stand the silence. "Master," he asked, "when am I going to learn something?"

"You'll learn," the expert replied and went about his business.

Several more days went by and the youth's frustration mounted. One morning as the expert approached and beckoned for him to hold out his hand, he was about to blurt out that he could go on no longer. But as the master placed the stone in the youth's hand, the young man exclaimed without looking at his hand, "This is not the same jade stone!"

"You have begun to learn," said the master. (Cavanaugh, *The Sower's Seeds,* pages 8–9)

Expecting the worst, Juanita braced herself as she was about to enter her new classroom. But instead of being greeted with judging stares and silence, Juanita was received with a huge handmade sign strung across the wall: "WELCOME, JUANITA!" All the members of the class had signed it.

- The summer was not turning out at all the way Rick had planned. Within the first two weeks of vacation, he had to go into the hospital and have his tonsils out. Exactly a week after he got home from that operation, he woke up in the middle of the night with an awful pain in his abdomen. An hour later, he was back in the hospital having his appendix removed.

  Rick was so mad when he woke up around noon the next day that he refused to eat or say anything. But later that day, Rick received a gift that helped turn his spirits around. After baseball practice that afternoon, the whole team—all of Rick's buddies—stopped by to visit: "We sure hope you get better soon, Rick. The team doesn't seem the same without you."

- Stephanie's mom got a new job about the same time school started. It was a big promotion, and Stephanie was really happy for her mom. Unfortunately, her mom often had to work late now. So the message on the answering

8. Recall a sacramental moment from your own life—an occasion when you felt especially attuned to God's presence. Write about your experience. Include some details and background.

machine didn't surprise Stephanie when she got home from school: "I won't get home till about eight o'clock tonight. I've called your grandma and told her to expect you for dinner."

At first, Stephanie resented not being able to spend as much time with her mom. They used to have a lot of fun getting dinner together and catching up with each other. These days, they did that twice a week if they were lucky. But as she was walking home from her grandma's house that evening, Stephanie realized just how lucky she was. Not only had she been able to get to know her grandma better since she had been eating there a couple of nights a week, but the times she and her mom could be together now seemed more special.

Though none of these examples may seem profound, they are, nonetheless, examples of sacramental moments— occasions in which God has graced a person's life.

Take a second look at the examples. Notice that what has been described in them echoes some of the sacraments of the Catholic church. Can you list them? It may surprise you, but in establishing the seven sacraments, the church has not created new events. Rather, it has taken a second look at some very natural, human events and has recognized and celebrated them as God's body language.

Recognizing sacramental moments means that we are listening to and responding to God's messages of love and concern. Although sacramental awareness requires some worked-at skills on our part, even our ability to listen and respond to God's gift of grace is itself a gift. That ability is what Christians call the gift of **faith**. Perhaps the surest sign that we have accepted the gifts of grace and faith is our willingness, like Jumping Mouse's, to let ourselves be transformed by the sacred in our life.

For Review

- How did Tony and Pat say yes to God's offer of friendship?
- List two skills necessary for sacramental awareness. Briefly explain why these skills are important for celebrating sacraments.
- What is a sacramental moment? Give an example.
- What do Christians mean by the word *faith?*

Sacraments Reveal God's Love

Christians believe that the primary message spoken by God is one of love. Consequently, the world is filled with meaning, charged with the Spirit, a revelation of God's presence as grace. In that sense, we are literally surrounded by sacraments.

Simply stated, the two dimensions of a sacrament are as follows: (1) God acts and is present as grace, and (2) we respond to God's presence in faith and friendship. The primary message of any sacrament, then, is the Good News that God is with us and for us, lovingly active in the affairs of human life. At the same time, we respond to that Good News in our relationships and celebrate it as a community using symbols and rituals—the topics of the next two chapters.

The primary message of any sacrament is the Good News that God is with us and for us.

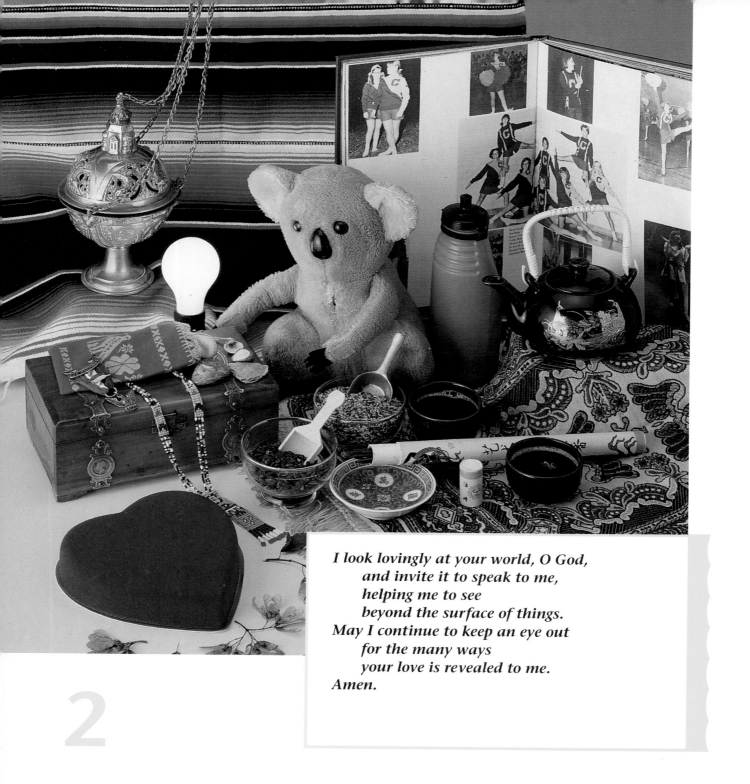

I look lovingly at your world, O God,
and invite it to speak to me,
helping me to see
beyond the surface of things.
May I continue to keep an eye out
for the many ways
your love is revealed to me.
Amen.

2

Symbols: Doorways to the Sacred

Chapter 1 of this course suggested that when we tap into the skills of listening and responding, we begin to see how actively present God is in the world. Through an increase in our awareness of the sacred, we can see that God is communicating with us all the time. This chapter looks at another skill that greatly enhances our sacramental awareness and thus our appreciation of the sacraments. This skill involves the human ability to communicate through the use of symbols. The following incident describes a particularly "enlightening" example of communicating through symbols.

During the visit of Pope Paul VI to the United States in 1976, thousands of people witnessed a marvelous occurrence. The pope was addressing a full house at the huge Madison Square Garden in New York City on a hot, steamy day. All of a sudden, the electricity failed, causing a blackout. The whole arena was in pitch darkness. You could not see your hand in front of your face.

After a few moments of restless reaction in the crowd, someone in one corner of the vast arena lit a match. Miraculously, it seemed, you could see throughout the whole arena, although dimly.

A murmur went up from the crowd. The symbolic impact of the moment was clear: In the darkest hour, even one small flame of hope casts a great light.

Communicating Through Symbols

Imagine that you were in Madison Square Garden when the incident in the opening story happened. Like everyone else there, you too would probably have realized the powerful symbolism of a small light illuminating such a large, dark space and carrying the meaning of hope. Communicating through the use of symbols is a universal human characteristic. It is something we do all the time.

Creating "Meaning Pictures"

Broadly speaking, **symbols** are observable, physical realities that represent invisible qualities or elements. The word *symbol* comes from the Greek root *symballein,* which means "to throw together." So to think symbolically means to take something tangible (something that we can perceive with our senses), like fire, and throw it together with something that has no material, physical form—like an emotion or a concept or an idea. Smells can be symbols. For instance, the smoke and flames of burning sulfur were traditionally associated with the Christian idea of hell. Actions can be symbols as well, but these are usually connected with rituals—the topic of chapter 3.

Symbols help us to see beyond the surface of things, to search for the deeper significance and levels of meaning in things, to take that "second look" mentioned in chapter 1. In a sense, symbols are "meaning pictures" that serve as doorways to the sacred.

Examples of Symbolizing

Take a few minutes now and try doing some symbolizing. Read each of the following exercises once or twice and then do what is suggested:

- Close your eyes, picture a river in your mind's eye, and say the word *river* aloud several times. Try to say the word in the various ways that a river itself might express its different moods. If the river you are imagining were human, what would be its attitude toward life? What qualities of the human spirit does a river represent for you?
- Close your eyes again and say the word *rock* aloud several times. Now picture a rock in your thoughts. Try to imagine the feel of a rock in your hands. Picture a person whom you would describe as "rocklike." Imagine yourself as a rock. If you were a rock, what attitude toward life would you have? What human emotions do you associate with a rock?
- Now close your eyes and picture a cat. In your imagination, follow the cat around for a while. What is it doing? How is it acting? How does it deal with things that cross its path? How does it view the world? What are "catlike" characteristics? If you told someone, "You remind me of a cat," what would you mean?
- Picture a dot, a straight line, a wavy line, and a spiral. If these figures could make noise, what sound would each one make? If you were to describe your life as one of these figures, which would you choose? Why?

When we look at some physical object like a river, a rock, or a cat and say, "There's more to this than meets the eye," then we are starting to see the object as a symbol. A river might remind us of the constant passing of time or conjure up images of things dark and mysterious. A rock might summon up positive images of someone who is strong and steady, or it might evoke negative images of someone who is cold and unfeeling. A cat might be used to symbolize sleekness, quickness, or a sense of independence.

1. Choose a symbol for your family and write a brief explanation for why you think that symbol is appropriate. For example, if your family does things together, you might pick a paper chain or a mobile. If your family is always on the go, a revolving door may be an accurate symbol for your family.

Simple Signs and Symbolic Signs

The words *sign* and *symbol* are often used interchangeably, a practice that confuses the precise meaning of both. For instance, we usually think of a stop sign as a symbol. Often, the insignia of a sports team is considered a symbol for that team. The images %, <, >, ÷, +, and = are math symbols, and the sequenced letters *t-r-e-e* are said to symbolize a tree. In each case, however, the word *symbol* is used too loosely to fit the concept as described so far in this chapter. The word *sign* is more accurately used in these examples.

A few distinctions between symbols and signs will help us arrive at the richer appreciation of symbols needed for seeing how symbols relate to sacraments.

Sign or symbol?

What Makes a Sign a Sign?

Sign, as a general term, refers to any object that represents something else. Thus, there are symbolic signs and signs that are less than symbolic. Simple, nonsymbolic signs are objects that have only one meaning. A yellow light at an intersection, for example, is a simple sign meaning "proceed with caution." A sign in a store window that reads "SALE" also has only one simple meaning. And a five-dollar bill is a sign of one particular monetary amount.

What Makes a Symbol a Symbol?

Although symbols, like all signs, represent something other than their physical realities, symbols have three main characteristics that distinguish them from simple signs.

A cat can symbolize sleekness or a sense of independence.

Symbols may have more than one meaning. Symbolic signs are much richer types of signs than simple signs. Recall the symbolizing exercises you did earlier with the river, the rock, and the cat. You probably came up with a number of different meanings for each of these images. Unlike simple signs, symbols may have more than one meaning.

What symbols stand for is connected to what they are. Symbols have certain meanings associated with them by their very nature. For instance, a rock, because of what it is, has many symbolic meanings very different from those of a cat. In other words, it is unlikely that we would choose a rock as a symbol for softness or quickness. In the same way, a cat, as a symbol, would not serve well as a sign of either unchangeableness or lifelessness.

In other words, we do not *impose* meanings on symbols. Rather, we *discover* meanings in symbols. To be precise, what we discover is a vital connection between the visible object and the invisible reality that it represents. A rock, for example, actually helps us to define our ideas of steadfastness, strength, and other qualities. The same is true for other symbols. What meanings do you connect, for example, with deserts? mountains? food and drink?

Discovering the appropriate symbols for our experiences can help us express the true significance of those experiences—a significance that might otherwise remain hidden. To say "Jesus is the light of the world," for instance, captures an aspect of the Christian experience of Jesus that cannot be reduced to a one-dimensional, factual description.

Symbols evoke more than one kind of response from us. Symbols speak to us in a more powerful and personal way than do other, simpler signs. When a sign speaks to only one dimension of our being, it cannot evoke a variety of responses from our many human dimensions—that is, from our mind, body, emotions, memories, senses, and spirit. Symbols, on the other hand, can touch us on many levels and dimensions. Symbols get us more totally involved; they spark a deep response. They touch our heart as well as our head.

For example, "light" can be viewed either as a simple sign or as a symbol. We generally treat a traffic light at an intersection as a sign with one narrow meaning. Yet we understand lights on a Christmas tree or Christmas candles as symbols with many meanings—perhaps as symbols of the brightness of the holiday season with its good cheer, perhaps as symbols of the coming of Jesus as the light of the world. And if we allow Christmas lights to speak to us symbolically, we may be touched by the memory of past Christmases, by

2. List, in writing, five symbols that you would use at your ten-year high school class reunion to remind your class members of their high school days.

3. Symbols often have emotional significance. For example, the sound of a siren might summon up the memory of a car accident. Recall an emotionally intense moment in your life. In writing, describe any symbols you associate with that moment.

the recognition of the many friends who act as "lights" brightening up our life, or by the light and warmth symbolized by the Christ Child in the stable. Indeed, lights are an essential part of what we think of as Christmas.

Symbols, by nature, can never be confined or reduced to narrow, one-dimensional meanings. What symbols are is intimately linked with what they represent. Symbols are thought-provoking and stimulating and soul-stirring all at once. All three of these characteristics of symbols contribute to their power as a means of communicating the sacred in our life.

Christmas lights can speak to us symbolically, touching us at the level of our spirit.

For Review

- What does *symballein,* the Greek root word of *symbol,* mean? How does this meaning relate to our present-day understanding of what it means to "think symbolically"?
- Name three characteristics that distinguish symbols from signs.

Different Kinds of Symbols

Although communicating through symbols is something all persons do, not all symbols communicate meanings that will be the same for all people in all places or times. Symbols that are closely dependent on a specific situation, place, or group might be called *cultural symbols*. Symbols that are clearly recognized throughout the world are called *universal symbols*. Let's take a closer look at the distinction between these two different kinds of symbols.

Cultural Symbols

Simply put, the meaning of a cultural symbol is tied to the situation the symbol is used in. Outside of that situation, a cultural symbol loses or changes its meaning, as the following story illustrates:

> We invited a newly arrived Chinese exchange student to dinner at a Chinese restaurant. At the end of the meal, we passed around the fortune cookies. When the plate reached her, she plainly blanked. We asked if fortune cookies weren't a custom in her country. She looked carefully at the cookies and replied, "I've never seen such a thing before."
>
> We all laughed at our presumption—not the first one we had made about her culture. We then showed the student the fortunes inside the cookies and read them all out loud. The student laughed with us but then leaned over to the person next to her and asked, "Does this have religious significance for you?"

As the Chinese student in the preceding story experienced, one of the frustrating things about moving to a different community or culture is that many of the symbols that are shared in the new community may not be familiar to us. North Americans who travel to Europe, for example, are often taken aback when they first encounter men kissing each other—a common symbolic gesture of greeting in southern European countries.

Cultural symbols also change in their meaning, or lose their meaning and die altogether. Did you know, for instance, that fifty years ago, shoulder-length hair on men was associated with classical musicians and conductors? "Longhair" music was classical music. Later, in the 1960s, long hair on men symbolized rebelliousness. Nowadays, long hair on men is perhaps more a matter of personal style than a cultural, symbolic style with a particular meaning.

4. Imagine that you are conducting a class for non-Catholics in which you want to explain five important Catholic symbols. Write down which symbols you would choose, and relate how you would explain them.

5. In writing, compare a symbol representative of today's teenage generation with a symbol representative of your parents' teenage generation. Explain how each symbol's meaning is tied to its cultural situation.

Wind as a symbol can be understood universally. A gentle wind stirring the grasses says "refreshment" to people of many cultures.

Universal Symbols

Universal symbols are unlike cultural symbols in that they are not tied to a specific situation, group, or place. The meaning of universal symbols can be understood by people of many different cultures.

For example, although people in the Sahara Desert have a greatly different experience of water from people in the Samoan Islands, water probably signifies "life" for both groups. A tree is a symbol for life in many different cultures. Another universal symbol might be fire, which people of many cultures could also understand as symbolizing spiritedness or destructiveness.

Sometimes, universal symbols convey complex or even contradictory meanings. Wind, for example, can be refreshing—a bringer of life-giving rain and relief from heat. Hurricane-like winds, however, can be a terribly destructive force. Likewise, hands can be seen as both creative and destructive. The heart is powerful yet vulnerable. Explosives are used in fireworks for celebrating and in bombs for killing.

Generally, symbols like water and wind are so rich in meaning and so much a part of human existence that they can be said to be universal.

6. Imagine that you are part of a study group made up of people from all the seven continents. You have been chosen to present to the group three symbols whose meaning you think all the members of the group will be able to understand. On paper, list these symbols and explain why you think they are universal symbols.

For Review

- Describe the differences between a universal symbol and a cultural symbol. Give an example of each symbol.

Symbols and the Natural World

Frequently, universal symbols come to us from the natural world. But in today's more urban and industrial culture, how many of us are in touch with the natural world enough to be able to appreciate the significance of nature-based universal symbols?

When most of the objects that surround our life come ready-made by machines, for instance, can we appreciate hands as symbols of creativity? When curative, medicinal oils come in spray containers, can we recognize oil as a symbol of healing? When microwave ovens cook our food, can we understand a hearthfire as a symbol of warmth and nourishment?

The natural world is one of God's primary means of communicating with us (the other way being our relationships with people). When we cut ourselves off from the natural world or do not cultivate a relationship with it, we are cutting ourselves off from God and from life itself.

Literal Thinking
Versus Symbolic Thinking

Communication by way of symbols is based on the human ability to think symbolically. But for a variety of reasons, modern Western people often have a hard time thinking symbolically. For example, when we think of the moon today, we often think of rocks in a museum or of spaceships or of some astronaut in a strange outfit bouncing around barren terrain. We tend not to connect the moon with the mystery of the night anymore—or even with romance.

Instead of seeing the moon in terms of symbols, we tend to think about it in more literal, obvious terms. When we only see things at their literal level, we endanger our ability to recognize the deeper meanings they can convey to us. We endanger our ability to recognize the sacred.

Literal Thinking: "That's All There Is"

Literal thinking involves considering something only at face value or just being concerned with the "facts." The attitude behind literal thinking reduces all of life to just the observable, measurable things and says, "That's all there is." Such an attitude is based on a belief that visible, measurable facts are the only valid foundation of knowledge. This attitude closes the door to the possibility of there being a deeper significance to something than just what our limited senses can detect.

Of course, literal thinking is often necessary. An airplane pilot, for example, must be more concerned about the speed and direction of wind currents than about the wind as a symbol of the Spirit touching human lives. Still, there is also something very natural, very human, and very necessary about symbolic thinking. Just think, without the willingness to communicate in symbols, we could not talk about our emotional, intellectual, moral, and spiritual experiences—all of which defy description in concrete terms.

For instance, consider for a moment the invisible realities we call love, hope, and faith. Would a person in love say, "She raises my heart rate five beats per minute, she increases my oxygen intake by twenty-five percent, and she and I scored 'compatible' on personality tests"? These statements may be literally correct, but they are lifeless. They certainly do not appeal to our emotions or spirit.

More likely, someone would use symbolic language to express his or her love, saying something like, "She's special—like one song is different from any other." Or, "He's

7. Using only literal language (that is, writing about measurable, physical realities), start a one-page essay that describes a close friend. Be as precise as you can. Then, after a couple of paragraphs, ask yourself if this description does justice to your friend's qualities. Finish your essay by explaining why such a description seems satisfactory or unsatisfactory to you.

pure treasure to me." Or, "She brings light to the darkness of my life." Only a symbolic language can help us to explain and fully experience these powerful realities.

Symbolic Thinking: "There's More Here than Meets the Eye"

The following story further illustrates the differences between literal thinking and symbolic thinking:

> One day, the English poet William Blake was looking up at the sun. One of his companions challenged him: "Surely when you look at the sun you see a round, golden globe shining in the sky." Blake responded, "When I look at the sun, I see choirs of angels singing 'alleluia,' and who are you to say that you are right and I am wrong?"

Blake's literalist friend tried to describe the sun in a simple, one-dimensional statement. Literalists generally look at things as objects isolated from everything else. They stick to the dictionary definitions of things. The symbolic thinker,

In Washington, D.C., the powerful reality of war is expressed both symbolically and concretely through this memorial wall, which is engraved with the names of over 50,000 U.S. soldiers killed in the Vietnam war.

on the other hand, sees things in relationship to all other things and as having meaning at many levels.

Some more examples might help to clarify this distinction. As you read the following statements, think about what they mean literally; then, think about what they mean symbolically:

- It's raining cats and dogs.
- He has a fiery temper.
- The movie is a watered-down version of the book.
- He was a cold shooter in the basketball game tonight.
- He's a real down-to-earth person.

Obviously, these statements are meant to be understood symbolically. Interpreted literally, they are silly or meaningless. Yet there is something about each of the images mentioned that makes them work as symbols.

Symbolic thinking helps us discover the many meanings that the things of our world can have. And because symbolic thinking helps us see the specialness of all things, it is a skill necessary for appreciating and celebrating sacraments.

8. Things can be viewed from both symbolic and literal perspectives. Choose three of the following four objects and write a literal description and a symbolic interpretation for each: (1) a rocky road, (2) a lightning bolt, (3) a seed, and (4) a roller coaster.

For Review

- What is "literal thinking"? When is literal thinking appropriate and when is it not?
- What is "symbolic thinking"? Why is symbolic thinking a necessary skill for celebrating sacraments?

Symbols and the Sacraments

The Language of Faith

As powerful conveyors of meaning, symbols are well suited for communicating experiences of faith. A quick look at the way Jesus preached his message testifies to the appropriateness of symbols as *the language of faith:*

- In the story of the prodigal son, Jesus described God as a forgiving father who rushes out to greet his wayward son.
- Jesus often called himself the Good Shepherd.
- Jesus likened God's Kingdom to the lowly mustard seed that becomes a tree with many branches, to a treasure hidden in a field, and to a wedding feast.

These are all uses of symbolic language that describe faith realities, which are not always easy to understand, in terms of more understandable, physical realities.

A church building is full of symbolism, in the art, in the furnishings, and even in the way the church is laid out.

9. Spend some time in a church observing its art and architecture. Sit down in a pew and write about the symbols and the meanings that you perceive from those symbols. Consider visiting a Protestant church, a mosque, a temple, or a synagogue for comparison.

The Christian church throughout its history has built upon and added to the symbols present in the Scriptures. Walk into any church building and you will be surrounded by symbols. The crucifix, candles, altar, tabernacle, assembly of people—all have symbolic meanings. Even the way a church is laid out, whether as a circle, a semicircle, or a long rectangle, communicates a certain message symbolically.

Sacraments as Symbols

The most important symbols of the Catholic church, of course, are the seven sacraments, which contain both universal symbols and symbols that are unique to the Christian community. Indeed, symbols are so commonly used in our attempts to recognize the sacred that it is almost impossible to talk about sacraments apart from symbols.

When the experiences we are trying to describe are our experiences of God's presence, then symbolic thinking becomes sacramental awareness and our symbols may become sacraments for us. To get a clearer idea of how sacraments are expressed through symbols, consider the following example:

> Suppose you fell in love. Imagine, too, that your love was so powerful that it seemed to you to reflect an infinitely greater love—that is, God's love that lights the whole world. Then any symbol of your love—a gift, a ring perhaps—might take on a genuine sacramental meaning because to you it would symbolize God's love.

The Catholic church's sacrament of marriage is based on just this sacramental understanding, as it is enhanced by Jesus' vision.

Earlier, sacraments were defined as God's loving presence made visible in our life here and now. Now, with an understanding of what symbols are, we can redefine sacraments as symbols of God's grace.

10. Draw or describe a symbol of *grace,* God's loving presence in the world.

For Review

- Explain why symbols can be thought of as the language of faith.
- When does symbolic thinking become sacramental awareness?

From Symbols to Rituals

Like the skills of listening and responding, symbolic thinking opens us up to the world of the sacred. Symbols enrich our experience of the world as sacred by helping us to look deeper at objects and to discover their different meanings. Thus, symbols also enable us to experience the sacraments of the church as fresh and alive, as avenues to deeper realities and meanings, and as places where God meets and speaks to us. Rituals, the topic of chapter 3, take symbols one step further by adding movement and gestures.

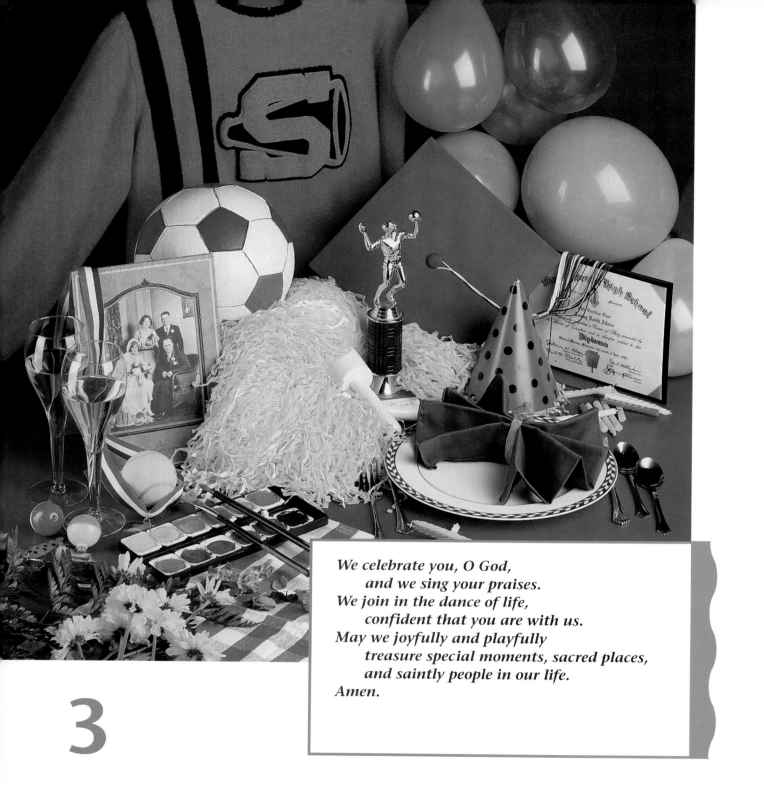

We celebrate you, O God,
    and we sing your praises.
We join in the dance of life,
    confident that you are with us.
May we joyfully and playfully
    treasure special moments, sacred places,
    and saintly people in our life.
Amen.

3

Rituals:
Conveying Meaning
Through Actions

Chapter 2 described symbols as "meaning pictures" that help us see beyond the surface of things. Rituals, or symbolic actions, take the notion of symbols one step further by adding movement and gestures to these "pictures." The role of rituals in life and their relationship to worship and sacraments are the subjects of this chapter.

Like symbols, rituals are a common part of human culture and communication. They help us express what is important to us, as the following story illustrates.

Carmen sat nervously, waiting to give her presentation on the culture of her home country, Mexico, to Ms. Halling's first-semester Spanish class. As an exchange student, Carmen knew that she would be asked to do this kind of thing once in a while—she just never expected to be doing it within the first two weeks of being at her host school. Fortunately, choosing what to talk about was easy; fiestas were such a common part of the life of her people that Carmen figured that describing one would give the class a good introduction to her country's culture.

Carmen began her presentation: "Celebrations, or fiestas, are an important part of my culture. Today I want to describe a very typical fiesta, a Mexican-style birthday party.

"Every year, parents try to have one big party for each child in their family. Up until the child becomes a teenager, the party usually celebrates the child's birthday—though sometimes the party is held on the feast day of the child's patron saint. In either case, the party is a major event that lasts for five or six hours. A birthday fiesta like this requires a lot of preparation.

"Many people are invited to a birthday fiesta: all of the extended family—grandparents, cousins, aunts and uncles; parents' friends and their children; and the child's own classmates and friends. Each family brings a gift for the child whose birthday is being celebrated.

"About an hour after the guests have arrived, everyone gathers for the breaking of the piñatas. A piñata is a decorated, breakable container filled with candy, fruits, toys, or other small gifts. It hangs from the ceiling, and blindfolded children take turns striking at it with a stick until it breaks. Then the children scramble to collect all of its fallen contents.

"At a party like this, everyone has a chance to get involved with the fun. Usually there are several piñatas for the different age-groups of children. The teenage boys get to move the piñata to a different spot once in a while, and the teenage girls are in charge of the blindfolding. The rest of the adults stand around the center of activity, throwing confetti and cheering for the children. In my culture, a birthday party—or any fiesta—would not be complete without a piñata.

"A large dinner follows the breaking of the piñatas and includes a birthday cake traditionally made by the child's grandmother. After dinner, the kids go off to play and the adults socialize. Or, if someone has a guitar, there is singing and dancing. The partying usually lasts until about midnight, and then everyone thanks their hosts and goes home.

"Fiestas like this are important to my culture because they bring all the different age-groups together. My culture stresses interaction between the generations very much. Fiestas often bring different social classes together as well, and give families and friends a chance to stay in touch with each other."

Rituals: Actions Serving as Symbols

Unless you are Mexican, the birthday party described in the opening story of this chapter is probably quite different from what you are familiar with. One striking difference may be the presence of so many people of all ages. When we put the differences aside, however, some common characteristics can be seen. Most obviously, both the birthday fiesta and a typical birthday party in the United States are celebrations of the life of the person whose birth is being remembered.

In many respects, a celebration like a birthday party serves no practical purpose; it is not necessary for human survival, nor is the reason for having one connected to producing something tangible, something that could be bought or sold. And yet, such an event is likely to be very important to the people involved, no matter what culture. The importance of a birthday celebration (or a pep rally, a graduation ceremony, and so forth) stems from the fact that the activity binds its participants together and gives expression to their identity as a family, a community, or a people.

Whether it takes place in a North American or a Mexican culture, a birthday celebration is an out-of-the-ordinary event. Celebrations lead people out of their daily business and their mundane concerns into a special time and a special way of being together. In short, a celebration such as a fiesta is an activity that functions as a ritual.

Simply put, **rituals** are symbolic actions that help us concretely, or physically, express our beliefs, values, and deepest concerns. So, like other symbols, rituals have deeper meaning than what immediately meets the eye. Rituals can be as simple as a handshake, a wave, or the sign of the cross; or they can be as complex as the Olympic Games, the celebration of a nation's founding, or the consecration of a

pope. All rituals serve as ways of communicating what is important to us, what has meaning for us.

Oftentimes, rituals help us express those things that are hard to express any other way but through symbolic action—like the bonding of two people who love each other (as in the sacrament of marriage) or the consecration of a person for special ministry within the church (as in the sacrament of holy orders). In any celebration of the sacraments, ritual actions serve as a vehicle for conveying the deeper meaning of the sacraments to those who participate in them and to the whole community of faith.

1. In one page, tell about a celebration you know of or have participated in that involved rituals. Include a discussion of the meaning behind the rituals—why were they part of the celebration?

Practical Actions Versus Symbolic Actions

Distinguishing the Practical from the Symbolic

By definition, all rituals involve actions. Obviously, however, not all actions are rituals, or symbolic actions. Actions that are performed only for specific, practical purposes are not rituals. Simply walking down the street to get to school, for example, is not symbolic and therefore would not be a ritual. On the other hand, walking down the street in a parade, a procession, or a protest march would be a ritual because these activities symbolize some important reality— things like community pride, the solemnity of an occasion, or the right to free speech and participation in choosing the policies and practices that affect people's lives.

Combining the Practical and the Symbolic

Fortunately, practical actions and symbolic actions do not necessarily exclude each other. They can be intertwined, and to good advantage. In China, some people do not just walk down the street on their way to work. They dance along the way, taking time to slay imaginary monsters in

2. Write down three practical actions you do regularly. Then, explain how you might intertwine each of them with a symbolic action.

intricate, ritual movements that provide exercise and entertainment for themselves and a free theatrical performance for onlookers.

Like walking, waking up and going to sleep are strictly practical activities; all creatures need rest. Morning and evening prayers, though, are symbolic actions that can bring deeper significance to our waking and sleeping. Saying grace before meals serves the same purpose for the practical business of eating. This brief ritual reminds us of the giftedness and beauty of sharing food—a significance that might not be called to mind if we just start eating.

Realizing the Practical Implications of Rituals

Although they are not practical actions in themselves, rituals can lead to practical action. For example, the people whom we honor in special ceremonies—sports heroes, Nobel Prize winners, or civil rights leaders—tell us about our values and serve as models for young people to imitate. Participating in such rituals may eventually result in practical actions like choosing a career in sports or teaching, voting in elections, or even running for public office. Praying before class or a game, if done attentively, can lead to a deeper, more genuine faith. Later, this course will discuss how the seven sacraments, as rituals, also have practical applications.

Rituals and Routines: A Popular Confusion

Confusion over what constitutes a ritual may come about because in popular jargon, an action that is repeated often or routinely is called a ritual. For instance, we talk about the "ritual" of brushing our teeth every morning or the "ritual" of riding the school bus every day. These are routines, however, not rituals, because they are not symbolic actions.

Rituals Have Meaning at Many Levels

The distinction between a routine and a ritual is similar to the distinction made earlier between a sign and a symbol. Routines, like signs, are one-dimensional in meaning, whereas rituals have deeper, multilevel meanings.

The contrast between a blink and a wink serves as a good illustration of the difference between a ritual and a routine: As humans, we blink regularly and routinely to keep our eyes moist. In contrast, a wink has public and symbolic significance. Although a wink is physically almost the same action as a blink, it possesses any number of symbolic meanings in a community. The next time you walk through the halls between classes, try winking at a few people to see how they react!

Keeping Rituals from Becoming Routine

Unfortunately, many gestures and actions that people perform regularly as rituals become so familiar that the distinction between the practical (routine) and the symbolic (ritual) can be blurred. We can forget what the ritual actions symbolize. Saying grace before meals can become simply another part of eating—rushed and hurried through without much thought about why we even do it. Even potent rituals like the Mass can be experienced as lifeless routines if they are repeated continually without any sense of their deeper significance.

Oddly enough, it is often when our rituals are disrupted or taken away from us that we realize what special significance they have. For example, imagine being at the funeral service of someone close to you and then suddenly hearing someone start to laugh. Imagine a group of noisy, enthusiastic basketball players chasing a loose ball into a church during the consecration of the Eucharist. Or imagine if Christians were denied celebration of Christmas for a year.

Rituals and Play

Rituals can also be distinguished from routines in that rituals are often playful activities. Connecting play with ritual does not mean that rituals are not serious. Rather, it means that they are not *work:* they are not done solely to provide physical, practical results. They are done for enjoyment. As

3. Write a brief description of a ritual in which you have often participated. Express what you get out of that ritual. Does it still have meaning for you, or has it become routine? Why?

4. Holidays, club meetings, induction ceremonies, and sporting events like the Olympics are filled with symbols and rituals. Choose a holiday, an induction ceremony, a club meeting, or a sporting event and jot down all the rituals and symbols associated with it.

playful activities, rituals enable us to pause from our daily routine. They free us up to pursue aspects of life that might otherwise be neglected—friendships, family relationships, physical and spiritual renewal, creative hobbies, and so forth. Birthday parties, fiestas, pep rallies, and graduation ceremonies, as well as drama, dance, opera, and athletics, are all forms of play in this sense.

Think about the people who put on school plays. They invest enormous amounts of energy in creating sets, acquiring costumes, and memorizing lines. Then the play is performed only four or five times. So why do they do it? For money? For experience? For fame and glory? For fun? The last reason is probably the most common answer. Leaving our "everyday" life and playfully entering another world is exciting. This kind of fun also expresses something very profound about life: Life is meant to be enjoyed. Through rituals, we can play at being bigger and better characters than the ones we usually portray in real life.

Athletic activities are another case in point. Sports are popular throughout the world. Many people, young and old alike, spend Saturday or Sunday afternoons playing or watching sports of one kind or another. We enjoy celebrating life in a way that involves friends, nature, exertion, and resourcefulness in a nonworking, playful atmosphere.

Margaret Mead, a famous American anthropologist, claimed that every culture develops rituals. Like symbols, rituals seem to be at the core of what it means to be human. Ritual celebrations open people up to the life-giving Spirit of God. They help people break through the barriers of isolation and boredom. Rituals are often public, community ceremonies symbolizing in word and action people's deepest hopes and dreams. Through rituals, people can re-establish their connection with the earth, the cosmos, and their Creator. In other words, rituals are symbolic actions that speak to and for people.

For Review

- Briefly explain what rituals are. Why are rituals important in celebrating sacraments?
- Describe the difference between symbolic actions and practical actions. Give an example of each type of action.
- How are rituals different from routines?
- What similarities exist between rituals and play?

Characteristics of Rituals

Many of the following characteristics of rituals have been referred to in one way or another in the previous discussion. They are highlighted in this section to add further insight into the importance of ritual for human life and celebrating sacraments. Of course, not all of the following characteristics are found in every ritual. Complex rituals, like Fourth of July parades and weddings, include more traits than simpler ones. And some rituals stress certain of these traits more than others do. When these traits are all viewed together, however, they make a powerful statement, not just about rituals but about what it means to be human.

Movements and Gestures with Meaning

The most basic characteristic of all rituals has already been mentioned in this chapter: Rituals involve movements and gestures that convey meaning. Shaking hands, kissing someone, waving good-bye, and clapping hands at a performance are all examples of simple rituals. They are acted out, and they have meaning beyond what they express as literal actions. For example, applause does not just make a lot of noise; it celebrates a performance. In religious language, we

Cheerleaders and spectators at a high school game use gestures to convey support for their team.

The Fox Explains Rituals

In Antoine de Saint-Exupéry's story *The Little Prince,* there is a classic passage in which a fox describes the value of repeating rituals to the little prince, a boy from another planet. As the fox explains, the repetition of a ritual does not necessarily make it routine.

The fox gazed at the little prince, for a long time.

"Please—tame me!" he said.

"I want to, very much," the little prince replied. "But I have not much time. I have friends to discover, and a great many things to understand."

"One only understands the things that one tames," said the fox. "Men have no more time to understand anything. They buy things all ready made at the shops. But there is no shop anywhere where one can buy friendship, and so men have no friends anymore. If you want a friend, tame me . . ."

"What must I do, to tame you?" asked the little prince.

"You must be very patient," replied the fox. "First you will sit down at a little distance from me—like that—in the grass. I shall look at you out of the corner of my eye, and you will say nothing. Words are the source of misunderstandings. But you will sit a little closer to me, every day . . ."

The next day the little prince came back.

"It would have been better to come back at the same hour," said the fox. "If, for example, you come at four o'clock in the afternoon, then at three o'clock I shall begin to be happy. I shall feel happier and happier as the hour advances. At four o'clock, I shall already be worrying and jumping about. I shall show you how happy I am! But if you come at just any time, I shall never know at what hour my heart is to be ready to greet you . . . One must observe the proper rites . . ."

"What is a rite?" asked the little prince.

"Those also are actions too often neglected," said the fox. "They are what make one day different from other days, one hour from other hours. There is a rite, for example, among my hunters. Every Thursday they dance with the village girls. So Thursday is a wonderful day for me! I can take a walk as far as the vineyards. But if the hunters danced at just any time, every day would be like every other day, and I should never have any vacation at all." (Pages 83–86)

might say that applause "blesses" the performer just as a priest blesses the congregation at Mass by raising his hands over them.

Repeated Actions

Ritual actions are often repeated—mostly because, as symbolic actions rich in meaning for us, they are worth doing more than once.

Sometimes the meaning of a ritual is in the repetition itself. Consider this example: Each year near the anniversary of their mother's death, Ron and his brothers and sisters join their father in attending Mass and visiting the grave site. Afterward, Ron, his father, his brothers and sisters, and all the grandchildren gather to picnic, play games, and reminisce.

By repeating this ritual every year, Ron and his family are reassured that their wife, mother, and grandmother continues to watch over and be present to her family. In turn, Ron and his family keep alive her memory in the way she would have wanted—by eating together, playing together, and enjoying one another's company.

Symbolic Celebrations

As the opening story about the birthday fiesta suggests, rituals are often closely tied to playful, lively celebrations. In this way, many rituals become more than just symbolic actions; they become symbolic celebrations that break us out of life's routines. Even simple rituals, such as prayer, can be seen as celebrations. In prayer, we are taking time out to rejoice in God's presence in our life.

When we use the term *celebration,* we often think only about laughter, partying, and general fun. Most celebrations, however, have their serious side. For example, the modern-day Olympic Games, with their opening and closing ceremonies paying tribute to all the participating athletes from around the world, bring a solemn purpose to sports. Embodied by the Olympic Games are values such as striving for excellence, commitment to a goal, respect for other cultures, and world unity. The Olympic Games would become mere routines if they did not possess meanings somehow related to human beliefs and concerns.

Important Events

Rituals are usually connected to important events in people's lives. Many rituals formalize our "firsts." The first ball of the baseball season, for example, is always thrown out by someone special. Turning the first spade of dirt on a building project, driving the first vehicle across a bridge, and cutting the ribbon during an "opening" ceremony—these are "new beginning" rituals.

Anniversaries, graduations, award ceremonies, or ceremonies to induct someone into a community illustrate some other types of important events that call for symbolic celebration. Did you celebrate your thirteenth birthday—your first day as a teenager? Have you celebrated a baptism in your family? Life would be pretty boring if we did not take time out to mark certain occasions for what they are—special!

5. Rituals celebrate special occasions. List five special events (either personal or communal) in your life, along with the rituals associated with each event.

The Power of Words and Deeds

Although words are not essential to ritual, using the right words can lend a powerful boost to one's actions. Even more striking is how the right actions can give life to what would otherwise seem like empty words, as the following true story demonstrates.

Chris froze as he opened the door to his cabin. It was a disaster. Clothes covered the floor, blankets were balled up in a heap, and a deck of cards was scattered across the table, along with the remains of a light bulb from the overhead fixture. Chris looked around the room at the ten junior high boys who had also frozen when Chris opened the door.

"Guys," Chris said sharply. "I leave for two minutes and the cabin is a complete mess." He shook his head.

Danny, a kid taller than Chris, stepped forward. He was the self-appointed leader of the group at the church Bible camp, and he stood looking boldly down at his counselor.

"We were only playing baseball," Danny said, turning and pointing to Bill. Bill nodded and picked up a sock and Chris's fishing rod, threw the sock into the air and smacked it across the room with the rod.

"Enough!" scolded Chris. "Let's get this place straightened up."

Chris, a college freshman, sat down on his bunk and began chewing his fingernails. He watched the campers' shoddy efforts at decluttering. They bickered among themselves, and punches were close to flying over who would scrub the bathroom toilets. Chris glanced at the clock. It was 10:00 a.m.

Camp rules said that Chris had to lead Bible study at 10:15 a.m. every day. This was the one time in the day when all the boys became united: They hated Bible study. In truth, Chris was not that keen on it himself. He had signed up as a counselor hoping that he could spend the summer taking kids canoeing on the white water rivers that he

loved. Teaching religion was an unfamiliar and uncomfortable experience.

Yesterday had been the worst. Chris had started by reading the story of Noah and his ark. Then each kid had taken a chunk of clay and molded his own animal. Chris had looked at their creations; none of them resembled any animal he had ever seen, except one fierce-looking dinosaur. Each kid had then put his sculpture on the wooden boat that Chris had fashioned. The whole group had walked down to the lake and launched the ark, which promptly capsized with all the monsters lost. Still, Chris had tried to close the lesson with prayer, but the kids just shook their heads and refused to contribute. . . .

Chris's daydreams were interrupted by a pillow fight between Bill and Danny. He broke it up and glanced at the clock: 10:13 a.m. Chris had no idea what to do. He was all out of gimmicks. Not that good ideas would necessarily work with these kids, most of whom came from rough, inner-city neighborhoods. They found hiking in the woods and canoeing scary and spent most of their time doing more familiar things, like bullying and hassling one another. Chris knew that some kept knives.

Chris had the boys drag their chairs into a circle, but when he finally got their attention, he still did not know how to get through to them. His silence grated on the boys, who had had a late night. "What?" "Speak up, Chris!" "We're being quiet," they whined.

Finally, Chris asked, "Did Jesus rule by force or love?"

That was easy enough. "Love," a couple answered.

"If Jesus ruled by love, was he a king or a servant?"

The boys gave both answers. Then, unsure, they looked to Chris for the right one. Instead of saying anything, Chris walked to his bed and grabbed a clean washcloth and towel from his bag. Next, he got a bucket from a nearby closet and filled the bucket with warm water. He then proceeded to kneel before the nearest boy and pull off his shoes. Wetting the clean washcloth, Chris carefully washed the boy's feet. After patting them dry with the towel, he looked up at the boy and said, "I am your servant." The boys were silent as Chris went around the circle, doing the same for each kid.

When Chris led the closing prayer and asked for contributions from around the circle, there were a few comments. Bill just said thanks, but Danny had more:

"Yeah, I've got something," he said. "Dear God, thanks for this Bible study and thanks for my servant. He's better than my own dad."

The prayer came back to Chris and he closed it: "Amen."

Significant Words

Rituals often include words that underscore the significance of the action. Drinking a toast is a good example of words combining with a gesture to make a symbolic statement: "May the best of the past be the worst of the future." Standing and reciting the pledge of allegiance, taking an oath of office, and making the sign of the cross also combine verbal with nonverbal actions.

Though rituals always involve actions, they do not always incorporate words. In rituals, words are typically secondary and supportive to the actions. Because a ritual is a physical, sensual activity, its power can be diminished by wordiness or excessive explanation. For example, to continually prompt the audience at an awards banquet by saying, "You may now applaud for this year's winners," would be unnecessary and even distracting, because spontaneous, heartfelt applause is normal and appropriate at such a ceremony. Choosing which words to use or not use in a ritual can make a great difference in terms of how effective the ritual is at conveying its intended message.

Celebrating the Chinese New Year in the United States reminds Chinese Americans of their roots.

Linkages to the Past

Rituals link people with their past. Fourth of July parades and fireworks displays are meaningful celebrations in the United States. Festivities like these speak to people about their past, reminding them of who they are.

As a more elaborate instance: In colonial times in South America, a group of African slaves defeated their Dutch masters. The slaves fled into the jungle, where to this day they have preserved their African heritage. The present community regularly re-enacts the revolt and victory of their ancestors. The ritual lasts for hours, until all the participants are exhausted. By the end of the celebration, everyone in the group not only knows the story—their history—but has ritually relived it. Through the ritual experience, they remember that their ancestors were a powerful and free people, and that they today are a powerful and free people. By partaking in the ritual, they seek to keep alive the inspiration and ideals handed down to them.

Communal Actions

Rituals are often communal actions; that is, they may involve a whole group of people at once. Christmas, New Year's Day, and graduations are just a few examples of events celebrated within a community setting.

In rituals, people come together to celebrate being a community with a common identity. For example, if U.S. citizens were in a foreign country during Thanksgiving, they would find it strange that no one around them celebrated the day. They might seek out other individuals from their homeland with whom to commemorate Thanksgiving. Even a simple religious ritual like private prayer can connect individual persons to a community when the ritual employs traditional prayers developed within that community.

Participation, Not Observation

People make rituals "happen" by participating in them. In other words, it is not enough merely to observe rituals. Nothing is more boring than being at a ritual and not understanding or being part of it. For example, an American once went to a Japanese tea ceremony, an ancient ritual founded upon appreciating the beauty in life's daily routines. From the visitor's perspective, the ceremony was a long, drawn-out way to brew a cup of tea. The Japanese attending it, however, were completely captivated during the hours that the ceremony lasted.

Even fans at a sporting event are not just spectators; they are actual participants. Sports analysts talk about a "home-crowd advantage" in most sports. What they mean is that an enthusiastic, supportive crowd can actually improve a team's performance.

When participating in rituals, we need not know all that they mean intellectually. But if rituals are to have any kind of meaning for us, we must be able to enter into their performance wholeheartedly.

In summary, rituals involve these characteristics:
1. They consist of movements and gestures that convey meaning.
2. They are often repeated.
3. They can be called symbolic celebrations because they break us out of life's routines.
4. They are usually connected to important events in people's lives.
5. They often include significant words that support the actions.
6. They link people with their past.
7. They are often communal actions.
8. They require people's wholehearted participation.

6. Using examples from your own experience, explain and critique the following statement in writing:
"All true rituals are memory-makers and memory-shakers. Good ritual is how we remember who we are and celebrate who we shall become." (Hixon, *RCIA Ministry,* page 35)

For Review

- List the eight characteristics of rituals. Give a short example of each.

Rituals and the Sacraments

Each of the characteristics of rituals described previously gives us clues as to the richness that rituals can have for our life. An appreciation for that richness is key to celebrating the sacraments of the Catholic church. As you probably know from experience or have gathered from earlier discussion in this course, all seven sacraments of the Catholic church involve a ritual of some kind. The importance of rituals to celebrating the sacraments can be more fully appreciated when we recognize that the roots of rituals are deeply connected to religion and worship.

The Roots of Rituals in Worship

The historical roots of rituals go back to the prehistoric era. From cave paintings and remains from early human communities, anthropologists (researchers who study ancient civilizations) have learned that after a hunt, not all of an animal was eaten. Apparently, early humans would save or burn certain parts, such as the brain. In many early farming cultures, the firstfruits (that is, the earliest portion of the har-

Native American paintings on cave walls indicate that early hunts were understood as rituals and that offerings from the hunts were probably made as religious acts.

vest) would also be burned, not eaten. Anthropologists interpret these early practices as ritual acts, and they feel that human society was performing religious rituals at its earliest stages of development.

"Doing the Holy"

For most ancient cultures, life necessarily centered on nature, and in these cultures, nature was believed to be controlled by both supportive and threatening spirits. Rituals functioned as the primary means of communicating with these spirits. Through rituals, people thanked the spirits of nature and attempted to keep them friendly.

From the beginning, then, rituals and ritual sacrifices were linked with worship. The word *sacrifice* comes from the Latin *sacrum facere,* which means "to make holy" or "to do the holy." Thus, when the early Israelites sacrificed the best young lambs of their flocks, they were doing the holy; they were performing acts of worship expressing their grateful acknowledgment of God's gifts to them. Likewise, Native Americans shared their peace pipe and lifted it up to the four corners of the earth in a gesture of gratitude—a ritual that is still practiced today.

Ritual Worship or Magic?

In discussions about the ritual practices of ancient cultures or contemporary cultures different from our own, the distinction between worship and superstition, or magic, sometimes becomes blurred. In actuality, a clear distinction can be made: Ritual worship is an attempt to get in touch with the spirit world, to put oneself in harmony with spiritual powers. Magic, on the other hand, is an attempt to manipulate spiritual powers. Magical actions and objects are believed to produce their effects on a person regardless of his or her motives or intentions. (If I stick a pin in this person's picture, harmful supernatural powers will be unleashed toward her. If a black cat crosses my path, evil forces will work against me.)

The ancients certainly had a keen eye for the world of the spirit. Many of their practices, labeled magic by us, probably served as worship for them.

7. Some rituals celebrate the cycles of nature. For example, flying kites is a way of celebrating spring. Describe in writing two nature-related rituals you have participated in.

Christianity and Rituals

Rituals have been a part of Christianity from its very beginning. In the Acts of the Apostles and Paul's epistles, we read that the early Christians gathered together for meals and broke bread and shared the cup as Jesus had instructed them to do. We read about converts to Christianity undergoing a

8. Do you agree or disagree with the following statement? State the reasons for your position in writing.

- Traditional rituals are no longer meaningful, and no new rituals have come along to take their place.

9. Imagine that you have been chosen to create a *new* way of celebrating an important event. Describe two symbols and two rituals to accompany the celebration. Choose one of the following events to work with: a basketball championship, a family reunion, a sixteenth birthday, a high school graduation, or a marriage engagement.

ritual washing that symbolized the change they felt inside. We also read about the laying on of hands, a practice that developed out of the Apostles' experience of receiving the Holy Spirit at Pentecost. Each of these rituals in the early church was closely tied to things that Jesus had said or done. This association, along with people's experiences, gave the rituals their meaning.

As the church grew and became a more complex community, rituals became more important to the life and identity of the church. And as the church became more complex, so did its rituals and the explanations of their meaning. Over time, the church also acquired more and more rituals, and many of these were called *sacraments*. Eventually, though, restrictions on which rituals were sacraments were set, and the sacraments themselves became more standardized. By the end of the thirteenth century, the term *sacrament* was restricted to the rituals of baptism, confirmation, the Eucharist, penance (now known as reconciliation), extreme unction (anointing of the sick), marriage, and holy orders—the seven sacraments still recognized by Catholic Christians today.

Chapter 6 will take a closer look at the historical development of the sacraments in the church, including why Catholicism has a more developed ritual system than most of the other Christian churches. Also, the chapters on the specific sacraments cover each sacrament's particular history. For now, however, simply note the following two points:

1. Rituals, whether formalized into sacraments or just into simple actions such as the kiss of peace, have been an important part of expressing Christian faith and community from Christianity's very beginning.
2. Someday, you may help plan a class or graduation liturgy, your own wedding service, or the funeral arrangements for someone close to you. By studying and knowing more about rituals, you can become a more creative participant both in your life generally and in your religion.

For Review

- Describe the connection between ritual and worship.
- What is the difference between ritual worship and magic?
- Name three rituals that have been a part of Christianity since its beginning.

Sprinkling the congregation with blessed water at Mass is a Christian ritual signifying renewal and purification.

Rituals, Sacraments, and the Christian Community

Rituals, rich and exciting symbols that include action and gesture, are of particular importance to human communities. Rituals help us keep alive our history, our values, our ideals—in fact, our very identity. As rituals of worship, the sacraments play a vital role in the life of the church as a community of believers.

Sacraments help Christians stay in touch with the Jesus Christ of the Gospels and with the experiences of the first Christians. The sacraments bring people into and keep them connected to the "body of Christ," the church, whose mission it is to carry on the work of Christ in the world. The sacraments enable Christians to express those experiences, values, and beliefs that are too rich and complex to express in any way but through symbolic action. The sacraments, as rituals, help Christians know for themselves what it means to be Christian and thus help Christians convey that meaning to others.

Sacramental awareness and an appreciation of symbols and rituals are two important elements in any celebration of the sacraments. A full experience of the sacraments is further enhanced by another element: an appreciation of prayer. In chapter 4, we will turn our attention to the role of prayer in celebrating the sacraments.

Word of God, teach me silence.
Lead me to that inner place
    where your presence brings peace.
From there, make all of my life a prayer—
    my thinking, feeling, sharing;
    even my hesitating, doubting, and fearing.
May the spirit of prayer
    always find a home
    in my heart.
Amen.

4

Prayer:
Worshiping in Word, in Act,
and in Silence

As we discussed in chapter 3, not all rituals are forms of worship. As simple religious rituals, however, prayers clearly are worship. This chapter offers information both on prayer itself and on specific ways of praying. Using a variety of prayer forms can give us much-needed breaks in our hectic routines and can enhance our appreciation of God's sacramental presence in our life.

To get an idea of the different ways some people pray and bring calmness to their life, reflect on the following personal sketches.

ill is sixteen years old. His main interest right now is getting a license to drive. He receives average grades in school, which is fine with him. He has a nice family, a crowd to do things with, and no particular plans for the future.

If Bill were asked about his prayer life, he would probably roll his eyes and look embarrassed. Bill was an altar boy for a number of years, a service he enjoyed. He believes that was prayer for him. He also appreciates the occasional times when classes stop and the school day is given over to prayer; these are times for a "breather," and he enjoys the peace they bring in a hectic day.

When Bill does stop and look inside himself, he often finds that he is carrying around many worries that burden him. At those times, he usually thinks of God and says a simple "Help!" as a prayer. On other occasions, he feels very grateful for his life, his family, and his friends. The words "Thank you, God" sometimes come to his mind. For the most part, though, Bill would have to say that prayer doesn't fit much into his life. He's all for it, but somehow it has gotten lost in other concerns.

*   *   *

Since she was eleven years old, Katie, now fifteen, has kept a diary. When she was younger, she filled it with accounts of what she had done all day, which friends she had walked home from school with, whether she had passed a test, and so on. As she has grown older, her diary entries have become more reflective. Now Katie does more than just describe things that happened; she finds herself pouring out her feelings in her diary, which she now calls her "journal." Whether she is hurt by a friend's remark, thrilled at a favorite team's victory, or torn in two directions by a difficult choice, Katie spills out her experiences on paper every night. It's remarkable how this process has helped her sort out some dilemmas, and it even seems to help her communicate with her friends better.

One night, Katie has an argument with her mother. She feels awful about it, and she's mad at her mother and herself

and confused about what she should do next. She sits down to pour out her troubles on paper. Ordinarily, she doesn't think of herself as a praying person, but to her surprise, she finds herself beginning the entry, "Dear God."

*   *   *

Joshua feels a lot of stress trying to balance the pressures of tough courses, basketball practices, and a part-time job. When Joshua feels really hassled, sometimes he just has to get away from it all and take a long walk by himself. These times alone help him clear his head and take away the sense of being overwhelmed by pressures.

Do these sketches remind you of yourself at times, or of how you pray? Almost all teenagers pray at least occasionally, but many may not recognize what they are doing as prayer. Like Bill, they may have had some positive experiences with prayer but seldom take the time to pray intentionally, except in a pinch. Or, as happened with Katie, they may discover that what they had been doing all along—writing out their thoughts and feelings to themselves—was really a way of talking to God. Joshua is like a great many teenagers, who may not recognize that taking time and space for solitude that renews them is actually a form of praying.

Thirty or more years ago, most Catholics had a fairly restricted notion of prayer. They believed they were praying only when they were at Mass, when they recited formal prayers such as the rosary, or when they simply talked to God during quiet moments. Today, Catholics understand prayer in a broader sense, recognizing that it occurs in many diverse ways of responding to God's gift of love.

Like any close relationship that we want to maintain, our relationship with God needs to be nurtured through conscious, intentional efforts.

Prayer is a wholehearted faith response to God, who loves us without conditions and is with us in every moment of our life. Because God is in every aspect of our life, we could offer our very living as a prayer, as a response to God. But there is something more intentional and conscious about the kind of wholehearted response that can be termed *prayer.* Suppose you had a friend whom you considered very important to you. Certainly you would not always need to be talking with or thinking of that friend in order for the friendship to be real. But if you *never* made contact with your friend or thought of him or her, the relationship would eventually wither. You need to intentionally nurture a relationship if it is to become a real friendship.

The same is true about our relationship with God. Although all living can be praying, moments of praying—intentional, conscious moments—give substance to prayer as a wholehearted faith response to God.

1. Write a one-page essay using either of the following titles as your topic: "The History of My Prayer Life" or "The Importance of Prayer in My Life Today."

Finding Sacred Time and Space

Reminded of God's Presence

Certain prayer rituals may be quite familiar to us:
- Classes in Catholic schools often begin with a prayer.
- Many people and families say grace before meals.
- Athletic contests, meetings, or ceremonial events often begin with a prayer.

What is the purpose of such ritual prayers? Even though everyone's attention is not necessarily focused on the words of the prayer, these little rituals can remind us of God's constant presence with us. All of life is holy, and God is never truly absent from us. But we need to carve out the time and space to make ourselves conscious of God-with-us, or we are like friends who never take the time to notice each other.

Just as the innings and the playing field remind us when and where we are in a softball game, so prayer reminds us that we are living in God's time and space—that is, all of time and all of creation. Even our briefest prayers, then, can enhance our sense of being in a sacred place at a sacred time.

A Time and a Place for Prayer: Essential to a Life of Love

A number of twentieth-century Catholics known for their wholehearted celebration and enjoyment of life, and equally for their commitment to justice for poor people, have emphasized the need to have sacred time and space.

Dorothy Day, the co-founder of the Catholic Worker Movement, often gave this advice to anyone who wanted to help provide shelter for poor people: Always leave room in the house for a place of prayer. Dorothy Day's houses of hospitality continue to provide shelter, food, and care to homeless people in many cities. And those who run Catholic Worker houses still see to it that prayer remains a vital part of their life together.

The L'Arche communities, founded by Jean Vanier and dedicated to caring for mentally handicapped adults, find their inspiration and strength in a life of prayer together. From his experience with these communities, Vanier writes: "Community life demands that we constantly go beyond our own resources. If we do not have the spiritual nourishment we need, we will close in on ourselves and on our own comfort and security, or throw ourselves into work as an escape" (*Community and Growth,* page 104).

Mother Teresa of Calcutta, India, has always had her Missionaries of Charity begin their day with Mass and end it with adoration before the Blessed Sacrament. During the day, the sisters care for the destitute poor and dying, hoping to communicate God's love to them through their own tender concern. Mother Teresa knows that beginning and ending the day in prayer creates the sense of sacred time by which the whole day becomes prayer.

In each of these examples, a certain time and place are designated as sacred, creating the awareness that other times and places are also sacred. Mother Teresa would not say, "I take time out to pray and then I go to work." To her, taking time out allows the rest of her day to be not only work but also prayer.

In the same way, morning prayer can be taking time out to welcome the day, the entire day. And it can help us be more welcoming throughout the day. Saying grace before a meal reminds us of God's presence during the entire meal. Praying before a game is taking time out to ask God to be with us for the entire game. Taking time out to pray in specific situations can create a time and place for prayer in all aspects of our life.

Silence as Inner Space

Besides needing actual time and physical space in which to pray, people need another kind of space—*inner* space, or the space within a person's consciousness that makes room for God. Such inner space can be cultivated by allowing silence into one's life.

2. Write a brief essay about someone—either a public figure or a person in your life—who is a prayerful person. Explain why you would describe this person as prayerful.

Designating a certain time and place as sacred creates the awareness in us that other times and places are also sacred.

Filling Up with Noise

We live in a world in which silence is a stranger. Our human habitat is filled with noise; silence can be a rarity in our life. And though we may complain about a noisy environment, the truth is that given a choice, we often seek out the noise. Rather than enjoy a bit of silence when we have it, we may turn on the radio, call a friend, or busy ourselves with activities that fill up our awareness.

Unfortunately, by running from silence and solitude, we deprive ourselves of the inner space needed for God to enter our awareness. It is important to ask ourselves, "Am I running away from myself, or am I moving toward greater intimacy with myself?" Because God is at the core of our true self, in the depths of our being, running away from ourselves through constant noise or activity is really running away from God.

A Way of Listening to God

Silence draws us inward. It enables us to listen to God, that is, to be attuned to what is going on inside us so that we can discover how God is present in our life at any given moment. "Listening to God" does not mean that we hear God speaking, as a voice, directing us to do this or do that. Instead, it means that we are quiet, receptive, and able to reflect on our own experiences in such a way that we can sense how God is present with us, even in troubling times.

Although we may go on a retreat for a day or two, during which we encounter silence, few of us will ever experience the life of solitude and silence found in a monastery. Nevertheless, we can seek to spend time daily alone with ourselves and with God.

Both Peaceful and Disturbing

Silence will not always be peaceful. Sometimes when we become quiet, we will be uncomfortable with our memories and emotions, or we will be just plain restless. No wonder we often want to flee from silence; it can be disturbing to us.

Yet God is present with us in disturbing encounters with ourselves as well as in peaceful times. An uncomfortable solitary silence signals us to pay closer attention to what is going on inside us, to feelings and fears that deserve to be taken seriously by us, just as God takes them seriously.

For Review

- How does the text define *prayer?*
- Why is taking time out to pray important to Jean Vanier? to Mother Teresa?
- What other element besides time and a physical space do people need in order to pray? How can this other element be cultivated?
- Explain how silence can be both peaceful and disturbing.

Paths to Intimacy with God

Three paths that Christians have traditionally taken to intimacy with God are vocal prayer, meditation, and contemplation (the prayer of simply "being with" God).

Vocal Prayer: Finding Your Voice with God

Talking to God, which is termed *vocal prayer,* is an ancient prayer form. For Christians, it often involves talking directly to Jesus. This sort of conversation is usually an interior kind of talk, something that anyone can do. Many believers over the centuries, whether educated in theological matters or not, have felt at home simply expressing their needs and hopes to God, through Jesus, in their own plain words.

Anthony de Mello, who has taught Christians much about prayer in recent decades, tells a story of a priest who went to visit a sick man in his home:

> [The priest] noticed an empty chair at the patient's bedside and asked what it was doing there. The patient said, "I had placed Jesus on that chair and was talking to him before you arrived. . . . For years I found it extremely difficult to pray until a friend explained to me that prayer was a matter of talking to Jesus. He told me to place an empty chair nearby, to imagine Jesus sitting on that chair, and to speak with him and listen to what he says to me in reply. I've had no difficulty praying ever since."
>
> Some days later, so the story goes, the daughter of the patient came to the rectory to inform the priest that her father had died. She said, "I left him alone for a couple of hours. He seemed so peaceful. When I got back to the room I found him dead. I noticed a strange thing, though: his head was resting not on the bed but on a chair that was beside his bed." (*Sadhana,* page 78)

Relating to Jesus or God as a real person who hears us, and not as an abstraction or an impersonal force, is the key to genuine vocal prayer.

Vocal prayer takes numerous forms. You may be familiar with the prayer of petition, calling upon God's help in time of need, because this type of prayer is part of the Mass. Prayers of praise, thanksgiving, contrition, and blessing are methods of vocal prayer also found in the Mass.

The fundamental form of vocal prayer is spontaneous prayer, in which we pour out our honest feelings and deepest concerns. Sharing the most personal part of ourselves in intimate conversation with Jesus means placing our concerns in his hands. Talking to Jesus opens the door to his saying to us, "Everything may not be okay, but that's okay. I am with you."

Meditation: Focusing Your Mind

The form of prayer that involves focusing your attention on an idea, a story, or a particular object is termed *meditation.* Focusing on something takes energy and concentration, so meditation does not come easily to most of us, but it can be learned. It helps to begin a time of meditation by trying to quiet the mind and the body, to become relaxed but alert. In this way, the noise that tends to fill us up and scatter our attention in everyday life will recede into the background, and God's presence can be better attuned to.

4. Think of a situation, issue, or person in your life that you would like to talk with God about. Dialog with God, and write down the conversation between you two.

In vocal prayer, we pour out our deepest concerns to God, knowing that God is there for us in our most difficult times.

Christian monasteries provide rich sources of learning about meditative prayer.

5. Research and write a brief report on the prayer traditions of a non-Christian religion or religious group.

The Christian tradition has a great history of experience with meditative prayer. Many saints, such as Teresa of Ávila and Ignatius of Loyola, have written extensively about meditation in works that have become spiritual classics. In recent decades, Christianity has also learned much from other religious traditions that emphasize meditation, such as Hinduism, Buddhism, Sufi mysticism, and Native American spirituality. Techniques like deep breathing, meditative postures, and repetitive chanting, which quiet the body and mind and thus lead to an inner experience of peace, have been integrated into Christian methods of meditation to enrich the prayer life of many Christians.

Contemplation:
The Prayer of "Being With"

There are times in a friendship between two persons when words, and even focused thoughts, are not all that necessary. In fact, words may even get in the way. The two persons may be happy just being in each other's presence, neither one talking and neither one thinking ahead to what either will do or say next. This is akin to the prayer of just "being with," termed *contemplation* in the Christian tradition.

A brief story illustrates this kind of prayer.

> An old man would sit motionless in church for hours on end. One day a priest asked him what God talked to him about.
> "God doesn't talk. He just listens" was his reply.
> "Well, then what do you talk to him about?"
> "I don't talk either. I just listen." (De Mello, *Taking Flight,* page 29)

This simple, mutual presence can be an extremely nourishing form of prayer, but it relies on a person's being receptive and open, able to quietly perceive and appreciate God's presence. For that reason, meditation, which quiets a person and allows the person's attention to be focused, can lead to the prayer of "being with," or contemplation. In fact, meditation and contemplation often overlap and cannot really be separated, just as vocal prayer often overlaps with meditative prayer.

The habit of engaging in contemplation tends to spill over into finding God's presence in the ordinary—in a tree, in a breeze passing over on a warm day, in a delightful time with friends, or in the hurt and loneliness of a classmate who feels like an outsider. This ability to be attuned to God's presence in all of reality is the sacramental awareness that was first discussed in chapter 1. So contemplative prayer and sacramental awareness are very much related.

The three paths to intimacy with God—vocal prayer, meditation, and contemplation—can take many different forms. The next section will look at a few possibilities.

For Review

• Identify and describe briefly three ways of praying traditionally used by Christians.

Praying "All Ways"

Saint Paul, in the Letter to the Ephesians, urges Christians to "pray in the Spirit at all times" (6:18). Of course, Paul, and Jesus before him, did not expect us to sit in silence all day. Nor did he expect us to use vocal prayer incessantly. What he did mean was that we are to pray in all the ways that we live our life: in our caring for pets, our visiting with relatives, our talking to friends and strangers, our attitude toward everything that comes our way. To pray "all ways" means to use all of ourselves—our senses and abilities—in prayer. If we limit prayer to an internal activity only, we risk missing out on the intimacy and vitality that come from seeing and celebrating God's presence in other people or in creation. A sacramental vision that sees God present not just within ourselves but outside as well opens up many worlds and many ways of praying. The following are some prayer forms that reflect the strong sacramental character of Christianity.

Praying with Our Imagination

One popular form of meditation is the method of praying with our imagination. This kind of prayer form is also known as "guided meditation," in which one's mind is led through a scene or an incident in order to imagine an encounter with God or a similarly significant experience. The person reads the meditation quietly or listens as the meditation is read aloud to him or her. Then the person fills in the details mentally at the pauses.

Here is a guided meditation to try (the pauses are indicated by ellipses, or series of periods):

> Picture yourself walking in a beautiful garden. . . . As you slowly move along the path, you take time to enjoy the many flowers, berry plants, and trees in the garden. . . . You savor each one and move on to other parts of the garden. . . . Eventually, you come to another section of the garden that has clearly been neglected. It is overgrown and tangled. You decide to walk through this section of the garden anyway, spending time with the weeds, bushes, and foliage found here, just as you did with the other, well-kept area. . . .
>
> Imagine that this garden is you. . . . How is this garden like you and your life? . . . What are the "well-kept, beautiful flowers" in the garden of your life? . . . What are the "weeds" hidden in the out-of-the-way reaches of your life? . . .

6. Using an image other than a garden, write a guided meditation that could help you pray. If you like, draw a picture to accompany your narrative.

Picture yourself in a beautiful garden.

Now you see a gardener across from you, in the nice section, wanting to join you but separated by the tangled weeds. As you see the tenderness in the gardener's eyes, you realize the gardener is God. . . . What does God have to say to you about the garden of your life, both the beautiful sections and the overgrown sections?

Guided meditation works best in a silent and calm setting, which enables us to relax enough to put imagination into the service of prayer. This activity is helpful in allowing God to touch us through the images that we ourselves create in our imagination.

7. Search through the Scriptures and select a passage you find insightful. Identify the passage and give it an appropriate title. Then, write down three questions to help you reflect on the passage. Finally, compose a prayer based on its message.

Writing in a journal not only records inner thoughts and prayers but also brings forth thoughts and ideas that we may not have even been aware of.

Praying with the Scriptures or Other Spiritual Writings

Another form of meditation uses the Scriptures or other spiritual writings as the stimulus for reflection. After reading a passage, the person can ask self-directed questions that relate the passage to his or her own life.

For instance, you might read this passage from the Gospel of Matthew:

> [Jesus said:] "The kingdom of heaven is like treasure hidden in a field, which someone found and hid; then in his joy he goes and sells all that he has and buys that field.
>
> "Again, the kingdom of heaven is like a merchant in search of fine pearls; on finding one pearl of great value, he went and sold all that he had and bought it." (13:44–46)

Then you might pose questions such as these to yourself for reflection:

- Is there a treasure hidden in my life that is worth the price of everything else in my life?
- What is the fine pearl in my experience, and what am I willing to give up for it?
- What is the treasure or the fine pearl that Jesus is talking about? Is it similar to what I consider to be a treasure, or is it different?
- How does Jesus' message apply to my life here and now?

Reading and reflecting on the Scriptures allows God to speak to us through the words of the Bible, and through this reading and reflecting, we gain an understanding of the Bible's meaning in our own life. God can also speak to us through other writings. Nowadays, there are many works that have been written specifically for aiding prayer. Some people have also found biographies, essays, poems, and fictional works to be pathways to prayer.

Praying with a Pen

Recall Katie's use of a journal in one of the brief sketches that opened this chapter. When she wrote "Dear God" at the beginning of a journal entry, she discovered that what she had been doing all along—expressing her thoughts and feelings to herself on paper—was actually a kind of prayer. She had been engaging in vocal prayer in a written form.

If you have never kept a journal for writing down personal thoughts and reflections, try keeping one. You should notice something exciting. In the very process of writing,

"Dear Diary": Journal Writing as Prayer

This journal entry of a sixteen-year-old girl gives a sense of how important an activity reflective writing can be for us:

> I had an awfully strange dream last night—that Mom and I were fighting. We weren't just yelling, but actually hitting each other too. We were outside in the backyard at high noon (like in one of those old Westerns); she would scream something mean, and then I would scream back. Then came the hitting. The really strange part was that the sky was clear, the birds were singing, and there was Muzak playing from somewhere. I woke up crying and went into Mom's bedroom and crawled into bed next to her.
>
> In school today, Beth told me that she had a fight with her mom. I told her that I never fight with mine and that she lets me do whatever I want. Beth said that's because I don't have a dad around to make my mom miserable and crabby. I feel sorry for Beth, because she just doesn't understand.
>
> Last weekend at Grandma's house, during Sunday dinner, Grandpa said that his son only married my mom because he had to and that they'd still be married if she weren't so immoral. I was so mad that I wouldn't finish my dinner or help with the dishes. He acts as if Dad is a saint. Truth is, they don't understand either, and even if I am mad at Mom, I'll never tell them. I don't know who I'll tell. I'll probably just write it down.
>
> The thing is, I don't know why I told Beth what I did, because I do fight with Mom. The things that she does make me mad; the guys that she dates are losers, and she's always down at the bar. I don't know why she lowers herself that way. I think it's disgusting and I never want to be like that. Sometimes I think I'd like her more if I didn't live with her. I told Beth's mom that, but she said I'd miss my mother, the way I miss my dad and don't really know it.
>
> The whole thing just confuses me, which makes me angry, because I want to understand everything and I don't want anyone to think I'm wrong. Mom and I heard a song on the radio called something like "Turn, Turn, Turn." She said it was popular when she was my age. Mom also said that the lyrics were quite "appropriate in these seasons of change" in my life. I just think that the more confused I am, the more I keep writing.

In what ways can this young woman's journal entry be thought of as a prayer?

insights will come to you. Writing is not just a record of inner thoughts and prayers. It is an activity that helps bring forth hidden thoughts and ideas. Taking time to write honestly and openly to ourselves is a way of entering that sacred place where we talk with God.

Praying with Our Body

Our mind and heart in particular are engaged during meditation and vocal prayer. But even more of ourselves can be engaged when we pray. Our senses and our limbs, even our whole body, can be involved in prayer. In fact, contemplation—the prayer of "being with"—often happens when we

get "out of our head" (in the sense of analyzing and questioning) and simply experience God present around us.

Spiritual writer Walter J. Burghardt calls contemplation "a long loving look at the real." By a look, he means more than simply gazing; he means taking in reality with all of our senses so that, in a way, we become united with that reality. We do not look at the real as something to be analyzed but as something to be appreciated and loved. In Burghardt's words:

> This real I *look* at. I do not analyze or argue it, describe it or define it; I am one with it. I do not move around it; I enter into it. Lounging by a stream, I do not exclaim "Ah, H_2O!" I let the water trickle gently through my fingers. ("Contemplation")

Let's consider some ways in which we can pray with our body, in order to bring our whole self to God.

Our Eyes

For meditation and for inner vocal prayer, we may be accustomed to closing our eyes to quiet our mind and prevent all kinds of distractions from entering into our attempts to focus. However, some of our most profound prayer can come through our eyes. In the Christian tradition, eyes are understood to be great gifts of God. They are meant to be instruments of prayer. We can pray by closing our eyes to gaze inward, but we can also pray by seeing God's splendor in the world around us. Try praying with your eyes:

> Visit a church—if possible, an old church. Look around at the statues, paintings, crucifix, stained-glass windows, candles. These objects can provide a rich feast for your eyes and mind, in what they communicate about the artist, about the world, and about divine realities and mysteries.
>
> Go to one of your favorite natural spots—perhaps a park, a beach, or a wide-open field. Take in the beauty and unite yourself to it in gratitude. Realize that you are praying with your eyes there as well as in the church.

Our Ears

Although silence is an important dimension of prayer, prayer sometimes involves attending to the sounds around us, whether the sounds are natural ones like rain beating on the ground or human-made ones like music. Attending to sounds can be a meditative and even contemplative experience, as the following story demonstrates.

> When Brother Bruno was at prayer one night he was disturbed by the croaking of a bullfrog. All his attempts to disregard the sound were unsuccessful so he shouted from his window, "Quiet! I'm at my prayers."
>
> Now Brother Bruno was a saint so his command was instantly obeyed. Every living creature held its voice so as to create a silence that would be favorable to prayer.
>
> But now another sound intruded on Bruno's worship—an inner voice that said, "Maybe God is as pleased with the croaking of that frog as with the chanting of your psalms." "What can please the ears of God in the croak of a frog?" was Bruno's scornful rejoinder. But the voice refused to give up. "Why would you think God invented the sound?"
>
> Bruno decided to find out why. He leaned out of his window and gave the order, "Sing!" The bullfrog's measured croaking filled the air to the ludicrous accompaniment of all the frogs in the vicinity. And as Bruno

Japanese Buddhist monks drum and chant to get in tune with the music of the universe.

attended to the sound, their voices ceased to jar for he discovered that, if he stopped resisting them, they actually enriched the silence of the night.

With that discovery Bruno's heart became harmonious with the universe and, for the first time in his life, he understood what it means to pray. (De Mello, *Taking Flight,* page 17)

To his amazement and delight, the monk had discovered the music of the universe.

Music is one of the most ancient prayer forms. Indeed, Hindus believe that creation began with the music of a drum. In the Christian tradition, we have the lovely story of the Nativity, in which Jesus' birth is accompanied by music; we also have the mythical description of the Second Coming of Jesus, which claims that Jesus' return will be announced by the sound of trumpets. Music can keep us "in tune" with the earth—even plants, it seems, grow better to the sounds of certain music.

Perhaps you have already had some meditative experiences through listening to music, though you may not have thought of your experiences as meditation at the time. Have you ever felt an emotional release from listening to a stirring, popular song that expressed a simple truth for you? Have you ever felt uplifted from listening to one of the great classical works? Try listening to a piece of reflective music or a song with strong, positive lyrics that expresses significant values for you, and think of your listening as a way of communicating with your inner self and with God.

Our Feet

"Remove the sandals from your feet, for the place on which you are standing is holy ground." (Exodus 3:5)

With these words, the Exodus account of Moses' first encounter with Yahweh reminds us that the ancient Israelites had a sense that certain places were meant to be savored as sacred—places where God was especially present.

We people in modern, Western societies are always on the go. In our comings and goings, however, we should try to be *involved* travelers, or "pilgrims," not simply detached "tourists." When we savor special places, we can allow God to speak to us through them.

The church teaches that all Christians are pilgrims on earth, in the sense of being people on a journey toward a destiny—both as individuals and as a community. Even in our everyday physical travels, we can think of ourselves as pilgrims searching for God. We can be somewhat like the pilgrims to the Holy Land or the people who visit shrines where Jesus' mother, Mary, is thought to have appeared. Travelers go to such places expecting to encounter God in a special way. God is present not only in the "official" holy places but everywhere in life. Our awareness of God in a certain place makes that place "holy ground" for us and reminds us that all the world is holy ground.

Here are some questions to consider about how you might pray "with your feet":

- Do you have any special places that you consider holy ground?
- Can you go to certain places in your neighborhood that bring back special memories?
- Do you connect certain places with people or events that you treasure?
- Are there places that hold spiritual significance for you or for your community?

If you thought of certain places in answer to any of these questions, visiting one of them could be a pilgrimage—a way of praying with your feet.

Our Whole Body

Incense, flowers, dance, and song—all suggest further ways of praying with the body. Our body itself is a sacrament of God's presence. Nothing could be more natural than to use the sacrament we are born with when communicating with God in prayer.

8. Compose a song, poem, or prayer that illustrates praying with our ears.

Native Americans use dance to create a meditative, prayerful spirit.

9. Reflect on ways you use your body—in athletics, in creative activities and hobbies, in helping others, or simply in communicating with body language. Try doing one of these activities in a spirit of prayer. Write down your reflections about the experience.

The Hebrew Scriptures and the Christian Testament present us with wonderful images of praying with the whole body through dance and song. In one account, King David, bringing the precious ark of the covenant back into Jerusalem, leads the crowd in rejoicing in worship:

> David danced before the LORD with all his might; David was girded with a linen ephod [apron]. So David and all the house of Israel brought up the ark of the LORD with shouting, and with the sound of the trumpet. (2 Samuel 6:14–15)

The psalms of the Hebrew Scriptures, too, give a sense of the joy, expressed through their whole bodies, with which the people of God worshiped:

> Praise the LORD!
> Sing to the LORD a new song,
>   his praise in the assembly of the faithful.
>
> . . . .
>
> Let them praise his name with dancing,
>   making melody to him with tambourine and lyre.
>
> . . . .
>
> Let the faithful exult in glory;
>   let them sing for joy on their couches.
>
> (149:1–5)

Writing to the early Christian community at Ephesus, Saint Paul remarks on how good it is for the people to express the Spirit of God in them through their singing:

> Do not get drunk with wine, for that is debauchery; but be filled with the Spirit, as you sing psalms and hymns and spiritual songs among yourselves, singing and making melody to the Lord. (Ephesians 5:18–19)

Until the last couple of centuries, the arts were closely associated with praising God. So it made perfect sense to the ancient Israelites that David was praying when he "danced before the LORD with all his might." The bodily expressions of drama and music-making were used by Christians to pray since early on; these expressions were likewise part of Greek, Roman, Hindu, and Buddhist worship. Even the Oriental martial arts, often cheapened into a form of violence, traditionally were forms of bodily meditation.

If quieting our body through silence and solitude can lead to "internal" meditation, then using our body creatively and expressively can be thought of as "external" meditation. Have you ever felt especially alive and in union with your surroundings while dancing, playing music, skiing, running, painting, or creating sculpture or pottery? Activities like these, done in the right spirit, possess a meditative quality. As such, they foster prayer and are themselves prayer.

For Review

- What did Saint Paul mean when he urged Christians to "pray in the Spirit at all times"?
- Explain how we can put our imagination to use in prayer. Why might this activity be helpful?
- Explain a common way of using the Scriptures or other writings in prayer.
- Summarize four ways that we can pray with our body. Give an example for each.

Being Rooted and Uprooted by Prayer

A few words from Malcolm X, a Black Muslim civil rights leader of the 1960s, serve to illustrate prayer's ability to both root us and uproot us:

> The hardest test
> I ever faced in my life
> was praying. . . .
> Bending my knees to pray—
> that *act*—well, that took me a week.
> (*The Autobiography of Malcolm X,* page 170)

Prayer as Changing Us

What could Malcolm X have found so difficult about praying? Isn't praying something one either does or doesn't do? It appears that Malcolm X knew that real prayer changes a person. Through prayer, Malcolm X was letting God into his life. Once that happened, he found he had to live life differently. He was uprooted from his everyday security and mind-set by prayer at the same time that he became more rooted in God's presence.

Paradoxically, prayer roots us more firmly into life and yet uproots us. It can fill us with confidence and humble us at the same time—as Malcolm X experienced in his life. Prayer makes us more clearly aware of God's presence in all of life. Once we are rooted in that awareness, we observe the world with a sense of its sacredness. That very likely will call

for changing our personal life—perhaps by simply growing out of bad habits, perhaps by taking a risky stand against injustice, or perhaps by committing our own time, energy, or even our life for a particular cause.

Toward a Deeper Security

This challenging, uprooting quality of prayer is exemplified in the life of Jean Donovan, who was once a lay missioner to El Salvador. Jean Donovan was killed by Salvadoran National Guardsmen in El Salvador in 1980 because the government there saw her work with poor people as threatening to its authority and power. Donovan realized that her life was in danger. But her awareness of the needs of El Salvador's poor people, especially the children, caused her to stay in that troubled land. She stayed even though she had a secure, comfortable, and happy existence that she could return to in the United States. Shortly before her death, she wrote:

> Several times I have decided to leave El Salvador. I almost could except for the children, the poor, bruised victims of this insanity. Who would care for them? Whose heart could be so staunch as to favor the reasonable thing in a sea of their tears and loneliness? Not mine, dear friend, not mine. (Carrigan, *Salvador Witness,* page 218)

10. Find out more about Malcolm X or Jean Donovan and summarize your findings in a brief essay. Conclude the essay with your impressions of the person.

"Who would care for them?"

Prayer in Jean Donovan's life both challenged her customary security and gave her the deeper security she needed to make difficult choices.

~~~~~~~~~~~~~~~~~~~

For Review

- With the help of an example from this book, describe the paradox of being both rooted and uprooted by prayer.

A Sacramental World Made Conscious

The first four chapters of this course have introduced the Catholic Christian vision of a sacramental world—a world alive with God's loving, active presence, or grace. Sacramental awareness, which is the ability to be attuned to this sacred presence, underlies the Catholic understanding of the seven sacraments of the church.

Sacraments can be broadly understood as God's loving presence made visible in our life here and now through the world around us—through people and the rest of the natural world. We can perceive God's action through symbols—concrete, visible realities that speak to us of deeper, unseen realities. And when symbols of God's activity are combined with rituals, or symbolic actions, the awareness of God's grace can be heightened. When we add prayer (a whole-hearted faith response to God) to these rituals, then we have a powerfully human means of celebrating and experiencing God's active love for us. Catholics have arrived at seven such rituals, the seven official sacraments. With these rich, significant expressions of the mystery of God's love for us, Catholics are enabled to see more consciously that the whole world and all the world's creatures are sacramental, full of God's grace.

Before moving on to consider each of the seven sacraments, this course will first reflect on how Jesus and the church can be considered sacraments, on how the seven sacraments of the church are essential to its mission in the world, and on the way the Catholic church developed and incorporated its seven official sacraments.

Compassionate God,
*   we thank you for your Word-become-flesh,*
*   Jesus, who walked the earth as one of us,*
*   teaching us about your love*
*   and about what it means to be human.*
Grant that we who are your church
*   may be faithful in bringing Jesus' message*
*   of your gracious love to the world,*
*   through our words, deeds, and sacraments.*
Amen.

5

Jesus and the Church: Sacraments of God's Love for the World

The broad understanding of the word *sacrament* discussed in the first four chapters suggests that there are many sacraments, or signs, of God's gracious offer of friendship to the world. Christians, however, believe that the clearest, fullest sacrament of God's love comes to us in the person of Jesus. Through his life and ministry, and through his death and Resurrection, Jesus shows the world who God is in a very tangible and complete way.

Christians also believe that the task of the church, the community of Jesus' followers throughout the ages, is to carry on the work of Jesus in communicating God's love to the world. The church does this by proclaiming the Good News, by "giving witness" (publicly affirming its faith) through its teachings and actions, and, in a special way, by celebrating the sacraments. The church, then, is to be a sacrament of God's love, as revealed through Jesus, for all of creation.

The mystery that God's love is revealed to the world in Jesus is not easy to grasp. The young woman in the following story discovers insight into the meaning of the mystery.

Tracy stretched out on the living room couch. She had been waiting all evening for her mom and younger sisters to leave for Christmas Eve Mass. At last, she could listen to her new CD on the portable compact disc player she had just received that evening as a Christmas gift.

Earlier that day, Tracy had informed her mom that she was not going to Midnight Mass on Christmas Eve, as was her family's custom after opening the Christmas presents. Trying the honest approach, Tracy had calmly told her Mom, "I just don't buy this business about God becoming human anymore. I'd feel like a hypocrite going to church."

And just in case her mom didn't go for her first reason, Tracy had added, "Besides, I heard it's supposed to be below zero tonight and really windy. With my cold, I probably shouldn't be going out."

To Tracy's surprise, all her mom had said was, "That's fine, honey. I guess you're old enough to make up your own mind. Now why don't you make that salad for dinner tonight?"

Finally, Tracy was alone in the house. As she reached for her headphones, Tracy could hear the wind howling through the trees near the house. She shivered at the thought of going out into such cold, and promptly covered herself with a blanket and took a good sip of her hot chocolate.

Then, just as she was about to push the play button on her new CD player, Tracy heard a loud thumping noise against the picture window on the west end of the living room, followed by tapping and scratching sounds.

Unwrapping herself from her warm nest on the couch, Tracy went to the window and discovered several small birds huddled outside on the ledge. They were pressing against and pecking at the glass, trying to get in from the frigid cold. An overwhelming desire to help the fragile creatures welled up in Tracy. Her immediate reaction was, "I should try to get them into the house."

First, Tracy tried leaving the door open, hoping the birds would take advantage of the opportunity and fly in. Instead, all that came in was the wind and some snow; the birds avoided the door and kept tapping at the window. Tracy's next tactic was to place pieces of bread in the snow leading to the open door. When she came back inside, two of the birds did hop down to eat some bread, but they didn't venture near the door.

By now, Tracy was getting frustrated. She wanted so much to help the birds, to let them know she was their friend and helper. But they were afraid of her. Tracy had never felt so powerless; she wanted desperately to help the birds but didn't know how to reach them.

"What can I do to show them they can trust me?" Tracy's mind raced. "If only . . . if only I could show them exactly what I mean, how much I want to help them. . . . If only I could spend some time with them on their own level, become one of them, just for a while. That would do it better than anything else! That would be perfect—if only I could become one of them."

Suddenly, Tracy remembered what night it was, and a strange realization came to her: "Maybe that's what Christmas is all about. If I want to become a bird so that I can let the birds know that I care for them, why should the notion of God becoming a human be so strange? If God wanted to communicate love to people in the clearest possible way, of course it would be by becoming one of us."

For Tracy, Christmas would never be the same.

Jesus: The Supreme Sacrament of God and Full Humanness

The Incarnation: "God Made Flesh"

The realization that Tracy came to in her efforts to help the freezing birds in the opening story of this chapter is none other than the Christian belief known as the **Incarnation**. The word *incarnation* comes from the Latin word *incarnare*, which means "to make flesh"; thus, the term *incarnation* describes God's embodiment, or "becoming flesh," in the person of Jesus. What Tracy wanted to do in the story— communicate her concern for certain members of creation by becoming one of them—God accomplished in the flesh-and-blood person of Jesus. In the words of John's Gospel:

> In the beginning was the Word, and the Word was with God, and the Word was God. . . .
>
> And the Word became flesh and lived among us, . . . full of grace and truth. (1:1,14)

The Christian understanding of Jesus as "God in the flesh" underlies the belief that Jesus is the fullest, most complete sacrament of God to the world. Although God does communicate with us directly in many ways, through many "sacraments," Christians consider the human person of Jesus to be the primary sacrament—the Sacrament of sacraments—because he most clearly communicates who God is. Jesus is the sacrament out of which all others flow and by which all others are understood. In other words, Christians believe that people meet God most clearly by meeting Jesus.

Jesus most clearly communicates who God is.
Art: "The Baptism of Christ," by seventeenth-century artist Nicolas Poussin

Jesus' Life and Ministry

We can see Jesus as the primary sacrament of God most tangibly through his life and ministry. What we read about Jesus doing and saying in the Gospels of the Christian Testament reveals to us the essence of God's love and concern. An encounter with Jesus is an encounter with God.

Encountering God in Jesus

Christians believe that by finding out how Jesus acted and treated other people, we can learn what God is like. So when we read that Jesus touched and cured ill or outcast people, or dined with despised tax collectors, or protected prostitutes from the scorn and violence of the self-righteous, we see him revealing a God whose love is all-embracing, whose concern is not limited by the standards and rules of society.

Jesus and the Reign of God

How Jesus treated people is inseparable from the whole purpose of his existence and inseparable specifically from his ministry—that is, his announcing of the Reign, or Kingdom, of God. Through his life and ministry, Jesus taught about God's loving relationship with all people and with all of creation. Jesus taught about a God whom he called "my Father," a passionately caring God whose love is unlimited, healing, tireless, and unreserved. By preaching and teaching about the Kingdom, Jesus spoke of God's desire for all of creation to experience the fullness of life in God.

In addition to teaching and preaching about the Reign of God, Jesus also invited people to participate in it by loving God and loving their neighbors. More will be said about this aspect of Jesus' teachings on the Reign of God in the following section on the church as a sacrament of Jesus. For now, simply note that Jesus embodied the Kingdom of God in a decidedly real sense. He believed that the Kingdom of God was being revealed in his own life and work.

Jesus' Death and Resurrection

The Christian church's belief that Jesus is the fullest sacrament of God to the world comes out of its understanding of Jesus' death on the cross, and his being raised from the dead.

The Paschal Mystery

From very early on in Christian history, the event encompassing Jesus' death and Resurrection has been understood as the **paschal mystery**. The word *paschal* means

1. Read one of the following passages: Luke 8:43–48 (about the woman with the hemorrhage) or Luke 19:1–10 (about Zacchaeus the tax collector). Go over the story several times, studying it carefully. You may even want to look up the story in a biblical commentary—ask your school librarian for recommendations. Then, write a short, reflective essay about why the story is of an encounter with God.

God frees us from the bonds of sin and death through Jesus' death and Resurrection.

"Passover" and can be traced back to the Jewish Passover experience recounted in the Bible, in which the angel of death "passed over" the homes of the Israelite slaves in Egypt. Consequently, all the firstborn of the Israelites were spared from death, the people of Israel were set free from slavery, and they passed over into new life in the Promised Land.

Starting with Saint Paul, Christians came to see Jesus' dying and rising in similar terms: God, through Jesus' death and Resurrection, frees us from the bonds of sin and death, and brings us into a new life with God. According to Paul, Jesus is the ultimate sign of God's gracious, saving love.

The Cross

The two dimensions of the paschal mystery, Jesus' death on the cross and his rising from the dead, each reveal specific aspects of the God that Jesus embodied while on this earth. Jesus' death on the cross particularly manifests God's care and concern for those who suffer. Indeed, the cross is a testimony to the reality that God is present with us in the midst of our suffering and pain. In a very real sense, God suffers with us.

2. Ending a friendship, quitting a job, moving to a new town or school, and graduating can be paschal-like events—that is, experiences of dying to one type of life and rising to another. Write about a dying followed by a new life that you have experienced. Describe your feelings about that change.

The Resurrection means that death in this world does not have the last word—that transformation is always a possibility.

The Resurrection

God is with us, even in our suffering—as powerful as that message of the cross can be, it is incomplete and makes little sense without the Resurrection. Jesus' being raised from the dead by God lets us know that God has the power and the graciousness to turn any kind of suffering—no matter how horrendous—into an opportunity for growth and transformation. This is the meaning behind many of Jesus' messages about "death":

"Very truly, I tell you, unless a grain of wheat falls into the earth and dies, it remains just a single grain; but if it dies, it bears much fruit." (John 12:24)

"If any want to become my followers, let them deny themselves and take up their cross daily and follow me. For those who want to save their life will lose it, and those who lose their life for my sake will save it." (Luke 9:23–24)

The Resurrection also reveals to us a God who created a world in which death is not the last word, a world in which goodness is more powerful and pervasive than evil, a world in which transformation is always a possibility. The God whom Jesus reveals to us through his death and Resurrection is truly gracious, loving, and powerful.

Jesus as the Sacrament of Full Humanness

Early in the church's history, some Christians denied the mystery of the Incarnation. They wanted an "either-or" explanation of Jesus—either he is God and not human, or human and not God. The church, however, has always held its ground. In its "both-and" vision, the Christian church declares that Jesus is both fully God and fully human. This means that Jesus is not only a sacrament of God but also a sacrament of full humanness.

As has been emphasized previously in this chapter, Christians believe that people meet God most clearly in Jesus. At the same time, the Incarnation also teaches that Jesus offers humanity a model of itself at its best, a picture of what we humans can be and what God desires for us. Additionally, Jesus as a sacrament of full humanness is a model for us in faithfully responding to God's offer of friendship.

Thus, when we hear the story of Jesus' life, ministry, death, and Resurrection, we are always hearing two inseparable messages: First, the story of Jesus is about who God is and what God desires for all people, all of creation. Second, the story of Jesus is also about how human beings are to respond to God—that is, by trusting God completely and by loving their neighbors as they love themselves. In other words, the story of Jesus teaches us how to be fully human.

3. Draw representations of the cross and the Resurrection that would speak to our contemporary world.

4. Imagine that you are a member of a panel addressing people who have never heard of Jesus. Their first question is, "What does Jesus' life tell us about God and about being human?" Write a brief response.

For Review

- What does the word *incarnation* mean? How does the opening story relate to the Incarnation of Jesus?
- What do Christians mean when they say Jesus is the primary sacrament of God?
- Summarize why Jesus' life and ministry are a sacrament of God. Use an example to illustrate your response.
- What is the paschal mystery? What do Jesus' death on the cross and his Resurrection tell us about God?
- What two things does Jesus' humanity model for us?

The Paschal Mystery and Everyday Life

Anyone who ever passes through a time of suffering and comes through it as a stronger, better, more compassionate person experiences the reality of the paschal mystery in everyday life. Jesus' death and Resurrection, then, were not some wild fluke in the history of the world. Instead, they definitively confirm what we can readily see in the world around us—that growth and rebirth can come out of pain and suffering. Consider the example given by a young man named Don:

> When I was twelve, my dad died of lung cancer. It all happened so quick. He first got sick in early May, and by the end of August he was gone. He was supposed to have coached my soccer team that summer. At first, I was really mad at him for getting sick, for letting me down. Mom had been pleading with him for years to quit smoking. But he always just said, "I'll try after I get finished with this project," or, "I'll quit after the holidays."
>
> Then, I just turned numb. I wouldn't hardly talk to anybody at home or at school. I just wanted to be left alone. By the time I was thirteen, I was drinking a lot—first beer, then harder stuff. The morning of my fourteenth birthday, Mom and Grandpa found me passed out in my room. Right away they got me into the chemical dependency unit at Saint Mary's Hospital.
>
> It's been a long two years. Every day I've had to come up with a list of reasons why I shouldn't drink. Those first lists were pretty short: Mom would hate me. And I'd have to go back to the hospital. But gradually, my lists started to get longer. The clincher just came to me the other day: I want to live. I don't want to kill myself like my dad did.

In our personal life, any time we experience a loss of something only to find new life or new meaning, we enter into the paschal mystery. Every time we witness the cycle of "life, death, new life" in the natural world, both human and nonhuman, we witness the paschal mystery. Christians can enhance their experience of Jesus as a sacrament if they reflect on and appreciate the dyings and risings, the crosses and the empty tombs, in their own lives.

The Church:
The Sacrament of Jesus
to the World

To many of the followers that he attracted during his lifetime, Jesus was someone who commanded great authority. Of greater importance to his followers, however, was the fact that they felt the presence of God in him. Yet Jesus also constantly challenged his disciples' comfortable images of him. When the disciples heard Jesus speak of God's Kingdom, for example, they envisioned royal robes and awesome power. What they got instead was common bread, talk of tiny mustard seeds, and lessons on being a servant.

Similarly, when Jesus was crucified, his followers felt betrayed and foolish, so they hid. Then the Resurrection brought renewed faith and joy. But soon afterward, Jesus ascended to God, and his disciples went back to fear and confusion. They had been offered hope, had had it snatched away and then miraculously returned—only to be left alone again. The disciples' frustrations were answered, though, by a key event in the history of the church: **Pentecost**.

A Greek Orthodox rendering of the Resurrection

Pentecost: The "Birthday" of the Church

After his suffering [Jesus] presented himself alive to [the Apostles] by many convincing proofs, appearing to them during forty days and speaking about the kingdom of God. While staying with them, he ordered them to not leave Jerusalem, but to wait there for the promise of the Father. "This," he said, "is what you have heard from me; for John baptized with water, but you will be baptized with the Holy Spirit not many days from now."

". . . You will receive power when the Holy Spirit has come upon you; and you will be my witnesses in Jerusalem, in all Judea and Samaria, and to the ends of the earth." When he had said this, as [the Apostles] were watching, he was lifted up, and a cloud took him out of their sight. . . .

When the day of Pentecost had come, they were all together in one place. And suddenly from heaven there came a sound like the rush of a violent wind, and it filled the entire house where they were sitting. Divided tongues, as of fire, appeared among them, and a tongue rested on each of them. All of them were filled with the Holy Spirit and began to speak in other languages, as the Spirit gave them ability. (Acts 1:3–9; 2:1–4)

5. Slowly and reflectively read the first two chapters of the Acts of the Apostles. As you read, imagine yourself taking part in the experiences described there. In a brief essay, write about your impressions of the church at its very beginning. Compare it with your current experience of the church.

What happened on the day Jesus' disciples were observing the Jewish feast of Pentecost had a powerful impact on them. Suddenly, everything began to make sense: By his leaving, Jesus had not abandoned the disciples. Rather, he had let go of them, like a parent lets go of a child so that the child can become an adult.

By his departure into heaven known as the **Ascension**, Jesus had shown that he trusted his disciples. He trusted them to represent him and to continue his mission. Jesus left his friends with the message of his life, with his sayings and stories, and especially with his Spirit. Although Jesus was no longer with the disciples "in the flesh," he was now present with them, and dwelled in them, through the power of the Spirit. (The titles "the Spirit" and "Jesus' Spirit" refer to what Christians commonly know as the Holy Spirit.)

Consequently, just as Jesus had preached, taught, and lived the Kingdom of God while he walked the earth, his followers—the people who were "the church"—were now to follow in his footsteps. Filled with the Holy Spirit, his disciples were empowered to go forth into the world and preach the Good News of Jesus. The church was charged on the day of Pentecost to be a full sacrament of Jesus to the world, a sign of Jesus' continued, real presence in the world. For this reason, Pentecost is often called the birthday of the Christian church.

Who Is "the Church"?

In order to grasp how the church is a sacrament of Jesus to the world, it is helpful to consider just *who* the church is; that is, *who* has the task of carrying on the message and work of Jesus?

All too often, Christians misunderstand the word *church* to mean something other than or outside of themselves. Phrases such as "the church teaches" or "the church says" conjure up the image of an institution that has a life of its own apart from the people in the pews, but whose authority they are under. Similarly, some people mistakenly identify the church primarily in terms of its hierarchy—the pope, bishops, and priests. A few people's notion of "church" extends no further than the building in which Christians worship. The church, however, is a much richer reality than any of these notions suggest.

The People of God

Wishing to put forth a rich, comprehensive understanding of what and who the Christian church is, Catholic church leaders at the Second Vatican Council during the mid-1960s spoke of the church as "the people of God." In its most inclusive or broad sense, the phrase "people of God" refers to the community of all people who acknowledge and serve God in holiness. Not only does this expression mean that all Christians—not just those ordained as pastors—are "the church," but it also suggests that even those who are not of the Christian faith can and do participate in the life and work of the church.

More specifically, however, the people of God can be described as a community of people brought together by their faith in and love for Jesus as the Anointed One of God. The church as the people of God is a community established by Christ to be, as the evangelist Matthew tells us, "the salt of the earth and the light of the world" (5:13–14). The church as a sacrament is to be a seed of unity, hope, and salvation (transformation) for the whole world.

The Body of Christ

In the First Letter to the Corinthians, Saint Paul "embodies" his understanding of what or who the church is as follows:

> For just as the body is one and has many members, and all the members of the body, though many, are one body, so it is with Christ. For in the one Spirit we were all baptized into one body—Jews or Greeks, slaves or free—and we were all made to drink of one Spirit. . . .
> Now you are the body of Christ and individually members of it. (12:12–13,27)

Members of a parish walk together to raise money for hungry people, expressing their unity with all members of the human family.

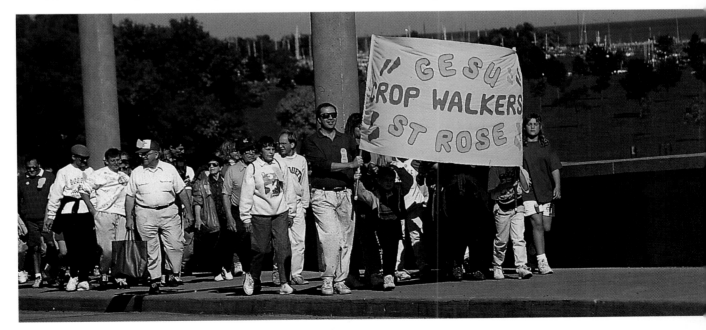

We Took Communion to the Nursing Home, My Friend and I

We took Communion to the nursing home,
my friend and I.

Bodies old, tired, worn out, broken, crippled.
Spirits old, tired, worn out, broken, crippled.
Some spirits very much alive.

We enter a room; he is in bed.
The once-virile body is faded, wasted,
seemingly asleep.
"Shall we pass him by?" we wonder.
But we ask, "Would you like to receive
   Communion?"
The eyes open. "Yes," he whispers.
"The Body of Christ."
"Amen." He opens his mouth, receives the
   host,
has trouble swallowing.
There is a cup of water by the bed.
I put the straw to his lips.
He isn't strong enough to suck.
I hold the cup to his lips and dribble some
   water
into his mouth. He swallows.
The faded eyes close, open again.
"Thank you," he whispers.

She is in a wheelchair in the hall.
"Would you like to receive Communion?"
"I don't know," she says wistfully.
"I haven't been to Confession lately.
   I'd like to,
but do you think I should?"
My friend assures her it will be all right,
and she receives gratefully.

She is in a wheelchair, alive, loud.
"Would you like to receive Communion?"
"Come here, let me kiss you." She kisses me.
"And let me kiss you." She kisses my friend.
"Would you like to receive Communion?"
"Yes!" she says loudly. "Amen."
"Come here, let me kiss you."
Her voice follows us down the hall.

We pass several rooms where the residents
are too frail and too weak to respond.

She lies in bed, staring at the ceiling.
"Would you like to receive Communion?"
Her eyes light up.
"Oh, yes," she breathes eagerly, "oh, yes."
"The Body of Christ."
"Amen," she responds, as her aging, wrinkled
   hand
makes a reverent, slow, deliberate
sign of the cross.
"Oh, thank you, thank you."

We have taken Communion to the residents
of the nursing home,
my friend and I,
and they have shown us illness, senility,
   sorrow,
suffering, tears, and weakness.

We have taken Communion to the residents
of the nursing home,
my friend and I,
and they have shown us acceptance, courage,
gratitude, reverence, faith, hope, and love.

We have taken Communion to the residents
of the nursing home,
my friend and I,
and they have shown us
the Body of Christ.

Ruth Kulas

Like the phrase "the people of God," the image of the church as "the body of Christ" suggests a community of persons who profess faith in Jesus. Perhaps even more vividly, however, the image of the body of Christ conveys the notion of a community whose members combine their individual gifts to work together to make Jesus alive and present in the world.

The church, then, is the continued embodiment of Jesus here on earth. Simply put, "Jesus is the head, the Spirit is our soul, and we are the parts. Jesus has no hands without our hands, no hearts but our hearts" (O'Malley, "Understanding Sacraments").

Building the Reign of God

The church is a sacrament of Jesus. Whenever and wherever its members act as Jesus acted, whenever and wherever they preach about and live out the Kingdom of God that is so dear to Jesus' heart, they make Jesus' presence in the world visible. Just as Jesus preached the good news of liberation to poor people and sinners, so must the church preach the Good News. Just as Jesus fed the hungry, so must the church feed the hungry. And just as Jesus cared for and healed the sick, so must the church care for and heal the sick.

The church is to be both a sign and an instrument of the Kingdom of God, as promised and delivered by God in Jesus. And as the body of Christ, the church, through its words and actions, is to carry on Jesus' work of building the Kingdom of God.

The Early Church

How strongly the early Christians saw themselves as carrying on Jesus' work can be seen in the following testimony, given by a non-Christian man named Aristides to the Roman emperor Hadrian:

> Christians love one another. They never fail to help widows; they save orphans from those who would hurt them. If a man has something, he gives freely to the man who has nothing. If they see a stranger, Christians take him home and are happy, as though he were a real brother. They don't consider themselves brothers in the usual sense, but brothers instead through the Spirit, in God. And if they hear that one of them is in jail, or persecuted for professing the name of their redeemer, they all give him what he needs. If it is possible, they bail him out. If one of them is poor and there isn't enough food to go around, they fast several days to give him the

6. First, read Saint Paul's description of the church as a body (1 Corinthians 12:12–26). Then, read the poem "We Took Communion to the Nursing Home, My Friend and I," on page 90 of this textbook. Finally, write an essay on how the poem and Saint Paul's words echo each other.

The church builds the Reign of God when it makes Jesus present in the world by carrying on his work.
Art: A Greek Orthodox rendering of Jesus' healing of the sick

food he needs. . . . This is really a new kind of person. There is something divine in them. (Balasuriya, *The Eucharist and Human Liberation,* page 26)

The Church Today

Examples abound of the people of God giving witness to Jesus and building the Reign of God today:

- Christians who work at food shelves and homeless shelters make Jesus visibly present to those they serve.
- Parish members who volunteer to bring confined or elderly persons to Sunday Mass are a sacrament of Jesus.
- Bishops and theologians who work together to issue statements on topics concerning peace and economic justice make Jesus' teachings about the Kingdom come alive in the present day.
- Employers who treat employees with fairness and provide them with safe working conditions and just wages are acting Christlike.
- Persons who reach out to hurting or troubled friends, even if only to listen or lend a shoulder to cry on, bring the healing power of Jesus to their friends.
- Families who gather together for times of celebration, sharing, and relaxation witness the fullness of life desired by God for all and revealed to us by Jesus.

Of course, many more examples could be given. The point is, however, that almost any situation Christians find themselves in offers them the chance to be a sacrament of Jesus—in both his divinity and his humanity—to those around them. Whenever persons love others as they love themselves, act with and promote justice, show mercy and compassion, celebrate and give thanks for the gifts in their lives, and so forth, they carry on the work of Jesus. In other words, people reveal to one another a God who is loving, gracious, and merciful, and they show by their example humanity at its best. By doing so, they in fact are being "the church."

The Church as a Sacrament of Unity

As a sacrament of Jesus to the world, the church has a specific task of reminding all the world's people that we have a common center—Jesus, whom Christians call Christ—and that we are one united whole. As the Second Vatican Council stated in its *Dogmatic Constitution on the Church,* the church, "by her relationship with Christ . . . is a kind of sacrament or sign of intimate union with God, and of the unity of all [humankind]" (no. 1).

7. Draw an image or a symbol that represents how you view the role of the church in the world.

8. Research one of the following people and the movement associated with that person. Write a two-page report on the person's efforts and their movement's efforts to build the Reign of God.

- Saint Francis of Assisi and the Franciscans
- Saint Elizabeth Ann Seton and the U.S. Catholic school system
- Cesar Chavez and the United Farm Workers
- Mother Teresa of India and the Missionaries of Charity
- Dorothy Day and the Catholic Worker Movement
- Martin Luther King, Jr., and the U.S. Civil Rights Movement

For the church, part of being a sacrament to the world means being an ongoing reminder that all the world has been saved by Jesus. The church, like Jesus, is a sacrament of God's compassion. The church proclaims that the Creator and Source of All Being is a loving God, and it points to the people, events, and places in the world where God's love can be found.

The church is a sign of intimate union with God and of the unity of all humankind. It reminds us of our ties to our sisters and brothers all over the world.
Photo: A street market in Guatemala

For Review

- Why is Pentecost often called "the birthday of the Christian church"?
- Identify two images that help Christians understand *who* the church is. Discuss why each is a helpful image.
- When or where is the church a sacrament of Jesus to the world?
- List three examples of how Christians can be a sacrament of Jesus to today's world.

9. What would you like the experience of the church to be like for the generation that would include your own children? In what ways would you like it to be the same as what you experienced? In what ways would you like it to be different? Write your reflections in a page.

Building the Reign of God: Bringing Water to the Slums

The following story is based on a real-life incident from the country of Uruguay in South America. Like the tiny mustard seed that grows into a large plant, the small actions on the part of members of the church can have far-reaching effects.

"The children come to school without washing because there is no water in the shantytown," the teacher explained to Teresa. "After nights spent trying to sleep on beds with no mattresses, no sheets, and with only rags for blankets, the children must get up very early just to get to school. It is a long way to fetch a bucket of water, and there is no time. So the children show up sleepy and without even having the chance to wash their face. No wonder they have a hard time paying attention to their studies."

All weekend, Teresa heard the same story as she worked in the shantytown with the volunteer youth service team from her middle-class parish, located in another part of the city: There was no water in the shantytown, and its lack was the cause of much hardship among its residents.

Her own privileged position had made Teresa feel uncomfortable—she had never thought twice about washing her face when she got up in the morning or getting a drink when she came in from the heat. Somehow, she sensed, she was responsible for the fact that there was no water in the slums.

"Surely something could be done," Teresa pondered out loud to her father, an engineer for the city's public works department. "How difficult would it be to provide the shantytown with its own water supply?"

Getting water to the shantytown would not be difficult at all, Teresa's father found out. And it would cost next to nothing. Indeed, one Sunday's worth of collections from her parish covered the amount the city was charging for laying the pipes to carry the water to the slum. However, to the shantytown residents, who had long ago unconsciously resigned themselves to the whole situation, such an expenditure of money would have been impossible.

Two weeks after Teresa spoke with her father, the shantytown had its water. Enough money was even left over to build a small community center that contained eight showers and a central water hydrant.

Soon, the life of the whole community and the character of the people were transformed. Now the children could come to school with washed faces; the old men who spent the day trudging around the garbage heaps could wash their weary feet at night; and the men and women, who before were easily irritated and hostile with one another because of being unable to find relief from the hot, midday sun, could refresh themselves with a cup of cool, clean water. Now life was a little easier, a little more bearable. (Adapted from Porcile, *New Eyes for Reading*, pages 35–36)

The Seven Sacraments of the Catholic Church

So far, the discussion of the church as a sacrament of Jesus to the world has focused mainly on the church's practical actions of serving and teaching others in the concrete, everyday world. But there is another way that the church, and specifically the Catholic church, sees itself as making Jesus fully present in our midst: through celebrating the seven sacraments of baptism, confirmation, the Eucharist, reconciliation, anointing of the sick, marriage, and holy orders.

In order for us to have an appreciation of each particular sacrament, we will spend some time looking at the role of the seven sacraments as a whole within the life of the Catholic church. Let's start by considering the following story:

> Kelly, Beth, Anita, and Cari had only begun to hang out together toward the end of their junior year, after they had been in the school play together. Early in the fall of their senior year, they discovered that all four of them arrived at school on Mondays about a half hour earlier than they showed up during the rest of the week.
>
> At first, the four girls got together just to pass the time. But as the girls grew to know one another better, their Monday morning gatherings changed. They began making sure they met where they could have some privacy, and started taking turns bringing something to eat

10. Write a brief story about an incident or situation in your own life that served as both a sign of something (like friendship) and as a source of renewal and nurturing.

and drink, surprising and amusing one another with homemade cookies or unusual snacks.

Their gatherings became something all the girls looked forward to and didn't want to miss. Sometimes, all they did was pass on the latest jokes or talk about what they did over the weekend. At other times they would be more subdued, especially when one of them was having a tough time at home or in school and needed the rest of them to offer support, or just to listen.

Late in the spring, with only three weeks left before graduation, the four friends realized just how much their Monday morning get-togethers meant to them. One morning, an unusual somberness permeated the room where the girls had gathered. Cari, in particular, was uncharacteristically serious.

"Can you believe it?" she said. "Only two more Mondays before graduation. Maybe we should plan something special for the last one?"

Beth sat picking at her doughnut, trying to avoid looking at her friends. "Let's not talk about it, Cari. Can't it wait till next week?" Though she tried, Beth couldn't keep her voice from cracking.

"What's the matter, Beth?" Anita, who was noted for her directness and not for timidity, put her hand on her friend's shoulder.

Like a dam too small to hold back the flood, Beth spilled over with emotion. "Oh, I don't know," she sobbed. "It's just that . . . well, you guys are my best friends. What're we going to do when we can't get together like this next fall? . . . Guess I'm just going to miss this, that's all."

Growing impatient—and uncomfortable—with the heavy atmosphere, Kelly got up to pour herself another glass of juice. "Well, we can still write each other and talk on the phone, can't we? Besides, we've got all summer before we leave for college. Let's save the tears for later and just enjoy these last few weeks as much as we can. What did you have in mind, Cari, for our last Monday morning?"

Though Cari and her friends might not have expressed their feelings in these terms, their Monday morning gatherings served as both a sign of their friendship and a time for renewing and nurturing it. Similarly, the seven sacraments of the Catholic church serve a twofold function. Through the seven sacraments, the Catholic faith community continues to express itself as a sacrament of Jesus to the world. In turn, the ritual sacraments of the church also build and continually strengthen the community and provide a spiritual basis for its witnessing efforts.

Jesus' Actions as the Basis of the Sacraments

As we saw earlier in this chapter, when Jesus charged his disciples at his Ascension to be his witnesses "to the ends of the earth," he did not leave them without some clue as to how to go about that task. Along with the promise that he would send his Spirit, Jesus left his disciples the story of his life and his example. The way his disciples would most effectively witness Jesus to others, then, would be to preach what he did and act as he did.

Jesus left us with the example of his own life, challenging us to act as lovingly as he did.

As the church grew and developed, Christians began to summarize Jesus' actions into seven primary ways in which he himself was a sacrament of God:

- He introduced people to new life.
- He forgave people's sins.
- He sacrificed himself out of love.
- He shared the power of his Spirit with others.
- He healed people's illnesses.
- He was faithful to the One he called "Abba."
- He ministered to people's spiritual needs.

Eventually, these seven types of Christlike actions were ritualized into what are now the official sacraments of the Catholic church. Through the seven sacraments, the Catholic church sees itself as continually expressing and bringing about the presence of Jesus in the world in a special and powerful way.

The Sacraments as Rituals of the Church

To appreciate the unique and powerful role the seven sacraments play in the life of the Catholic church, recall the importance of symbolic actions as discussed in chapter 3. A number of insights can be drawn from that discussion:

The sacraments ritualize the concrete. The seven sacraments ritualize the Christian community's experience of living out the commandment of Jesus to continue his work of announcing and bringing about God's Kingdom. In a sense, the sacraments are the ways the church solidifies its work of initiating and instructing, forgiving and reconciling, sacrificing and building community, sharing and maturing, healing and comforting, faith-keeping and loving, and serving and ministering. Thus, the ritual sacraments and the church's practical actions flow out of and support each other.

The sacraments embody what the church is and is becoming. All rituals help people express who they presently are and who they seek to become. When the church celebrates the sacraments, it is embodying the reality of what it is—a sacrament of Jesus—and the values it is committed to. By making such a statement about itself and its values in the sacraments, the faith community reminds itself that it can always do a better job of making Jesus real to the world.

The sacraments reveal the extraordinary in the ordinary. Like most rituals, the sacraments lift up or magnify many common, fundamental human experiences—being born, passing into adulthood, falling in love and getting married, experiencing illness, and so forth—and help Cath-

olic Christians see the deeper meanings of these events. The sacraments remind us that God is found in the midst of life, and they offer us a chance to give thanks to God for the everyday happenings of our world.

The sacraments show us the extraordinary nature of our everyday, ordinary life.

The sacraments keep alive the mysteries of faith. Rituals often help people express thoughts and experiences that are too big for words and that are not totally understandable. The seven sacraments help Catholic Christians express the mysteries of their faith—such as the Incarnation and the paschal mystery. The sacraments enable their participants to acknowledge the truth of these mysteries without trying to explain them. Through the sacraments, Catholic Christians are invited to enter into the mysteries and to be transformed by the experience.

The Sacraments:
Grounding Points for the Christian Life

The seven sacraments play a vital role in the church's fulfillment of its mission to be a sacrament of Jesus to the world. They are the rituals by which the church continually symbolizes, celebrates, and brings about the mysterious reality of God's loving action in our life and in our world.

Thus, the sacraments also serve as the grounding points of Christian life for Catholics, providing a fertile soil for faith to grow and thrive. Just as all creatures need food, water, and a healthy environment, so too do Christians need their faith to be fed and nurtured. The seven sacraments offer Catholic Christians a way to satisfy these needs. Therefore, if individuals and communities truly let the sacraments become grounding points for their lives as Christians, they will be empowered to be living examples of Jesus to others.

In summary, the connections between the sacraments, Jesus, and the church can be stated in the following way:

1. A sacrament is a symbol of God's presence, or grace.
2. Jesus is the fullest sacrament of God and full humanness in the world.
3. The church is a sacrament of Jesus to the world.
4. The seven official sacraments of the Catholic church are a special way of symbolizing, celebrating, and bringing about Jesus' real presence in people's lives and in our world.

For Review

- What twofold function do the seven sacraments serve in the Catholic church?
- What is the most effective way for Christians to witness Jesus to others?
- Correlate the seven actions of Jesus listed on page 98 with the seven sacraments of the Catholic church.
- List four insights about the role of the seven sacraments as rituals. Elaborate on two of these insights.
- Explain the following statement: "The sacraments are grounding points for the Christian life."
- Summarize the connections between the sacraments, Jesus, and the church.

The Sacraments in History

Sacraments, or symbolic actions that embody and convey God's grace, have historically played an essential role in the life of the church. However, the seven sacraments celebrated by Catholic Christians today have not always been the only rituals acknowledged by the church as sacraments. Nor have the seven sacraments of today's church been celebrated or interpreted the same way throughout the church's history.

Although each sacrament's particular history will be covered in an individual chapter on that sacrament, the next chapter, chapter 6, will take a look at how the sacraments as a whole developed in the church. As you will see, the sacraments changed as the church itself changed.

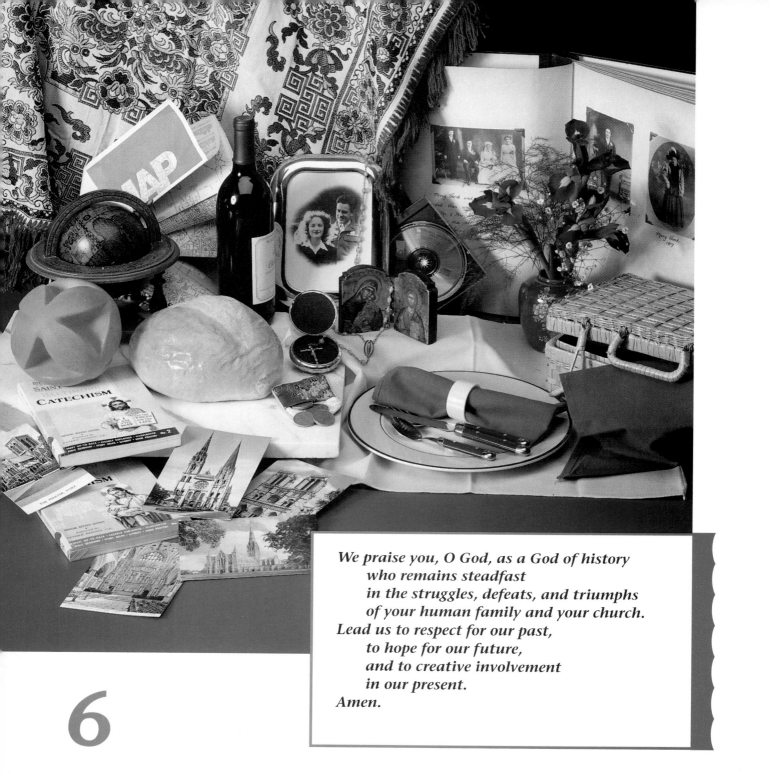

We praise you, O God, as a God of history
    who remains steadfast
        in the struggles, defeats, and triumphs
        of your human family and your church.
Lead us to respect for our past,
    to hope for our future,
    and to creative involvement
    in our present.
Amen.

6

The Sacraments in History: Changing Church, Changing Sacraments

If we are to understand the seven sacraments today, our knowing something about the Catholic church's history of formation and reformation is necessary. Upcoming chapters on each of the seven sacraments will discuss their historical development individually. This chapter will look at four major time periods in the church's history and examine how the significant changes that occurred during these periods affected the church's understanding of the sacraments.

The seven sacraments of the Catholic church, as we now experience them, did not suddenly materialize in the life of the early church. Nor was, or is, the sacraments' existence stone-unchanging. Rather, the church's understanding and awareness of God's presence in the world went through changes, just as family members and their circumstances go through changes—as the following story illustrates.

Sitting out on the deck of their parents' house, three out of Tom and Kate Delaney's six adult children tried to break some unusual news to their parents as gently and honestly as possible. The traditional family get-together at Christmas had become unworkable, and the children wanted a summer gathering at their parents' home instead. Because Tom and Kate would probably be able to hear Sam's "excuse" the easiest, the task of starting things fell to him.

"Ma, we're sorry. I know it means a lot to you and Pa when we come back for Christmas—and it does to us, too—but . . . I don't think we're going to make it this year. Between eight hours in a car with screaming kids and never knowing how bad the weather will be, it's just too much of a hassle. We don't want to get caught spending Christmas in a little podunk motel halfway between here and home like we did that one year—it's really hard with the kids. We're really sorry.

"We were figuring that it might be a lot easier to have everyone get together in July or August instead of at Christmas. What do you think?"

Sam's younger sister, Audrey, spoke up as soon as Sam had finished, knowing that a blow like the one Sam had just delivered needed to be followed up quick with something positive. "Even Marilyn said she'd come home every year if we held our family reunions in the summer," Audrey noted. "We've been lucky to see her every other Christmas."

Piping in to confirm what his sister Audrey had just said, Loren added, "Yeah, Ma. Coming home in the summer's a lot easier and a lot more enjoyable for everyone. We don't have to worry about the weather, and we're not all crammed into the house getting on each other's nerves like when it's zero degrees outside. You know how cranky you get, Pa, when that happens.

In the summertime, when things get too noisy, you can kick us all outside to the yard or onto the deck, like now. Besides, I like it when we go play ball at the schoolyard like we did last night. Can't do that in the winter in Iowa!"

Figuring her father was starting to see the sense of their suggestion, Audrey wanted to slide in an extra bonus. "Just think, Pa—you and Ma not having everyone at home for Christmas means you could come visit Ken and me and the boys in Oklahoma, where it's a lot warmer."

Change and Opportunities for Renewal: Part of Everyone's History

As hard as it was to face their parents, Sam, Audrey, and Loren recognized that things had changed a lot for their family over the past few years. Now that all of them were married, starting families, and living long distances from where they had grown up, trying to get together at Christmas no longer seemed workable. The commitment to getting together once a year was still strong; it was simply time to change when they did it. Now, instead of gathering at Christmastime, the Delaney family would reunite during the summer.

In spite of the loss that they would feel with this change in the "ritual" of their family get-togethers, the Delaney children anticipated the opportunity for renewal for their family. Without having to deal with the stresses of traveling over the holidays and during the winter, they would once again be able to look forward to coming home—rather than dread-

As an essential part of life, change offers opportunities for growth and renewal. Childhood is full of change and thus full of growth.

ing it as they had begun to do. Family get-togethers would once again be appreciated as special and meaningful.

Change: A Fact of Life

As a young person going through a number of changes at this stage in your life, you are probably aware of the fact that life is full of changes and opportunities for renewal and growth. As you grew out of childhood and into adolescence, how you acted, how you dressed, and how you related to others most likely changed considerably. In turn, all these changes allowed you many opportunities for renewal, such as the following:

- letting go of things that were no longer appropriate for you in your new time or place
- confirming or rediscovering what was most important to you
- deepening your understanding of who you are
- establishing new relationships and enriching old ones

Recognizing change and renewal as part of the "facts of life" provides a helpful basis for understanding history— whether we are looking at our own personal "history," the history of our family, school, or country, or even the history of the Catholic church and its sacraments.

1. Describe in writing a major change that you or your family experienced. How did this change offer an opportunity for growth or renewal?

Change, the Church, and the Sacraments

As you read the following broad summary of the history of the church and its sacraments, keep in mind the perspective that change is a fact of life. Although the church is guided by the Holy Spirit and acts as the body of Christ, it is also a human organization. Like any other human organization, the church grew and changed with the passage of time. Change also came for the church when it found itself in new cultural environments and when it was faced with situations where the traditional ways of doing things did not work.

Likewise, change and opportunities for renewal were sometimes deliberately sought by the people of God, particularly when the church realized it had lost touch with some of its original roots. With all the various changes in the church throughout its history, there also came changes in how it expressed itself, particularly in its sacraments.

For Review

- With what perspective can we view change in the church?

Phase One: Church and Sacraments Before 400 C.E.

An Early Convert

This section's glimpse at the Christian church and its understanding of the sacraments during its first four hundred years begins with an imaginary personal sketch of a woman named Paulina, who converted to Christianity. The date for the sketch is around the year 250 C.E.

Paulina lived in a Greek-speaking section of Asia Minor north of Palestine. Religion meant little to her. On occasion, she attended religious services—usually associated with a festival for one of the many popular gods worshiped in her area—out of a sense of civic duty. She did know of groups for whom religion seemed more meaningful. Often these were sects with secret rites.

One such group was the Christians. As an offshoot of Judaism, the Christian religion was known for its strong belief in one God and its high moral standards. Yet Christians also believed the human-divine Jesus had come to usher in a new age. Moreover, they seemed especially concerned about the people who were overlooked by the rest of society: widows, orphans, slaves, foreigners, poor people. Christians' enthusiasm about their religion was even more remarkable considering their religion had been declared illegal. Christians of the time always lived with the possibility of persecution.

Paulina heard stories about a mysterious Christian rite that some claimed was cannibalism and others said was a drunken orgy. Whatever these Christians were doing on Sunday mornings, however, clearly left an impact. The people that Paulina knew to be Christians were joyful in the face of murderous threats. And they promoted a unity and equality in a world where boundaries were solidly built between rich and poor, citizen and noncitizen, free and slave, man and woman.

One day, Paulina heard some Christians preaching in the marketplace. They spoke of their former lives and of how their accepting Jesus as Lord had changed them. Paulina chatted with one of the women in the group, who took the time to tell her the story of Jesus and explain his teachings. The woman then invited her to attend one of their gatherings, which she called an *agape* (pronounced *ah*-gah-pay), or "friendship meal."

Partly out of curiosity, Paulina accepted the invitation and went. She noticed that the small group of people greeted one another warmly, sang psalms with enthusiasm, and listened intently to readings about Jesus that a bishop then applied to their present lives. The woman who had spoken to her earlier then took Paulina aside and explained that the remainder of the celebration was only for baptized members of the community. Through the sharing of bread and wine, the woman explained, Christians believed they shared Jesus' body and blood. She said that by doing this they would enter the mystery of Christ's dying and rising, and it would remind the participants of their commitment to sacrifice themselves in Jesus' name and for his truth.

Paulina was impressed, though still confused. The woman volunteered to be Paulina's sponsor if Paulina wished to begin initiation into the community. The woman used the word *sacrament* for this process of initiation.

Paulina decided to begin. She recognized the risk in becoming a Christian, but the joy, mutual caring, and inner peace that she saw in the community seemed worth the price.

The early Christians gathered regularly for a joyful "friendship meal," at which their sharing of bread and wine became for them a sharing of Jesus' body and blood.

2. If Christianity were illegal in this country today, do you think the church would be stronger or weaker than it is now? Explain your answer in writing.

In Paulina's lifetime, Christianity was a prohibited organization composed of small, secret communities, and it had been illegal since the reign of Roman Emperor Nero (54–68 C.E.). In spite of its illegal status and the periodic persecutions that came with it, the church managed to survive and spread throughout the Mediterranean area from the foundations laid by the Apostles. Increasingly, converts came from the non-Jewish (Gentile) world. Evidence suggests that early Christian missionaries even made their way as far as India!

Early Christian Worship

Christians during Paulina's lifetime would have gleaned their models for community life and ritual celebrations from the examples set by the very first Christian communities described in writings such as Saint Paul's epistles and the Acts of the Apostles. These rituals included baptism, sharing the Lord's Supper, and the laying on of hands.

Formality Begins to Emerge

By the time Paulina sought to become a Christian, around 250 C.E., the church had already become somewhat formal in its worship and ministry. In the sketch, we read about a gathering called a "friendship meal," which has many similarities to today's Mass. There was singing, reading

Because Christianity was prohibited in the early centuries of the church, Christians had to meet secretly to avoid the periodic persecutions by the Roman government. They often gathered in catacombs, or underground passageways with recesses for tombs in the walls.
Photo: The tomb of Saint Callistus, bishop of Rome from 217 to 222, in a catacomb

from the Scriptures, the preaching of a "homily" by the bishop (the ordained leader of the community who presided at its liturgical celebrations), and a sharing of bread and wine. Evidence of formality can also be seen in the sharing of the bread and wine, which was done only by the baptized members of the community. All those who were still preparing to become Christians were taken aside during this time. In Paulina's day, the church also had a formal initiation process for those who wanted to join.

Christian and Pagan Rites Mingle

When new cultural groups converted to Christianity, their traditional religious rites were often mingled with those already in use by Christians. For example, the early church borrowed popular pagan festivals and Christianized them into Christmas and other annual holy days. Likewise, much of the wedding service as we know it originated in common Roman practices. Rings, the mutual kiss, the exchange of promises, and the wedding banquet were all typical elements of weddings in the Mediterranean area before the appearance of Christianity.

The early church's openness to adapting to other cultures is also evident from the fact that the prayers and procedures used at the celebration of the Eucharist differed according to local custom.

3. Imagine that you have been asked to create church customs or celebrations that would reflect current North American teenage culture. List three changes in church practice that you would make.

Early Church Teachings on Sacraments Emerge

About forty years before Paulina became interested in the church, around the year 210, a Christian writer named Tertullian first used the Latin word *sacramentum* in a sense similar to how Catholic Christians use the word *sacrament* today. At the time, Roman religious rites—such as the initiation ceremony for young Romans entering the army—were called *sacramenta*, the plural of *sacramentum*. In his writings on baptism, Tertullian borrowed the word to describe this Christian ritual. Eventually, *sacramenta* was used to describe a whole variety of religious rituals practiced by Christians.

As mentioned earlier, Christians of this historical period looked to the very early church writings (Saint Paul's epistles, the Acts of the Apostles) to find models for their rituals, faith, and practices, including those practices that were now being called *sacramenta*. They wanted to know what these rituals and symbols meant. Based on their own experiences and on what they read in the Scriptures, these Christians began to see the connections between the sacraments and the mysteries of Christian faith. And they began to recognize that these rituals and symbols were true encounters with God.

After Christianity became legal in 313, Christian communities could move "above-ground" to practice their faith openly. Before long, they were building magnificent churches.
Photo: The interior of Santa Maria Maggiore, a basilica constructed in Rome from 432 to 440

Christianity Becomes the Official Religion of the Empire

The prospects for the Christian church's continued survival and growth were given a large boost in the fourth century. First, the emperor Constantine lifted the ban on Christian worship in the year 313. Christians could now gather openly and freely without fear of persecution from government authorities. Then, by the end of that century, Christianity was declared not only legal but the *official religion* of the Roman Empire—a far cry from its previous persecuted status.

Unfortunately, Christianity's big chance came at about the same time that the Roman Empire was in a serious state of decline—both culturally and politically.

For Review

- What were some formal elements present in the church's worship and ministry by around 250 C.E.?
- Who lifted the ban on Christian worship in 313, and what effect did lifting the ban have on Christians and Christianity?

Phase Two:
Church and Sacraments
During the Dark Ages

The period of Western history from about 400 to 1000 C.E. is often called the Dark Ages. The Dark Ages were brought about by the fall of the Roman Empire in the West.

The Fall of the Roman Empire in the West

In the year 326, Constantine, the same emperor who had made Christianity legal, angered the citizens of Rome by refusing to participate in a pagan procession. Subsequently, in the year 330, he moved the Roman Empire's headquarters eastward from Rome to the city of Byzantium—or Constantinople, as the city was renamed. When a succeeding emperor died in 395, the Roman Empire was split in two, never again to be reunited.

Over the next century, the Western Empire was constantly being attacked, first by the Huns from central Asia and then by the Vandals, who sailed across the Mediterranean from North Africa. In 476, the last Roman Emperor in the West was killed. The collapse of the Western Empire soon followed. In the political and cultural chaos resulting from this collapse, the church and its popes would play an increasing role in governing the West.

4. Focus on a time of chaos in the history of your own family, community, or nation. Recall the changes in customs and practices that came about during that time of chaos, and explain in writing how the chaos may have contributed to the changes.

Saint Augustine:
"Administering and Receiving" Sacraments

The general anxiety caused by the decline and fall of the Roman Empire spilled over into the church. By the time Augustine became bishop of the North African city of Hippo in 395, controversy and division plagued the church.

Saint Augustine introduced a way of talking about the sacraments that is still sometimes used today. For Augustine, the sacrament of baptism imprinted a new *character* upon the soul of the person, a character that could not be taken away. (Later on, the same would be said about confirmation and ordination into the priesthood.) This character was said to be "administered" through the sacrament and thus "received" by the person. Eventually, other sacraments were spoken of in "administering and receiving" terms as well. Today there is a move away from this way of talking about the sacraments. Instead, Christians speak about participating in or celebrating the sacraments.

A baptismal font from the Eastern Christian tradition

The Eastern Churches

In 451 C.E., the Council of Chalcedon (the fourth ecumenical, or general, council of the Christian church) declared that the bishop of Rome was the highest authority in the church. At the same time, the patriarch of Constantinople (the head of the church in the East) was named second in authority. Because of the split in the Roman Empire between Rome and Constantinople, relations between the church leaders of the two cities were frequently strained. Eventually, the tensions between western and eastern Christians resulted in a formal split between the churches led by the bishop of Rome and those led by the patriarch of Constantinople.

Today, some of these Eastern Christian churches, which have their roots in Asia, northern Africa, and eastern European countries, are officially united with Roman Catholicism. These are called *Eastern Catholic churches.* But those churches called *Eastern Orthodox churches* are not officially in union with Rome, although relations between the two are more friendly than they have been in the past.

This course only examines the sacraments as they developed in the Western or Roman Catholic tradition, but be aware of the existence of Eastern Christian churches. They too practice the sacraments in their own unique fashion.

"Onion-domed" churches are a familiar sight in Moscow. The Russian Orthodox church is one of the Eastern Christian churches that is not officially in union with Roman Catholicism.

A Broad View of Sacraments

Although Augustine began to narrow down the church's understanding of what constituted a sacrament, he still thought of sacraments in the broad sense as "signs of a sacred thing." To him, sacraments included not only rituals such as baptism but also the sign of the cross, the Lord's Prayer, and the oil used for anointing. In fact, Augustine believed that almost anything could be a sacrament, or a sign of God, because all of creation was a reflection of God.

Some Sacraments Seen as More Important

While believing that many things could be sacraments, Augustine also believed that some sacraments were more important to the church than others. He listed these sacraments of greater importance in two categories: "sacraments of the word," such as sermons, prayers, reading of the Scriptures; and "sacraments of action," such as the various symbols and rituals used in Christian worship. It would be more than eight hundred years before the church restricted its use of the word *sacrament* to the seven official rituals celebrated by Catholic Christians today.

Sacramental Practice in the Dark Ages

After Augustine died, very little new thinking about the sacraments took place until about the eleventh century, largely because of the social and cultural upheaval of the Dark Ages.

During the five hundred years or so following the fall of Rome, the church continued to spread across Europe. With that spread and growth, numerous developments in sacramental practices took place as well. Examples include these developments:

- Confirmation became separated from baptism.
- Public penance was replaced by private confession.
- Lay involvement in the eucharistic liturgy (the Mass) decreased significantly.
- Marriage came to be seen as a sacramental rite.
- Anointing of the sick became anointing of the dying.
- Presbyters were ordained, as well as bishops, to take care of the liturgical functions in the church, doing so as the bishop's representatives.

By the year 1000, social and political stability began to return to Europe, the world of the Roman church. The stability brought with it a revival of activities centered on studying the Christian faith. Once again, the climate was ripe for looking at the meaning of sacramental symbols and rituals.

The exterior of a baptistery in Florence, Italy, built about 1100. An entire building was set aside specifically for baptisms.

For Review

- How does the terminology about sacraments that is encouraged today differ from the terminology introduced by Saint Augustine?
- List three developments in sacramental practices that took place during the Dark Ages.

Phase Three: Church and Sacraments in the High Middle Ages

A Medieval Christian

Whereas growth, formation, risk, and turmoil characterized much of the church's first one thousand years of existence, formality and relative stability were the hallmarks of the period between the years 1000 and 1300, a period often referred to as the High Middle Ages. Let's explore the church's history and its understanding of the sacraments during this period with the help of another imaginary personal sketch, this time of a medieval Christian named Hugh of Lyons.

One thing about Hugh—he knew his place. He was a serf, tied to the land and to his local lord. He was also a Christian; everyone was, except for the pockets of Jews and the infidels across the seas. As a citizen both of his city and of the universal church community known as Christendom, Hugh knew his place.

Hugh had been baptized as an infant and later confirmed by the local bishop. He attended Mass regularly at Lyons Cathedral, which Hugh and his forebears had helped build. The cathedral was a showplace of beauty and splendor and a storybook of stone statues and stained-glass windows. The cathedral contained the tombs of former bishops who had supervised its construction. It also housed numerous relics of saints regarded with respect by the townspeople. Naturally, it attracted pilgrims from great distances.

The cathedral itself was a symbol of harmony and symmetry, giving a clear impression of an orderly universe. Within its walls, statues of the twelve Hebrew prophets faced statues of the twelve Apostles. Pictures of the seven deadly vices were balanced by those of the seven virtues. Everything about the cathedral assured Hugh that the world was united under God. And everyone worshiped there, from bishop and lord to lowly serf.

Hugh's Christian responsibility, as Hugh perceived it, was to obey his local lord and his bishop. At liturgies and other religious events, he was a silent spectator, not a participant. Nonetheless, Hugh was awed by the richness of the ceremonies.

Hugh's identity was intimately linked with being a Christian. He could not conceive of a life apart from Christianity. The vast array of Christian symbols and rituals, and Christianity's dominance in Hugh's society, supported Hugh in this identity. Although he was a mere serf, he fit into his world. At the same time, his work in building up God's Kingdom on earth—for instance, his work on the cathedral—was thought to assure him of a lordly place in heaven.

A Different World

Note the striking contrast between the circumstances experienced by Hugh and those experienced by Paulina, for whom joining the church meant going against the dominant political and cultural forces of her day. For Hugh, to have gone against the dominant culture would have meant *not* being a Christian. In fact, in Hugh's time, the culture of medieval, feudal Europe and that of the Christian church of the West

were pretty much the same. Because most political rulers in medieval Europe were Christian, so were their subjects. Not being a Christian meant not being a citizen. In effect, the church was the center of life for the ordinary citizens of Europe.

Also different for Hugh were his experiences of the church's rituals, which had become much more formal and elaborate in style. By Hugh's time, the friendly informality of the Mass that Paulina attended had long been replaced by grand ceremonies in enormous cathedrals.

In fact, the sacraments in the medieval church had accumulated quite a few "extras" in terms of ornamental details. Part of this accumulation happened because the ceremonies used in the royal courts were often adapted for religious purposes. For example, if, as a medieval person, Hugh had to kiss the ring of an earthly king, he would have felt it only proper to kiss the ring of the Heavenly King's representative, the bishop. Once again, in interacting with its surroundings, the church was naturally influenced by them.

The medieval cathedral was a showplace of beauty and splendor, and a storybook of stone statues and stained-glass windows. *Photo:* A stone archway of the Notre Dame Cathedral in Paris, including statues of the saints

5. Would you rather have been a Christian in Paulina's time or in Hugh's time? State your reasons in a paragraph.

A typical church of the Middle Ages

The Middle Ages: A Significant Time for Sacramental Theology

Part of an explosion of intellectual interests during the High Middle Ages included a renewed interest in the sacraments by Christian scholars. In many ways, the medieval period was a pivotal time, one of the most significant periods of growth and change in the Catholic understanding of sacraments.

Seven Sacraments Made Official

Up until—and into—the twelfth century, Christian writers shared Augustine's broad view of the sacraments; that is, many symbols and rituals were considered sacraments. In fact, one twelfth-century document listed thirty sacraments. By this time, however, the rituals Catholics now know as the seven sacraments were gaining prominence. Then, in the thirteenth century, the Second Council of Lyons affirmed that there were only seven official sacraments of the church, basically those that Catholics celebrate today.

With the word *sacramentum* being restricted in application to the seven rituals of baptism, confirmation, the Eucharist, penance (today called reconciliation), anointing of the dying (now more broadly understood as anointing of the sick), marriage, and ordination into the priesthood, other changes came as well. Rituals became more standardized, and the theological explanations of them became more uniform.

Thomas Aquinas and the Sacraments

The medieval church's understanding of the sacraments reached its peak in the work of Saint Thomas Aquinas. One of the most significant contributions by Thomas Aquinas to the Catholic church's understanding of the sacraments came from his discussion of the sacraments as *causes* of God's grace. That is, not only were sacraments *signs* of sacred reality, as Augustine and others had taught, but the sacraments also served as instruments that actually *brought about* God's grace.

An Emphasis on Correct Form Emerges

Over the years, persons concerned with standardizing the practices of the church (to prevent abuses) picked up on and perhaps overemphasized Thomas Aquinas's idea of sacraments as *causes* of grace. This led to an insistence on the proper performing of the rituals. Guidelines were then set as to the minimum requirements needed for a sacrament to be valid and therefore effective.

Literal Thinking Leads to Magical Thinking

The emphasis on "correct form" in ceremonies encouraged literal thinking. As a result, many people put their faith in proper performance of the externals rather than in any meaning or experience underlying a ritual.

A magical attitude in general: A magical or superstitious attitude toward religion in general invaded many of the church's practices. "Correct forms" and the proper performance of certain actions or rituals were thought to make those rituals effective. Recall the example of Hugh of Lyons, who was thought to have earned a place in heaven because of his work on the cathedral. Here are some more examples of people's magical thinking:

- Special prayers to the Blessed Virgin or the saints were certain to be answered.
- Staring at the Communion host or crucifix guaranteed that a son would be born.
- Touching relics of martyrs or saints assured miraculous healings.
- Making a pilgrimage to Rome or a famous shrine earned merit in heaven.
- Reciting certain prayers at proper times canceled any punishment after death.
- Making a donation to the church released a soul from purgatory.

The Sacred Heart Cathedral in Paris

A magical attitude toward the sacraments: Inevitably, the sacraments were affected by this magical attitude. Merely following the correct forms, it was believed, automatically guaranteed special graces: The priest's words of absolution immediately washed away one's sins; the anointing of a dying person assured him or her of going directly to heaven; and so forth.

Certainly, it was necessary for the church to affirm that a sacrament's power and grace did not rest on the worthiness or holiness of the priest who was its minister. There was much corruption in the clergy at the time, and people needed to know that God's grace, strength, and transformation would be available to them in the sacraments regardless of their priest's personal life.

However, in the process of re-emphasizing this truth, a distortion crept into the popular thinking about the sacraments. The importance of the intent or disposition of the person *receiving* the sacrament was overlooked. It was assumed that the sacrament always "took" in the person regardless of whether the person's heart was receptive to it or whether the person had faith in Jesus as savior. Note that the church never officially promoted such a magical approach to the sacraments. It has always taught that a sacrament will have an effect in a person *according to the person's disposition to it*. But that official teaching did not stop a magical attitude from flourishing among the people.

Setting the Stage for a Religious Revolution

There is something to be said for the spirit of wonder and awe underlying an emphasis on objects and actions properly performed. "Magical" attitudes and practices like those mentioned earlier certainly communicate the awesome power of God and of those persons and things viewed as God's intermediaries—priests, sacred objects (such as the relics of saints), and of course, the elements used in the sacraments. However, a superstitious attitude suggests that God's power can be bought, bargained for, or manipulated to suit one's own ends. Superstition fails to distinguish magic from religion; it represents an attempt to control rather than accept God's power.

Although the superstitious, magical attitude toward the sacraments was never part of the church's official teachings, it was enormously widespread during the Middle Ages. By the late fifteenth and early sixteenth centuries, abuses concerning the sacraments and other church practices were so

6. What do you think is the appeal of magic or superstition? Would you consider yourself superstitious? Explain your answer in writing.

out of hand that the situation was ripe for a religious revolution. In 1517, a monk named Martin Luther publicly protested these abuses, and a religious revolution indeed took place. The movement that Martin Luther sparked was soon known as the Protestant Reformation.

For Review

- Contrast the circumstances experienced by Paulina in the early church with the circumstances experienced by Hugh in the church of the High Middle Ages.
- List the seven sacraments that were affirmed as the official sacraments of the Catholic church in the thirteenth century.
- What significant contribution to the Catholic church's understanding of the sacraments was made by Saint Thomas Aquinas?
- Describe a magical or superstitious attitude toward religion in general and specifically toward the sacraments.

Martin Luther

Phase Four: Church and Sacraments After the Council of Trent

Early Attempts at Reform Fail

As suggested by the prevalence of a magical view toward the sacraments and many other pious practices, the stability and optimism of the High Middle Ages had declined during the two centuries preceding the Protestant Reformation.

Martin Luther's call for church reform, a protest that by then was firmly entwined in the politics of Europe, was by no means the first. In fact, between 1123 and 1517, church leaders officially gathered nine times to deal with clerical and political abuses in the church. By and large, however, these attempts at reforming the church were to no avail.

What came to be called the Protestant Reformation started out as an attempt to reform the Christian church from within. For reasons having as much to do with politics as with religion, the reform movement eventually organized itself into various Protestant denominations that denied the central authority of the pope, the bishop of Rome.

Common Sacramentals After the Council of Trent

In the centuries that followed the Council of Trent, an interesting side effect developed from that council's teachings, in part because of the imposition of uniform practices and uniform theology for the seven sacraments. This side effect was the increased use of unofficial sacraments called *sacramentals,* devotional or pious practices and symbols that helped people get in touch with spiritual realities. Most likely, either your parents or your grandparents, if they were raised as Catholics, will be familiar with some of the following sacramentals.

Prayer books: Prayer books containing devotions, prayers, and reflections on some aspect of the Catholic faith (such as the suffering and death of Christ) became a standard part of Catholic piety.

Devotions to Mary, the Mother of God: Devotions and shrines to the Blessed Virgin, which had long been part of Christianity, gained new momentum in the post-Trent period. Ringing the church bells at noon and praying the Angelus became common practices. Praying the rosary, a practice that began in the Middle Ages, picked up considerable popularity after the Council of Trent. Organizations or religious movements devoted to Mary, such as the Legion of Mary, became commonplace.

Litany prayers: Although its origins were in the Middle Ages, the litany became a more widely used form of communal prayer in the centuries after the Council of Trent. A litany consisted of a list of such things as titles of Christ—or of Mary—or names of the saints. These were read aloud by a prayer leader, and after each one, the congregation would respond with a phrase such as "Pray for us."

Devotion to the Sacred Heart of Jesus: A sacramental image from the sixteenth century that became quite popular during the eigh-teenth century was the Sacred Heart of Jesus. From that time on, it was not uncommon for Catholics to have pictures or statues of the Risen Jesus with his heart exposed from under his garment and enlarged with burning love.

The way of the cross: Another sacramental that gained popularity during the post-Trent period was "the way of the cross." Even today, most Catholic church buildings have fourteen stations of the cross on their walls depicting the suffering and Crucifixion of Jesus. Making the way of the cross is still a part of the Catholic observance of Lent—in particular, the Good Friday observance.

Devotion to the Blessed Sacrament: An extremely popular and widespread devotional practice following the Council of Trent was the adoration of the Blessed Sacrament. The term *Blessed Sacrament* refers to the consecrated Communion bread that is stored in the tabernacle in the church sanctuary; Catholics believe that the consecrated bread is the body of Jesus Christ. Originally, a forty-hour period of continual prayer and devotion to the Blessed Sacrament was part of the Holy Thursday observance during Lent. At the time of the Council of Trent, in the sixteenth century, this devotional practice began to be employed outside of Holy Week as well. Eventually, a shorter ritual called the Benediction of the Blessed Sacrament became a common religious practice in Catholic parishes. Today, for many Catholics, this practice is still a much-loved way to revere the Eucharist.

The Council of Trent: The Catholic Church's Reformation

Although leaders in the Catholic church felt attacked by the reformers, they also recognized that many of the grievances were legitimate. To respond to these grievances, as well as to the doctrinal challenges of the reformers, the Council of Trent was convened in 1545 and met off and on until 1563.

Addressing the Major Complaints

One of the major complaints of the reformers was that the church took a casual attitude toward the popular superstitions previously mentioned. As a result, essential beliefs such as grace and faith in God had become distorted.

To accomplish reform, the Council of Trent first legislated practical changes aimed at eliminating abuses. Second, it reaffirmed the belief that although the importance of performing good works cannot be denied, grace is an unmerited gift from God that cannot be bargained for.

Focusing on the Sacraments

The Council of Trent gave much of its attention to the sacraments. In fact, over half of the doctrinal teachings put forth by the Council of Trent dealt with the sacraments. The council participants felt the need to be very exact about the

Saint Peter's Basilica in Vatican City, Rome, which houses the tomb of Saint Peter, was renovated and added to around the period of the Reformation to become the structure familiar to us today.

church's beliefs and practices pertaining to the sacraments. Otherwise, the sacramental rituals and practices would have little consistent foundation, and people might interpret or recognize them differently. Many Protestant groups, for example, recognized only baptism and the Eucharist as sacraments; other groups taught that there were no sacraments.

Two main points stressed by the Council of Trent about the sacraments are as follows:

1. There are seven—and *only* seven—sacraments. Council leaders declared that there were "not more nor less than" seven sacraments. Other devotions, like the rosary, were termed *sacramentals*. (*Sacramentals* are religious practices, or holy objects used in religious practices, that can be spiritually enriching but that are less central to Catholic Christian faith than the seven official sacraments.)

2. The church approves a scholastic understanding of the sacraments. The theology of Thomas Aquinas and his successors, which was known as Scholasticism, was deemed the official Catholic interpretation of the sacraments. In particular, the council picked up on the idea of the sacraments as causes of grace and declared that the sacraments were necessary for salvation.

The Council of Trent: Its Impact on the Church and the Sacraments

The two major emphases of the Council of Trent on how the sacraments would be understood and practiced, as well as the other teachings that came from the council, literally defined Catholicism for the next four hundred years. Further changes were not made until the Second Vatican Council met (from 1962 to 1965). In particular, the Council of Trent had these two effects:

1. Because the Council of Trent approved only a scholastic understanding of the sacraments, no new ways of thinking about or different ways of talking about the sacraments were permitted.

2. Soon after the Council of Trent, the official Roman missal for the Mass and an official book on the rites of the other sacraments were published. Both of these publications, which had to be used by all Roman Catholic dioceses throughout the world, imposed greater uniformity in how the sacraments were practiced—including the language used (Latin), the words said, the actions used, and the performance of these actions. Neither book underwent substantial changes until the 1960s.

Pope John XXIII, 1958–63

In short, the trend toward standard practices and a unified understanding of the sacraments that began in the Middle Ages became solidified with the Council of Trent.

Much of this uniformity was done to protect the sacraments from the kinds of abuses that came about prior to the Council of Trent. As a result, however, Catholic Christians were given very little room to adapt the symbols and rituals of the sacraments to fit their changing culture or time period. Thus, a Mass in South America prior to the mid-1960s would have been nearly identical to one celebrated in Italy or the United States.

Nearly four hundred years passed before the Catholic church made any significant changes in its official sacramental teachings and practices. This was part of the challenge that Pope John XXIII asked church leaders to address at the Second Vatican Council.

7. In two columns labeled + and –, list what you think would be the pluses and minuses of standardizing the Mass and other rituals of the Catholic church, so that a Mass in one area of the world would look and sound just like a Mass in another region.

For Review

- Briefly explain why the Protestant Reformation came about.
- What two main points about the sacraments did the Council of Trent stress?
- Define *sacramentals*.
- Describe the trend regarding the sacraments that became solidified with the Council of Trent.

A 1950s Teenager's Experience of the Pre–Vatican II Church

You may have heard your parents or other relatives talk about how different being Catholic was before Vatican Council II. The following story offers a glance at what the pre–Vatican II Catholic church was like from the perspective of a teenager in the 1950s.

As you read Jerry's story, notice how many of the practices date back to the period in the church immediately following the Council of Trent in the sixteenth century. Although the piety and the devotional practices described may seem strange to persons who have grown up in a post–Vatican II church, these things were nonetheless important and familiar to many generations of Catholics.

Jerry hated to hear his mom yell "Rise and shine, rise and shine!" so early on Sunday morning. He wanted to sleep in. Last night, he had gone to the sock hop after the season's final basketball game. Then he, Charlie, and Scott had driven to the local Howard Johnson's for a bag of fried clams. Following their usual ritual, they had cruised over to Duck's Drive-in for dessert, but two guys were punching each other out at Duck's, so they headed home.

In any case, Jerry knew he had to roll out of bed for 8:00 a.m. Mass. He knew he didn't dare miss going to Mass. As his parents and the nuns at school had drilled into his head, "It's church law. If you miss Mass, it's a mortal sin." Although Jerry didn't quite understand why not going to Mass was a mortal sin, he had just enough fear of eternal fire that he followed orders. One thing Jerry did know was that going to "first Friday" Masses was worthwhile. He wanted to make sure he had enough indulgences stored up to keep himself out of purgatory.

"Hurry up, Jerry, for Pete's sake!" his mom yelled from the back door. "And wake up! You have to serve Mass this morning, remember?"

Jerry and his family drove to Mass. His dad listened closely to a funny sound coming from the engine, shushing Jerry's mom, who was wondering aloud who would be saying Mass. Jerry wondered himself, feeling the butterflies start up in his stomach at the thought of serving for Monsignor Kearney. His mother often complained about Monsignor Kearney. "He just isn't pious enough," she would harrumph. This was true, Jerry reflected. The monsignor was known for zipping through even Solemn High Mass in a blur of fuzzy Latin and frenetic blessings.

As usual, Monsignor Kearney led everyone in praying the Litany of the Saints before Mass began. When Mass was under way, Jerry—dressed in his black cassock—forgot his butterflies. He had to be on his toes serving High Mass. Between switching the missal from the Gospel side to the epistle side, saying the Latin responses correctly, hurrying to get the cruets of water and wine, and washing Monsignor's hands, Jerry didn't have time to be nervous. He didn't even get much rest during Monsignor's sermons, which were never long. They were also predictable. Monsignor had two favorite topics: the need to give money to the church and the need for constant vigilance against the devil's wiles. Both were necessary, Monsignor continually reminded the people, so that they "would not lose their souls to eternal damnation." At the end, he exhorted the congregation to pray to the Virgin Mary for intercession.

The biggest challenge Jerry faced when serving for Monsignor Kearney was keeping up with him as he distributed Communion. Monsignor gave out Communion so fast that Jerry could barely back up quick enough. People knelt at the altar rail, stuck out their tongues, received Communion, and got up hurriedly. They filed back to their pews with their hands folded in church steeples and eyes cast down. All that could be heard during Communion was the shuffling of the communicants' feet and the occasional rattling of rosary beads on the wooden pews. The kneeling communicants said their prayers silently.

When he wasn't serving Mass, Jerry liked to gaze at his favorite stained-glass window—the one of the prodigal son being forgiven by his father—after receiving Communion. Just looking at the scene calmed him. He had heard that the story was really about God's forgiveness toward sinful humans. Jerry liked to think that God would always be merciful with him.

"Ite, missa est," Monsignor intoned. *Go, you are dismissed.*

"Deo gratias," the congregation responded. *Thanks be to God.*

As Jerry snuffed out the altar candles after Mass that morning, a strange and disconcerting thought swept over him. He actually enjoyed going to Mass, especially serving for it. Somehow, he felt part of a fascinating mystery that went beyond not completely understanding all the Latin.

Almost as quickly as this strange thought popped into his head, Jerry looked around to make sure no one was watching him. He knew he had best keep such thoughts to himself or his friends would start calling him "Father Jerry."

Phase Five: Church and Sacraments in the Twentieth Century

The Church Rediscovers Its Roots

By the late nineteenth and early twentieth centuries, the Catholic church's defensive stance toward the emerging modern world began to subside. Among the many contributing factors to the church's more open attitudes were several developments happening within the church. Around this time, Catholic scholars began to look closely at the teachings of Thomas Aquinas, the worship practices of the early church, and the biblical roots of the Christian faith.

When people began looking back into the history of the church in the Middle Ages and earlier, they discovered that church practices and ways of expressing its theology had not

Pope John XXIII called for an ecumenical council, Vatican Council II, to "open the windows" of the Catholic church and "let in the fresh air"—that is, to examine all aspects of church teachings and practices in an open, forthright manner.

always been the same as they were at the present time. Although this may seem like an obvious fact to us living in the 1990s, it was a liberating realization at the time. Eventually, these new developments within the church led Pope John XXIII to call the Second Vatican Council in the 1960s.

The Second Vatican Council: A Call for Change and Renewal

By calling the Second Vatican Council, or Vatican Council II, Pope John XXIII declared that it was time to examine all aspects of church teachings and practices in an open and forthright manner, using the best information and insights of modern thought. He wanted to open the windows and let in fresh air, so to speak.

Reclaiming the Past

Chief among the concerns at Vatican Council II was helping the church get back in touch with those aspects of its tradition, especially from the early church, that had been lost or neglected over the centuries. Regaining such elements, the bishops felt, would help the church better respond to the contemporary world.

Unlike previous councils in the Catholic church, Vatican Council II questioned the appropriateness of continuing the Council of Trent's rigid approach to the sacraments. Given the social and cultural changes that had occurred in the world and within the church itself since the Council of Trent, the church recognized the need to open itself up to other ways of thinking about and practicing the sacraments. Delving into the past and seeing the differences that existed there helped everyone in the church realize that the church's theology and sacramental practices had been changing all the time.

Keeping the Clear, Letting Go of the Cloudy

In the Second Vatican Council, the church committed itself to renewal based on a fresh look at its origins and its long history. It saw that over the years, many of the changes had helped bring out the true meaning of the sacraments. These changes, the council leaders decided, were worth keeping or reinstating. Other changes were not necessarily for the better. For instance, over the centuries, many unwanted practices and notions had "crept into" the sacramental life of the church and were clouding the true spirit of the sacraments. These other changes, the council leaders decided, should be discarded.

A Continuing Challenge

With Vatican Council II, the Catholic church entered a new phase in its history and understanding of the sacraments. Once church leaders had studied the historical development of the sacraments, they saw that change and renewal were necessary and even natural. At the same time, they also realized that a great challenge faced the church. This was the challenge of keeping the church's teachings on the sacraments in line with the Spirit of Jesus and allowing the church's sacramental practice to be an effective instrument of God's grace in the world.

Since the Second Vatican Council, the seven sacraments have undergone changes for the specific purpose of pointing more clearly to the one sacrament who is the center of Christian belief: Jesus. This focus continues today, over thirty years later. The Second Vatican Council also serves as a reminder to the church that the challenge of growth is to remain true to one's spirit while facing the changes that inevitably come along.

8. Interview a Catholic person old enough (forty-five or older) to remember the early changes in the sacraments that occurred following the Second Vatican Council. Find out how he or she reacted to the changes at the time. Write up the results of your interview.

For Review

- How did leaders at the Second Vatican Council decide which changes in the rituals of the church should be kept and which should be discarded?
- What challenge regarding the sacraments did the church face after the Second Vatican Council?

Mariama—
The Church of the Future

During the past few decades, the number of Catholic churches has been growing rapidly in the southern half of our world. These relatively young churches with youthful members typically exhibit an enthusiasm for and a delight in the Christian message. Their members—Asian, African, or Latin American—bring unique cultural expressions to their celebrations of the sacraments.

In large part, the vitality of these young churches is possible because of the openness reintroduced to the church by Vatican Council II. Here is the story of one modern Christian who is helping to shape the church of the future.

Mariama has been active in her local Christian community ever since her baptism four years ago. Like many people in her village, Mariama has found in Christianity a cause for hope in an often bleak existence. In particular, she finds the Masses held in her simple village church to be moving experiences. She appreciates how the Masses blend the beauty of the Catholic liturgy with elements from her own African and tribal customs. The festive atmosphere that surrounds the Christmas season is a special source of joy and excitement for her and her community. The story of the Christ Child coming into the world to bring peace and good news to poor people is a story she enjoys hearing over and over.

Mariama has five children. She performs regular household chores, along with tending a small stand at the village market. Yet she still finds the time to attend meetings and prayer sessions at the local church hall. For Mariama, spending time with other Christian women provides the spiritual support and physical contact that keep her spirits up.

When Mariama was a small child, she saw Christianity as the religion of the white European and American missionaries. Now, members of the local Catholic Christian communities and most of their leaders are native Africans. Mariama has seen a growing number of young African women becoming religious sisters working in schools, hospitals, and community centers. Although books and other educational materials are scarce, a real hunger for learning more about the Christian religion exists, especially among the young people in her village. For Mariama and her friends, a discussion about Bible stories often becomes the starting point for similar discussions about family or community events.

Mariama lives a simple life in which basic necessities are barely met—or sometimes not met. Being Christian has helped her question the injustice of her poverty, given her confidence and a community with which to work for change, and provided her with hope for a brighter future.

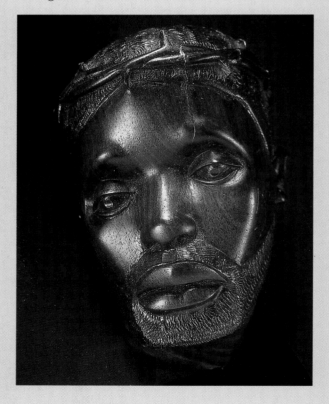

An African wood sculpture of Jesus

The Seven Sacraments

In one of his novels, writer Kurt Vonnegut introduces an alien being who can see forward and backward in time—just as we might look out over a range of mountains, seeing behind us and in front of us. If we could see our own life this way, all at once, it might look very much like a mountain range with peaks and valleys. And at the bottom of each valley, there is often a stream or a river or a lake. To get to the next mountain, we have to make a crossing. Some of these crossings are just simple jumps across narrow streams. Others are frightening voyages across wide lakes or wild rivers.

The seven sacraments point to the fact that we have many such crossings in our life. For example, we face many new beginnings or rebirths, as symbolized by baptism. We confront other crucial crossings related to belonging, caring, forgiving, serving, healing, and worshiping. The next seven chapters will deal specifically with each of these crossings. By celebrating all of these important crossings, the seven sacraments reflect the whole range of human crossings—from birth to death.

At the same time that the sacraments echo life's crossings, the sacraments' strong connection to the paschal mystery suggests that people can get through life's crossings. At those moments when they feel daunted or trapped by hazardous crossings, Catholics can look to the sacraments to remind them of a mysterious, miraculous truth: Jesus' crossing was a journey through death to new life.

Let's turn our attention now to the seven sacraments celebrated by Catholic Christians.

Like a mountain range, life is full of crossings that can present us with great challenges. The seven sacraments celebrate those crossings and help us find meaning and purpose in them.

Giver of Life, be born in me.
I welcome you as you welcome new members
    into your church at baptism.
May my life say welcome to all those
    who cross my path.
May my life become new
    as I open myself
    to your Spirit.
Amen.

7

Baptism: Celebrating Welcome and Rebirth

We have arrived at the first of the seven official sacraments of the Catholic church. Baptism is one of the three sacraments of initiation, which celebrate a Christian's transformation, entrance, and lifelong growth in the community of Jesus' followers, the church.

In the early centuries of Christianity, the other two sacraments of initiation—confirmation and the Eucharist—were united with baptism and celebrated in one ritual as part of the process of becoming a Christian. Today, adults who join the Catholic church go through a process similar to what the early converts experienced, celebrating all three sacraments together. But for small children and infants entering the church, baptism is celebrated as a separate sacrament, with confirmation and the Eucharist following at a later age. The significance of baptism is best explained by the adult experience of this sacrament, the "original" version. So let's begin our study of baptism by considering a different but related kind of adult initiation.

David couldn't believe it: He really was in a new world, at a college halfway across the country from his home. He had dreamed of this day since ninth grade. Now he was at his first day of college orientation in a city he had never been to, in a college he had only read about, in a building he had seen only in pictures. David was trying to appear cool and calm, to pretend it didn't bother him not to know anyone on campus. He wanted to act like he knew exactly what he was doing and where he was going, but he knew his act wouldn't be much of a success. He couldn't even find his assigned dorm.

Lining up in a gym with four hundred other new students, David waited to pick up his packet of information on the orientation and the college. When he was handed his packet, a guy came forward, a good-natured grin on his face. "You're David," he said, shaking David's hand. "Yeah, I'm Tony. I'll be showing you around this week. You got any questions, just ask me. This is my third year here. I know how it feels to be in your shoes—just starting out. It's pretty overwhelming at first, but I think you'll get to like it here. I do. Say, where are you from, anyway?"

David and Tony swapped stories about backgrounds and interests as they walked across campus to David's dorm, stopping first to see the Student Center and the cafeteria.

"The food's not terrific," Tony said. "For lunch I usually go to the snack bar and get a sandwich. That way I know it's fresh. Desserts are good—especially their homemade ice cream." Somehow, David no longer felt the need to act cool and experienced. Here was someone who expected him to be curious about everything and would just be a friend while he got used to things.

We have all experienced feeling welcomed, as well as feeling isolated or left out.

Before the first day of the week-long orientation was over, David was more at ease. Not only did he have Tony to show him the ropes, but he had been teamed up with five other first-year people to talk about what the transition from high school to college meant to them. Already David was making friends.

By the end of the week, David felt much more at home, and his enthusiasm had soared. Now he knew lots of people, both newcomers like himself and upper-level students like Tony. He had heard talks from student leaders, teachers, and administrators, and he had registered for classes. The risk he had taken by plunging himself into his new world was beginning to pay off. Already he could sense the great transformation that college life held in store for him.

Many factors were contributing to David's transformation: the independence of living away from home, the new and exciting relationships, the sense of purpose he felt about his classes and his future, the feeling of belonging to a great college and sharing in the college's own special spirit. . . . David was amazed: He felt like a brand-new person!

Despite all of his internal and external changes, David realized vaguely that his transformation had just begun. But he was ready for more growth. He couldn't wait to get on with it.

The changes David went through during his college orientation week were just drops compared to the ocean of changes he would go through in the next four years. David could not possibly anticipate all the highs and lows, the achievements and disappointments, the undreamed-of adventures that were to come. But he had already opened himself to these experiences.

Welcome or Alienation?

In the near future, you may face challenges similar to the challenges faced by David in the previous story. Someday, certainly, you will find yourself at a crossroads, perhaps feeling isolated and in need of friends, support, and reassurance. In fact, you may already be familiar with that experience.

Which comes closer to your experience of the world—a world of alienation and cold stares, or a world of friendliness and welcome? You have probably encountered the world as a lonely, impersonal place at some times; you have likely found it warm and welcoming at other times. Both portraits of the world are real.

Most of us were born into a welcoming family filled with smiles, support, and sharing. Every human baby needs at least some touching and affection just to survive, so our needs were met in a survival sense. At the same time, however, we were born into a world in which alienation and imperfections exist and are inevitable. A baby's complex physical and psychological needs cannot always be met (or understood!), even by the best-intentioned parents, so every child is bound to feel lonely or abandoned at times. We all discover that the world can be an unfriendly or even hurtful place beyond the security of home or loved ones. And from an early age, most of us have cautionary messages drummed into us: "Stay away from that part of town." "Don't talk to strangers!"

Thus, from birth on, we all have experiences that parallel David's experience of walking through a threshold into a new life, experiences where we face either alienation or welcome.

1. Write about a situation in which you felt uncomfortable and unwelcome. Then, write about a situation in which you felt at ease and welcome. Focus on what made the difference for you.

What Does Baptism Celebrate?

David's initiation into the world of college had these characteristics:
- He was welcomed into the college community.
- He began the long-term process of learning and growing in a new, transforming way of life—college life.
- He left behind an old identity (high school graduate) for a new one (college student).
- He took on a new sense of purpose connected with being in college.
- He felt the spirit that energized the college.

The initiation into the Christian faith highlighted by the sacrament of baptism has certain parallels with David's journey from alienation to belonging through his college orientation. Christian initiation, and baptism in particular, celebrates these realities for the Christian:

- being welcomed into the community of Jesus, the church
- beginning a lifelong conversion process of learning and growing in the Christian way of life
- being reborn to a new identity as a Christian
- sharing in the mission of Jesus and adopting it as one's own life purpose
- receiving the gift of the Spirit of Jesus that animates the Christian community

A Welcome into Jesus' Community

Most of us have experienced feeling both welcome and unwelcome in a group. When you have to linger around the edges of a group, hoping to be noticed and subtly trying to be accepted, you probably do not feel welcome, even if the group members do not reject you outright. People do not have to be cruel to be unwelcoming toward others; they just have to fail to take initiative with others. David, on his first day at college, faced the unknown with fear and insecurity. He began to feel more comfortable when Tony noticed him and made an effort to help him feel like he belonged.

God Takes the Initiative

Baptism celebrates the good news that God takes the initiative with us human beings. We do not have to do anything to be "noticed" by God. God is always pouring out love and acceptance to us personally, inviting us to share in God's own life of love. God's ever-present, inviting love for us, personally, is another meaning of the term *grace*.

Through baptism, the Christian community—on Jesus' behalf and thus on God's behalf—takes the initiative in welcoming persons into a life of loving relationships, whether these persons are infants or adults.

A Warm and Welcoming Church

Ideally, local Christian churches would be such warm, welcoming communities that outsiders would sense something remarkably alive about them. People would feel accepted, embraced by the inclusive love of God's open heart. Most people are hungry for that kind of experience, and when they see a spirited community, they feel drawn to it. In fact, the parish and school communities where teenagers and adults are coming into the church in great numbers are characteristically vital, caring communities; they are a sign of God's outstretched arms.

2. If you were to create an entrance-way banner welcoming people to a local parish church, what would your banner look like? Draw a sketch of your banner and include your written message of welcome.

The Old Life of Sin	The New Life in Christ

Sin	Grace
Death	Life
Fear	Courage
Slavery	Freedom
Alienation	Welcome
Isolation	Community
Hoarding	Sharing

A Lifelong Conversion

Turnabout and Transformation

Christians believe that an experience of the unconditional welcome extended by God leads to making a turnabout in one's life, to reorienting one's life and seeing and acting in new ways. The world looks different to those who experience God's love: They become aware of the bonds that unite them with every other human being, and they believe that life asks something more of them than a humdrum, "same old thing" existence.

David, in the opening story, experienced a turnabout in his first week at college. He went from the familiarity of living at home, going to high school, and socializing with his high school buddies to a new life of more independence, more responsibility, and new ways of relating with friends. He felt transformed, even after a single week, and he had opened himself to further changes on the horizon.

In a similar way, Christian conversion marks a profound change in the way people perceive themselves, other people, and the world. Baptism celebrates this turnabout, not with the expectation that the profound change is once-and-for-all accomplished but with the hope that it has just begun and will be a lifelong process.

From an Old Life of Sin to a New Life in Christ

God created people free to accept or reject love, free to choose good or bad. History's wars, persecutions, discrimination, and exploitation give testimony to the fact that people have not always made good choices.

The human tendency to make shortsighted and self-serving choices over grace-filled, wise, and generous choices has been termed *original sin.* The destructive effects of this tendency to choose evil are evident as far back as human beings can recall (as represented by the story of Adam and Eve in the Garden of Eden).

Christian conversion reorients people's lives, changing the way people see themselves, others, and the world.

The conversion of baptism does not happen all at once. Rather, it is like looking through mist that only gradually rises from a lake; we see more clearly over time.

In the Rite of Baptism, an adult says no to sin and yes to God's life of grace, which is more powerful than any sin or any destruction wreaked by sin over centuries. For children too young to comprehend the choice, their parents and sponsors say yes by renewing their own baptismal promises, with the understanding that they will try to guide the children toward grace and away from sin. This yes implies that the person believes and will try to live out these truths in the world:

- Grace can overcome sin.
- Life can triumph over death.
- Courage can banish fear.
- Freedom to live joyfully in God can overcome slavery to destructive patterns.
- A spirit of welcome can banish alienation.
- Community can replace isolation.
- Sharing can dissolve hoarding.

Baptism is not magic. Saying yes to God's life of love will not make sin disappear or melt away the legacy of sin's tragic effects. The conversion to a new way of life, which is symbolized and celebrated in baptism, will go on for a lifetime.

3. Reflect on the list of truths in the adjoining column—the truths that Christians try to live out in the world. Choose the statement that most appeals to you and explain its appeal for you in writing.

Born Again to a New Identity

To appreciate baptism as an opportunity for rebirth, we need to know something about the life that is left behind and even more about the life that is embraced in this sacrament.

An incident from John's Gospel describes some puzzling remarks that Jesus made about the "rebirth" of baptism:

> Now there was a Pharisee named Nicodemus, a leader of the Jews. He came to Jesus by night and said to him, "Rabbi, we know that you are a teacher who has come from God; for no one can do these signs that you do apart from the presence of God." Jesus answered him, "Very truly, I tell you, no one can see the kingdom of God without being born anew." Nicodemus said to him, "How can anyone be born after having grown old? Can one enter a second time into the mother's womb and be born?" Jesus answered, "Very truly, I tell you, no one can enter the kingdom of God without being born of water and Spirit. What is born of the flesh is flesh, and what is born of the Spirit is spirit." (3:1–6)

Nicodemus at first did not understand what Jesus meant when he said we must be "born anew," or "born again." Nicodemus heard the phrase literally, not symbolically. So what did Jesus actually mean?

Born into Risen Life

In speaking of being born anew, Jesus was referring to the inner transformation that comes from people's experience of God's Spirit in their life. Instead of experiencing a new physical birth, people would experience a birth into the Spirit, a rebirth into God's life after passing through a kind of "death." Imagine what rebirth into God's life might mean:

- We notice our parents arguing with each other more and more. Their divorce seems almost certain. Can we survive a family breakup? Rebirth into God's life reminds us that Jesus journeys with us through all the suffering and dying in our life.
- We struggle with decisions about our priorities in life, about how to balance looking out for ourselves with giving ourselves to others. Remembering that we are born anew into God's life colors the way we look at our life decisions. We try to see things as Jesus would.
- We think back on our childhood experiences and recognize that we carry within us many old wounds from disappointments or mistreatment. The rebirth of baptism affirms that Jesus the healer shares our life. In the end, we are never alone.

4. Imagine how rebirth into God's life might affect a troubling situation in your own life. Describe one possible outcome of that situation in a paragraph.

Baptism, then, plunges a person into the paschal mystery. Through baptism, Christians are united with Jesus in his life, death, and Resurrection.

Dying and Rising: An Ongoing Process

Recall again the story of David's entering college. After his first week there, David had a sense of a new identity, but his identity would develop and grow throughout his years in college. Just as David's experience of growth was gradual, the process of rebirth into Christian identity does not happen all at once. Baptism celebrates the mystery of our being continually reborn, every day of our life. We do not "die and rise with Christ" once but over a lifetime of many "deaths and resurrections," of losses followed by new growth, of failures followed by deeper understandings and victories of the spirit. Our rebirth is ongoing; we are never finished being born again until we reach our eternal destiny of union with God.

Perhaps you have heard the phrase "born-again Christian" and wondered what it really means. Some people may ask you pointedly, "Have you been born again?" and they may even want to know exactly *when* in your life you were born again. When these Christians use the phrase "born again," they are referring to a one-time-only, supposedly life-changing event in which a person accepts Jesus as Lord and Savior. It is obvious that this notion differs significantly from the Catholic understanding of rebirth. Baptism itself celebrates a process of dying and rising to new life within a community, a process that happens over and over again in a person's lifetime.

Sharing in the Mission of Jesus

In the opening story, college-newcomer David finds a new sense of purpose in his life during his orientation. He may also at times wonder about his purpose beyond college.

A Life Purpose

Many of us ask ourselves big questions like these:
- What am I going to do with my life?
- What am I here for?
- What's my life all about, anyway?

When we ask ourselves these questions, we are considering our basic purpose in life.

Jesus' Priority: The Reign of God

With initiation into God's life, the Christian shares in the larger life purpose that Jesus calls his followers to. For instance, Christian initiation challenges Christians to look at

5. Choose one of the questions in the adjoining column on this page, reflect on it, and write down your reflections.

war with a different attitude, to show concern for people who are different or distant from themselves, and to think critically about the values that are popular in a culture.

In Jesus' set of priorities, life is not simply about taking care of our own needs and wants and those of our family. Jesus' life purpose, and therefore his followers' life purpose, is to usher in the reign of God's justice and peace in the world. The Christian's personal life goals are still important—like getting an education, finding meaningful work, and raising a family. But these goals become just part of the larger life purpose—carrying on Jesus' mission, a task Jesus entrusted to his church. In identifying with Jesus' life purpose, Christians will no doubt encounter suffering, but they will also experience a deeper, more-lasting happiness than the kind that can be attained through success or money.

Conversion and rebirth, as described earlier, do not happen suddenly and completely. Likewise, a person's commitment to Jesus' life purpose does not happen instantaneously with baptism, even for adult converts. That commitment takes a lifetime of growing into it. Baptism—and indeed, the whole process of initiation—celebrates that the commitment has begun.

Christians share in the larger life purpose that Jesus calls his followers to—building the Reign of God through a compassionate, inclusive lifestyle.

Receiving the Gift of the Spirit of Jesus

Recall that one outcome of David's college orientation was that he shared in a certain spirit of the college. That spirit was apparent in the enthusiasm and the interest of individuals he met that week, but it was bigger than just personal attitudes. It seemed to characterize the college as a whole. Your high school probably has its own "school spirit." Sports teams, too, are said to have "team spirit." Becoming part of those groups entails catching the spirit, energy, and vitality that seem to breathe life into the groups.

For the Christian, initiation also involves "catching the spirit" of the Christian community. But the "spirit" that enlivens, moves, and guides the community at the deepest level is Jesus' own Spirit, poured out on the disciples at Pentecost, after Jesus' Resurrection, and continually poured out in history even to the present moment. To become a Christian is to become a "Spirit-ed" person, living in Jesus' risen life, because the person shares in the Spirit-life of the Christian community and is thus enlivened, moved, and guided by that Spirit.

In summary, baptism, as the first of the sacraments of initiation, celebrates these realities in the new Christian's life: welcome, conversion, rebirth, commitment to Jesus'

6. In writing, describe what you like best about your school's or your team's spirit. Illustrate your description by recounting at least three concrete incidents in which that spirit was displayed.

mission, and the gift of Jesus' Spirit. Initiation, however, is not a one-time-only event; it is a lifelong process. Christians are always being initiated more profoundly into the mystery of Christ; they are never "all the way there." The sacrament of baptism celebrates that this process has begun and that it will continue every day.

For Review

- Name the three sacraments of initiation. In general, what do these sacraments celebrate?
- What five realities for the Christian are celebrated in baptism?
- What is meant by the term *original sin?*
- What did Jesus mean when he spoke of being "born anew"?
- How does the Catholic church's understanding of the phrase "born again" differ from some other Christians' interpretation of that phrase?

Baptism's Symbols and Rituals

In baptism, as in all the sacraments, the Christian community—the church—is the primary symbol. In welcoming new members, the Christian community represents God, who takes the initiative in inviting us into divine life. In addition, four symbols in the Rite of Baptism express different realities of the sacrament. These special symbols are water, oil, a white (or new) garment, and a lighted candle.

Each of these symbols is rich in meaning, and any discussion of their symbolic power is bound to be incomplete. So before reading on, take a few moments to make a list of the meanings that you associate with each of these symbols.

Water: Cleansing and Life-giving

A Natural Symbol

For refreshment or recreation, we often use water. We can drink it, swim in it, ski on it, walk near it, listen to it. Water can restore our energy by cooling us on a hot day and by cleansing us when we are dirty or sweaty. We also get some of our food from fresh and salt waters. And without rainwater, most of what we eat could not grow.

Water is vital for human life: We cannot live without it for more than five days. And although we ourselves did not actually come from water, we do have evolutionary relatives who lived in the sea. It seems, too, that we may not have left the sea far behind; the human body is over 70 percent water.

Of course, water can be destructive as well as creative. Persons who live in places liable to floods know this only too well, as do swimmers and sailors. Being plunged into water can be a deadly experience.

Scriptural Meanings

Water has special meaning for the Christian community. In the Hebrew Scriptures, in the very beginning of the Book of Genesis, God breathes on the waters to bring order to Creation. Later, in the story of Noah, the world of sin is destroyed and washed clean through the waters of a flood.

In the Book of Exodus, Moses leads the Israelites out of slavery in Egypt by guiding them miraculously, with God's power, through the great "sea of reeds" and toward freedom and new life in the Promised Land. That sea-crossing was the first step in a long journey for the Israelites. On the way, God provided them with life-giving water just when they were feeling hopeless, afraid they would die of thirst wandering in the desert.

In the Christian Testament, too, water has great significance. Jesus himself is baptized in the water of the Jordan River. Later, Jesus would refer to the life he offers people as the "living water." It is no wonder that water is the essential symbol of Christian baptism.

Taking the Plunge

In the early years of the Christian church, baptisms were performed in rivers and streams. The converts would be plunged into the water to symbolize their being cleansed of sin and their dying to an old way of life. Their coming up again would show that they were rising to a new life, a new identity, in Christ. Even when baptisms moved indoors, new Christians were immersed in a pool of water as a sign of embracing the mystery of Christ's death and Resurrection. Their plunge into the waters also reminded them and the gathered Christian community of how God had rescued the Israelites from slavery, taking the Israelites through the waters of the "sea of reeds" and bringing them out safely to freedom on the other side.

A Powerful Communicator

For many centuries, Catholics have not seen any dramatic use of water in their baptismal rites. Typically, water is poured over the candidate's forehead. In the last two

Plunging into the water and coming up again symbolizes dying and rising with Christ.

decades, however, many Catholic churches have begun to use the symbol of water in a more powerful fashion in the Rite of Baptism, as it was originally intended, either by immersing the whole person in water or by submerging just the person's head. Some Protestant denominations today baptize only by immersion. Consider how much more the symbol of water can communicate about baptism when it is used this fully.

7. If you were invited to teach a class of first graders about the symbolism of water, how would you do it? Outline a brief lesson you would give.

Oil: Healing, Strengthening, and Being Chosen

Oil has been used on persons for thousands of years in a variety of ways, many of which find echoes of meaning in the Catholic sacraments.

At the time of the Roman Empire, gladiators and soldiers prepared for battle by covering their bodies with oil for protection against abrasions and infections. Oil was known for its healing qualities. Greek athletes, too, were rubbed with oil as a means of strengthening them. On beaches during the summer months, present-day people guard against the sun's rays using oils from squeeze bottles. Swimmers and other athletes also use protective and healing ointments.

Mixed with perfume, oil was used in ancient times for anointing a person as royalty; anointing was a sign of making the leader sacred for a sacred responsibility. The title *Christ* actually means "the Anointed One," the Messiah long awaited by the Jews.

In the baptismal rite, anointing with oil on the breast or on both hands occurs before the water ritual of baptism. This anointing is associated with asking God for strength for the person. The anointing of the new Christian on the crown of the head with chrism (special consecrated oil), which takes place after the water ritual, signifies being chosen and anointed as Christ was chosen, to share in his risen life and to receive the Spirit through him.

A White Garment: Becoming a New Creation

Treating ourselves to new clothes can help us feel renewed inside. Dressing up on Easter Sunday or for a school prom goes naturally with the freshness of the season and with the excitement of the occasion.

To symbolize the radical newness of a life in Christ, of being "clothed in Christ," the baptized individual receives a white (or new) garment or a white cloth to wear after the

Baptism in Words and Symbols

Litany of the Saints

Holy Mary, Mother of God,
   pray for us. . . .
Saint Peter and Saint Paul,
   pray for us. . . .
All holy men and women,
   pray for us. . . .

Blessing of the Water

Through the waters of the Red Sea
you led Israel out of slavery
to be an image of God's holy people
set free from sin by baptism.

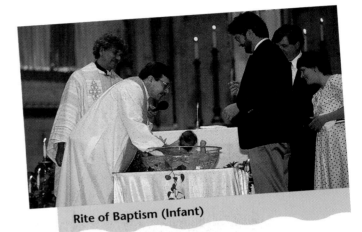

Rite of Baptism (Infant)

Rite of Baptism (Adult, Full Immersion)

Renunciation of Sin

Do you reject sin so as to live in the freedom of
God's children?
   I do.
Do you reject the glamour of evil and refuse to
be mastered by sin?
   I do.

Anointing with the Oil of Catechumens

We anoint you with the oil of salvation
in the name of Christ our Savior.
May he strengthen you with his power,
who lives and reigns for ever and ever.

Profession of Faith

[Name], do you believe in God, the Father
almighty, creator of heaven and earth?
   I do.

Rite of Baptism

[Name], I baptize you in the name of the
   Father,
and of the Son,
and of the Holy Spirit.

Anointing After Baptism

[If there is no sacrament of confirmation after
the Rite of Baptism, an anointing is done.]
As Christ was anointed Priest, Prophet, and
    King,
so may you live always as a member of his
    body,
sharing everlasting life.

Anointing After Baptism

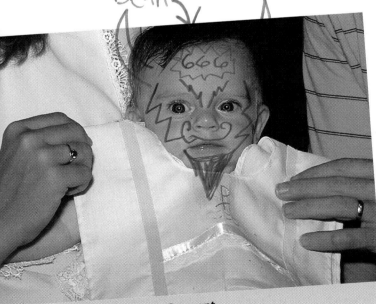

Clothing with the White Garment

Presentation of the Lighted Candle

Clothing with the White Garment

[Name], you have become a new creation
and have clothed yourself in Christ.

Presentation of the Lighted Candle

Walk always as a child of the light
and keep the flame of faith alive in your heart.

water ritual. In appearance as well as in spirit, the person is a "new creation." In the early church, newly baptized people wore this garment the whole week after their baptism, as a constant reminder, to themselves and the community, of their new life and Christian dignity. (In some cultures today, colors other than white are used, because in those cultures white signifies death, not life.)

A Lighted Candle: Sharing in the Light of Christ

Imagine yourself in a vast, totally dark room that you have never been in before. You have no idea what awaits you in the room, what you might stumble on, or how you might find your way around the room. You are anxious, even fearful. Then imagine being handed a candle that is suddenly lit. The light from even this small flame fills the corners of the room. You are relieved and glad to carry the light, and you do not want it to be snuffed out.

The burning of a single candle, especially in darkness, fascinates and captivates us. Light dispels darkness. It guides the lost. It wards off danger and exposes evil. Light is warm, inviting, comforting. Where there is light, there is life. Jesus called himself "the light of the world."

At baptism, the newly baptized person is given a lighted candle to hold. (In the case of an infant or small child, a godparent holds the candle.) The flame of this candle is re-

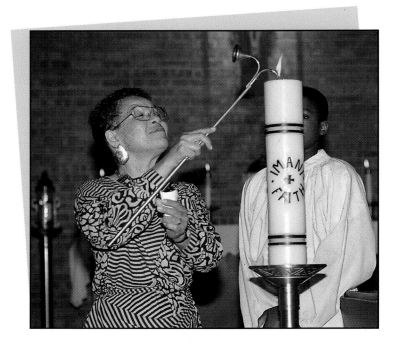

The large Easter candle, or paschal candle, which signifies Christ, is the source of the light shared with new Christians in baptism.

ceived from the large Easter candle, which signifies Christ, the light of the world. In this way, the newly baptized person shares in the light of Christ, the hope and warmth of the world, and is encouraged to always walk as a "child of the light."

The baptismal ritual, with its rich symbolism, has intensely individual meaning: For an adult, it celebrates a person's decisive break with the past to enter a new way of life. But it is also strongly communal, with its emphasis on the significant role of the community—sponsors or godparents, family, congregation, and leaders—in welcoming newcomers and in helping them to grow into the Christian life they are embracing.

8. Focus on one of the primary symbols of baptism—water, oil, a white (or new) garment, or a lighted candle—and complete one of the following two exercises:
(1) Write a poem or an essay about an experience you had involving that symbol.
(2) Make a collage or draw a picture illustrating the practical importance of that symbol.

For Review

- List three symbolic mentions of water in the Hebrew Scriptures.
- What do the two anointings with oil during baptism signify?
- What is the significance of the white garment worn in baptism?
- Why is a lighted candle given to the newly baptized person?

Baptism's History

The First Baptisms

The very first Christians were the Apostles. Recall that after Jesus' Resurrection and Ascension to God, the Apostles huddled together in an upstairs room in Jerusalem, fearful that their lives were in danger. But on the day of Pentecost, they were filled with the Holy Spirit. They had been "baptized" by the whole experience of Jesus' life, death, and Resurrection, and now they were filled with the new life of God.

The Apostles then wanted to share this Pentecost outpouring of the Spirit with others. So Peter and the other Apostles boldly went out to convert and baptize all who would hear the Good News and believe in Jesus. Following the example of Jesus' own baptism, they baptized with water, which symbolized receiving the Spirit of Jesus as they had received it at Pentecost.

This simple act of baptism with water later developed into a complex ceremony of initiation, full of the rich symbolism discussed earlier. Let's see how the process evolved.

In the Early Church

As the fledgling community of Jesus' followers grew and broadened to welcome Gentile (non-Jewish) converts, the church discovered that it needed a more thorough way to prepare persons to become Christians.

The Catechumenate

From the second century (the 100s) into the fourth and fifth centuries, a process of baptismal preparation called the **catechumenate** developed and flourished, along with the beautiful, powerful rituals of initiation.

As illustrated in the story of Paulina's conversion in chapter 6, becoming a Christian was quite a risky step to take in the earliest centuries of the faith. With Christianity officially illegal, the religion existed "underground"—in secret. Bloody persecutions by the Romans were a constant reminder that becoming a Christian could bring martyrdom. One did not decide lightly to become a Christian.

A person desiring to become a Christian needed to find a Christian who would be a sponsor, who would vouch for her or his character and help the person during the two- to three-year preparation for baptism. About forty days before the person was to be baptized, the final preparation took place during the period that later evolved into Lent. This preparation consisted of intensive instruction, prayer, fasting, and liturgies involving the group of candidates, or catechumens, with the whole community, led by the bishop. The final step was the Easter Vigil—the only time baptisms were performed.

At the Easter Vigil

The Easter Vigil ceremony was preceded by a ritual bathing on Holy Thursday and by two days of fasting. On the Saturday night of the vigil, all the candidates were brought together, men in one room and women in another. Their sponsors—the persons who had guided them toward their new birth—were there. The sponsors were called "fathers" and "mothers" by the candidates because sponsors performed a parental role. (Later, sponsors would become known as godparents.)

At the start of the ceremony, the candidates faced the West, the place of sunset and darkness. They stretched out their arms and denounced Satan. Suddenly, they turned to

Just as it began in the early Christian church, the Easter Vigil today begins with the lighting of the Easter fire and a chant of praise to "Christ our light."

the East and shouted their attachment to Christ. This physical turnabout by the candidates marked their spiritual turnabout or conversion. The East was considered the place of light, of the rising sun, and of new life.

Next, the candidates went to a room where there was a pool, often modeled after the Roman public baths. They stripped off their old clothing. Oil was poured over the candidates, who then stepped down into the waist-deep waters. One by one, the bishop submerged the candidates into the water, usually three times—in the name of the Father, the Son, and the Holy Spirit. After the candidates emerged from the other side of the pool, the bishop anointed them with oil, and they donned new white linen robes, signifying their new life in the Risen Jesus. They were embraced in a sign of peace and welcome, and each was handed a lighted candle.

Finally, the candidates were led into the room where the Eucharist was celebrated. By now, dawn had come. For the first time, on Easter Sunday, they participated in the total eucharistic celebration. Prior to their baptism, the catechumens attended Mass only up to the completion of the sermon. As a matter of fact, the first part of the Mass was called the Mass of the Catechumens because the prayers, readings, and sermon were intended to give instruction to the catechumens. What a joy it must have been for the newly baptized, after three years' preparation, to share the Eucharist with their friends for the first time! It must have been a similar joy for the rest of the community to welcome these long-awaited newcomers to their special Easter meal.

9. Imagine that you live in third-century Rome and that you were recently baptized at the Easter Vigil along with two other candidates. Write a letter to a friend describing your experience of the ceremony. Include details: Was the ceremony held in a remote location out of fear of persecution? Did the aura of secrecy make it more sacred? Was the water cold? And so on.

Mystagogia

After the Easter Vigil baptisms and the Easter Eucharist, the new Christians would go through another period of study and intense involvement with the community as they learned more about the mysteries of the faith. This period was known as the **mystagogia.**

Becoming a Christian required abandoning pagan ways and renouncing many comforts, conveniences, and privileges of the time. And before Christianity was made legal in 313 in the Roman Empire, being Christian presented a great risk of martyrdom. Initiation meant sharing one's fate and faith with the Christian community. Considering all that initiation involved, a lengthy process for acceptance into the community certainly made sense.

At the same time, the early Christian leaders realized that baptism was meant to be a sustained joy, not just a moment of excitement. Developing a joyful, loving community demanded a profound initiation of its newcomers. Today, the church has revised the Rite of Baptism, along with the other sacraments of initiation, to recapture the spirit, joy, and meaning of the rites in the early church.

An Evolution into Three Sacraments

The process of initiation just described was appropriate for the adult converts who were joining the faith in the early centuries of Christianity. But later on, so many candidates sought initiation into the church that the bishops had difficulty officiating at all the ceremonies. Yet it was considered essential that the bishops conduct the rites.

A Delayed Anointing

To handle the increased numbers of converts, in the Western church, priests of a given community performed the baptism with water but delayed the rest of the baptismal ceremony (the anointing with oil by the bishop) until the bishop could get around to the church to "confirm" the initiation at a later time, sometimes even years later. This ritual of anointing and laying on of hands by the bishop became known as *confirmation*, and was gradually accepted as a separate sacrament.

Infant Baptism

By about the year 200, some children of Christian parents were being baptized into the church without going through their own conversion process. By the year 500, when almost everyone in the empire was Christian, infant

baptism was, almost without exception, the way one became a Christian. Baptizing infants as soon as possible after birth became the norm because it was thought that an unbaptized baby who died would not go to heaven. With such an urgent time frame, it became impossible for confirmation by the bishop to take place at the time of baptism.

In addition, with the practice of infant baptism, children did not receive the Eucharist until they were old enough to understand the sacrament. Eventually, in the Western (Roman Catholic) church, the baptized members began to participate in the Eucharist before they were confirmed, and they became confirmed at an even later age. Until recently in Roman Catholicism, these sacraments of initiation remained separate and were celebrated in this sequence: baptism, the Eucharist, and then confirmation. Even today, debate is going on in the church about how and when in a person's development these sacraments should be celebrated.

The Eastern Church Practice

In the Eastern churches, the original sequence of initiation was kept. Priests were allowed to baptize, confirm, and offer the Eucharist to the initiates. Today in the Eastern Orthodox churches, and in some of the Eastern Catholic churches, babies and little children receive all three sacraments at one time.

Most Catholics today are baptized as infants.

Since Vatican Council II

After the Second Vatican Council of the 1960s, the church developed two main procedures for baptism:

1. a ceremony specifically for young children
2. an initiation process for adults (and a parallel process for older children) modeled on the process used in the early church

For Young Children

Before the special rite for baptizing children was developed, the words of the baptismal ceremony were addressed to the child as if he or she were an adult. Therefore, when infants were baptized—which accounted for the majority of baptisms during most of Christian history—the adult godparents responded for the children.

Baptism not consciously chosen: Today's distinct baptismal rite for young children acknowledges that the awareness and experience of the sacrament differ between adults and small children. For adults and older children such as adolescents, initiation is consciously chosen and experienced. For infants, baptism is not "conscious" (personally felt) or chosen by the children. So during the baptism of an infant or small child, the parents are addressed rather than the child. No one speaks "for" the child, as the godparents used to do. The parents are recognized as the primary community of the child and as the ones who seek baptism for their child and want to raise the child in the Christian faith.

As with adult initiation, the new baptismal rite for an infant involves the entire community, not just the child being baptized and the child's close family and godparents. The whole community is reminded of its role in helping the parents raise the child in the faith. All who are present also recall the significance of their own baptism and their own ongoing initiation into the mystery of Christ.

"Initiated," one way or another: In a concrete way, the practice of infant baptism acknowledges the fact that from our earliest experiences, we are being "initiated" into *some* way of viewing ourselves and our world. From infancy on, we are influenced by the people around us, by our physical environment, and by all of our internal and external experiences. Parents can choose to let "initiation" for their child just happen through exposure to the images, stories, and values communicated by the popular culture and media, like television. Alternatively, parents can put their hopes in the images, stories, and values of the Christian vision as the context for raising their child.

10. If relatives of yours asked you to help make their newborn baby's baptism a true community celebration, what would you suggest to them? Describe in writing at least three recommendations.

Through baptism, an infant is welcomed into a community that claims as its own the simple beauty of the Christmas story and the dramatic realities of Holy Week. Through baptism, the community celebrates a baby as a child of a loving God, someone whose family ties extend to heaven. Thus, infant baptism signifies the crucial roles that the family, the church community, and the Christian story play in developing within children the Christian view of life.

For Adults and Older Children

Since 1972, an official process of initiating adults into the Catholic faith has been in use, and it is modeled after the process the early church used in initiating its new members. The official process today is titled the Rite of Christian Initiation of Adults. Popularly called the RCIA, it takes into account these realities:

- Becoming a Catholic Christian is a process that takes time.
- Becoming a Catholic Christian means joining a community.

11. Do you agree or disagree with each of the following statements? Explain your answers in writing.

- When I have children, I won't have them baptized as infants. They can decide for themselves when they grow up.
- If I were running a parish, I would not be willing to baptize children of parents who did not practice their faith.

Children baptized as infants are brought up as members of a community that shares the Christian vision and values, exemplified, for instance, in the simple beauty of the Christmas story.

Christian Initiation, 1990s-Style

Jay's family was not religious. In fifteen years, Jay had never known his family to attend any religious services. A few of his friends did attend church regularly—the Catholic church not too far from school. They seemed to take their religion seriously, and Jay was impressed.

One day, Jay accompanied his friends to their church. Everything seemed strange, but his friends tried hard to answer all his questions. Jay soon started to join his friends in their parish youth group activities. For a while, he enjoyed his role as the outsider, but eventually he realized, "I want to belong."

One of Jay's friends, Maria, told him that if he wanted, he could join a group of people who were interested in becoming Catholic. She said that Mrs. Hernandez was in charge of the program and would gladly explain it to him.

Jay met with Mrs. Hernandez and talked about his desire to feel closer to Jesus, to know and share the life his friends seemed to share. He also expressed his fears about whether or not he could live up to what it meant to be a Catholic. After conversations with Mrs. Hernandez and then the pastor, Jay decided that he wanted to join the group of nine people who were beginning preparation for initiation into the church.

Jay's friend Maria agreed to be his sponsor, accompanying him to meetings, prayer sessions, and social events. Once Jay heard the others in the program tell their stories, he became more and more convinced that becoming a Catholic would connect him with a group of people who trusted in Jesus and who shared their life with one another through Jesus.

Jay went through many steps on the way to initiation into the church. He met many people who helped him feel welcome and who explained what being Catholic meant to them. Each ceremony of the preparation period, or catechumenate stage, moved Jay closer to what

he realized would be a very special event for him—his baptism, confirmation, and first Eucharist at the Saturday night Easter Vigil.

When the Saturday of the Easter Vigil arrived, Jay was nervous and excited, but he knew that he was not alone. Thanks to his sponsor, the youth group members, the people from the parish who helped out with the program, and his fellow catechumens, Jay felt that he was joining a community of friends and a church with a long and special association with Jesus. When he celebrated the Eucharist for the first time after his baptism, Jay knew that Jesus was with him forever.

A similar rite is specifically designed for older children—that is, children old enough to learn about and choose the faith.

The RCIA is also used to welcome and initiate into full union with the Catholic community those persons who have previously been baptized. These persons could be Catholics who have lost touch with the Catholic church, or they might be Protestants. The Catholic church recognizes the baptism of other denominations as valid, so baptism would not be repeated for them.

As a process, the RCIA has a number of stages to help interested persons move along to becoming informed and active members of the Catholic Christian community:

1. Inquiry: Before someone enters a formal initiation program, during the phase when she or he and the church are getting to know each other, the person is called an "inquirer." When both parties are satisfied that they want to continue with the initiation process, the individual enters the catechumenate stage.

2. Catechumenate: A catechumen studies the Catholic faith, accompanied by a sponsor or sponsors, ideally within a community of other catechumens. The catechumens also participate with their sponsors in certain rites that bring them more deeply into the faith and the community. Ideally, this period lasts from about one to three years. All during this time, the catechumens attend Sunday Mass, but leave the church after the homily in a formal Rite of Dismissal. This reminds them and the assembly how important full participation in the Eucharist is for Christian life. Toward the end of the catechumenate stage, on the "day of election," the community chooses each candidate to be among the "elect," provided he or she has shown sincerity as a catechumen.

3. Period of enlightenment or illumination: The season of Lent preceding the Easter Vigil, when the elect will be baptized, is a period of intensive preparation with its own particular rites, consisting of questioning those to be baptized and hearing their profession of faith. As in ancient times, this season gives everyone, the already-baptized members and the elect, the chance to reflect on the mystery of the Resurrection, which they are soon to celebrate at Easter.

Of course, the major event for the candidates and the community is the Easter Vigil. The Easter Vigil service is filled with baptismal imagery so that the new and longer-standing members of the Christian community can reflect on the relationship between the Resurrection of Jesus and the sacraments of initiation. During the service, the new members, accompanied by their sponsors, may be baptized and are confirmed. Later in the liturgy, the new members receive the Eucharist for the first time.

4. Mystagogia: The process of initiation does not end with baptism, confirmation, and the celebration of the Eucharist at Easter. Naturally, new members of a group have special needs. During the time from Easter to Pentecost Sunday, new members and their sponsors reflect together on their experiences of being Christian. The term applied to this period is *mystagogia,* a word related to the word *mystery.* Mystagogia is a time to understand and appreciate more deeply the Christian mysteries.

Throughout the Rite of Christian Initiation of Adults, the church community plays a significant role. Persons are usually drawn to Catholicism because they see some evidence of the life of Christ present within a local Catholic community, or within individuals who have cared about them. During the RCIA process, the catechumens and sponsors gather regularly as a community to share their own life stories and faith stories, and the candidates are affirmed in their journey of faith. The various rites throughout the catechumenate stage are celebrated with the whole gathered community. In fact, where the RCIA is experienced as a dynamic process with the involvement of the community, the growing faith of the catechumens presents church community members with a challenge to their own faith. The community members are challenged to not be complacent about their faith and to foster the bonds and commitments that build a genuine faith community. Thus, the RCIA has the potential to renew local churches in their spirit.

For Review

- Briefly describe the process called the *catechumenate* in the early church.
- Why did the ritual of anointing and laying on of hands, or *confirmation,* become separate from the ritual of baptism?
- What reminder does infant baptism place before the Christian community?
- Name and briefly explain the four stages of today's RCIA process.

12. Interview someone who became Catholic as an adult. Ask why he or she made this decision, what the initiation process was like, and how the person's life has changed since joining the church. Write a brief summary of your interview.

Lifelong Initiation, Lifelong Baptism

At each Sunday Mass, Catholics are reminded that their own initiation into the paschal mystery will be a lifelong process.

If you were baptized as an infant, the community of your family and your parents' friends would obviously be significant in your growth as a Christian. But as we have seen, adult baptism also relies on the community to help new members grow into a Christian life, and it builds up the bonds and commitments in the community.

Baptism is not unique among the sacraments in its emphasis on the crucial role of the community. Each of the seven sacraments is celebrated on behalf of and for the good of the whole community, not just the individuals who are obviously involved.

Each time members of the community witness a baptism, at the Easter Vigil or at Sunday Mass, they are reminded that their own initiation into the paschal mystery is not yet complete. Initiation will be a lifelong process, a lifelong baptism in Christ, open to ever-deeper consciousness of the mystery of Jesus and to commitment to his mission.

Breath of Life,
    may I give witness to your Spirit
    and light up my corner of the universe
    by creatively working with others.
And may I, like your Son,
    continue to grow
    in wisdom and age and grace.
Amen.

8

Confirmation:
Celebrating Growth
in the Spirit

Confirmation, the second of the three sacraments of initiation, celebrates and acknowledges that the Spirit of Jesus given in baptism is truly alive and at work in the Christian. Originally celebrated as a part of the early church's initiation ritual, which included baptism and the Eucharist, confirmation later developed into a separate sacrament.

Today in Roman Catholicism, confirmation is celebrated at the time when a Christian is able to be conscious of the Spirit's life in him or her. For people baptized as infants, this means that confirmation must come at a later age, the "age of discretion." (This term is used in Roman Catholicism to describe the age when a person is able to make moral judgments. In practice, the age of confirmation varies across countries and regions, anywhere from age seven to age eighteen.) For older children and adults being baptized, confirmation is celebrated at the time of initiation, with baptism and the Eucharist. In either case, confirmation is a sign of growing in the Spirit of Jesus.

Like all the sacraments, confirmation celebrates a transformation so profound that its meaning can never be captured in any simple description. In confirmation, Christians acknowledge all the wonderful, usually subtle ways that Christ's Spirit is with them—affirming, strengthening, and challenging them. The following story hints at the many ways that the power of the Holy Spirit can be confirmed in a person's life.

Emily wondered if her life would ever take off—if she would ever have the excitement in her life that seemed to come naturally to other girls in her class. She thought about Mia and Jenna, whose conversation she had just overheard. Mia and Jenna had been going on about the great weekend they were each going to have. Mia and a new guy she was interested in were going to meet at the basketball game that night and then go out later for pizza. Jenna's plans were to go skiing with a couple of her girlfriends; they would probably meet some guys at the ski lodge and have a great time.

Emily considered her own "plans" for the weekend. Well, there would be the usual farm chores, which had to be done every day. Life on a dairy farm was pretty predictable. Milking twice a day, without fail, was the essential feature.

What else would go on this weekend? Emily thought about how she might watch some TV shows, baby-sit her little brothers and her sister while her parents went to an auction, and do her homework. The biggest issue of the weekend would be whether to go to Mass Saturday night or Sunday morning. And that would be decided by when there was a car free to go. In a large family

like Emily's, there was plenty of demand for a car, because the family lived so far from town.

"What a boring life," Emily sighed inside, careful not to let other kids see how down she felt. "My problem is, I'm just a dull person. I never do anything, I never go anywhere. I just exist."

Emily wanted to leave school after the last class and get home on the early school bus. Then she could settle down in front of her favorite talk show before chore time.

As Emily rushed for the door, Mrs. Daly, the speech teacher, motioned for her to come over. Emily did not want an encounter with such a vigorous, demanding teacher at that point, when she already felt so low. "Oh, no, what did I do now? Maybe she thinks I should change the way I did my speech for class. Like I haven't already put enough time into it!"

But Mrs. Daly was beaming. She didn't look ready to pounce on her with criticism. "Emily, you did some job on that speech today. Marvelous expression—so much feeling you put into it, and in just the right rhythms!"

Emily put her head down and smiled shyly. "It's easy when you've got Kennedy's words to work with." She had chosen to deliver John F. Kennedy's inaugural address as her major project.

"I've heard students give that speech a hundred times. And believe me, Emily, I never heard it like I heard it from you today."

Emily lifted her head up slightly and caught a glimpse of Mrs. Daly's animated face. "I felt a lot when I was giving it. I guess it showed."

"You bet it did. You know, Emily, you sit there in class so quietly, and I don't often hear from you. Today you amazed me with that speech."

"Yeah, well, I don't usually have much to say. I guess I'm just not very interesting."

"Now that's where you've got it all wrong! You are interesting. You're passionate, Emily; you're full of life inside you that's just begging for a chance to come out."

Emily took in Mrs. Daly's words like a parched field soaking up a gentle rain. Yes, Emily knew she had a lot going on inside her, a lot of vitality; she just never seemed to have an outlet for it. So she felt dull. Now here was someone who recognized what had been in her all along—her tremendous feeling.

"Emily, I would love for you to join the speech team. You've got so much to give."

The early bus was now pulling away from the curb. Emily realized that it would be 4:30 before she could leave, getting her home just in time for chores. No talk show for her this afternoon. But taking the late bus and missing her talk show didn't bother Emily like it ordinarily would have.

Looking up into Mrs. Daly's eager eyes, Emily grinned. "I'd like that. Yeah, that might be real neat."

Emily discovered a gift within herself—her own deep feeling, her own inner life. Until Mrs. Daly recognized it, this gift had gone largely unnoticed and unrealized. Emily herself was only dimly aware of it as a gift. Channeling that immense inner vitality into a great, passionate speech, and having someone notice her rendering of that speech as special, gave Emily the sense that there was more inside her than met the eye.

What Does Confirmation Celebrate?

Lifelong Growth in the Spirit

Like Emily in the previous story, all people carry within themselves great gifts that are not necessarily apparent to themselves or others. Growth in such gifts does not happen all at once. For their part, Christians need to "grow" their way into grace, into living in the Spirit of Jesus. The Spirit is given in baptism, certainly. But the Spirit needs plenty of time to be discovered and to grow if grace is to come to fullness in a person.

Through the sacrament of confirmation, the church affirms the view that growth in the Spirit is a continuing, lifelong journey. In recognizing the impact that an individual's faith community can have on his or her journey, the church also affirms the following:

- The Holy Spirit operates in subtle ways throughout people's lives.
- Confirmation itself is one special moment when Christians consciously acknowledge the presence of the Holy Spirit.
- Caring people are bearers of God's Spirit and "confirmers" of one another's gifts.

The Breath of God

Holy Spirit is the translation of an old Hebrew term that means "wind" or "breath of God." In the Scriptures, people experienced the Spirit sometimes as a powerful wind, other times as a gentle breeze or a whisper, and still other times as God breathing life into persons or events. On Pentecost, the Apostles felt the Spirit in a dramatic way, as wind and fire. Often in life, however, the Spirit is revealed in the subtle ways—more in the breezes than in the strong winds. The Spirit at work in us may become apparent in a simple, gentle moment, like being affirmed by a friend or being moved to tears of sympathy.

1. In writing, tell about a gift you have that you were not aware of until another person or an occasion brought it out. Compare your experience with Emily's.

We need a lifetime of learning and maturing in community to "grow" into living in the Spirit of Jesus.

2. After looking up the various dictionary meanings of the word *spirit,* write about what you think the name *Holy Spirit* tells us about God. List five ways that you think the Holy Spirit is at work in the world today.

Taking Flight

The following story, based on an African folktale, gives us a way to consider the meaning of confirmation.

Once upon a time, while she was walking through a forest, a farmer found an eagle tangled in a bush, an eagle too young to fly. She took the young eagle home and put him in the stockyard, where the eagle soon learned to eat chicken feed and to behave as the chickens did.

A month or so later, when the farmer was in the stockyard, she saw the eagle awkwardly pecking at kernels of corn. The farmer thought to herself, "This eagle needed to be here for a while. But now, it is sad to see this king of all birds living in a stockyard with chickens."

"He has never learned to fly," the farmer remarked to her husband. "He behaves as chickens behave. You might say that he is no longer an eagle."

"Still, he has the heart of an eagle and can surely be taught to fly," suggested the farmer's husband.

After talking it over, the two agreed to find out whether this was possible. Gently the farmer took the eagle in her arms and said, "You belong to the sky more than to the earth. Stretch forth your wings and fly."

The eagle, however, was confused, not knowing who he was. Seeing his friends the chickens, the eagle jumped down to be with them again.

On the following day, the farmer took the eagle up onto the highest cattle hut and urged him again, saying, "You are an eagle. Stretch forth your wings and fly." But the eagle was afraid of his unknown self and jumped down once more to the chicken yard.

On the third day, the farmer rose early, took the eagle out of the stockyard, and climbed with him to a high mountain. There she held the king of birds high above her and encouraged him again, saying, "You are an eagle. You belong to the sky as well as to the earth. Stretch forth your wings now. Fly!"

The eagle looked around, back toward the stockyard and up to the sky. Still he did not fly. Then the farmer lifted him even higher, straight toward the sun. And it happened that the eagle began to tremble. Slowly, he stretched his wings. At last, with a triumphant cry, he soared away into the heavens.

It may be that the eagle still fondly remembers his friends the chickens. Yet, as far as anyone knows, he has never returned to the chicken yard.

Becoming Conscious of the Gift

In the opening narrative about Emily, Emily became aware of her gift of speech when Mrs. Daly commended her for it. In a similar way, if young Christians are to become conscious that Jesus' Spirit is truly alive and at work in them, then other people in the community must take the time to recognize and nurture the young persons' growing gifts.

The sacrament of confirmation provides an opportunity for persons to consciously claim as their own the gift of the Spirit given at baptism. Confirmation recognizes that the Spirit is bearing fruit in a person's own emerging talents and personal qualities. Confirmation also "confirms" that the person's initiation into Jesus' life at baptism is now consciously being embraced. The Spirit can more readily flourish in a heart that willingly accepts the Spirit's gifts.

Needing Other People

Notice that in the opening story, Mrs. Daly did not try to make Emily into something she was not. Rather, she recognized Emily's wonderful gift and realized that nurturing it was necessary. Likewise, all of us need such "confirmation" throughout life. When others act in our life as Mrs. Daly acted in Emily's life, they confirm our identity and encourage our growth in the gifts we have been given.

Reflect for a moment on your own life, and ask yourself:

- Which persons have confirmed my identity and encouraged growth of the gifts I have been given?
- Who have been the primary revealers of the Spirit to me?

The people you thought of in answering these questions have been channels for God's grace in your life. In a way, they have been your *sponsors*—a term used in the sacraments of initiation to describe people who encourage and nurture the faith of the person being initiated. For example:

- Our parents provide us with food and clothing.
- Our relatives visit our home and take an interest in us.
- Our teachers give their time to help us learn.
- Our friends share their lives with us.
- Many other people whom we meet are friendly to us.

These are some of the sponsors through whom God's grace acts in our life. In preparation for confirmation, young people usually choose one such person to be their sponsor, to accompany them through a particularly significant time of growing in the Spirit.

Learning in Community

As chapter 7 discussed, adults and older children who are initiated into the church today through the Rite of Christian Initiation of Adults are confirmed as well as baptized,

3. Are there certain people through whom God's grace acts dynamically in your life—people who encourage and inspire your faith? Think of specific examples of these people's positive influence on you, and write an essay entitled "The Sponsors in My Life."

Many persons, including our friends, confirm our identity and encourage our growth in the gifts we have been given. We can think of these people as our "sponsors."

The gift of reverence can be seen in the compassion we show toward ourselves and others.

and they receive the Eucharist at the Easter Vigil. Their celebration of these sacraments follows an extensive period of preparation known as the catechumenate. With other catechumens and their sponsors, they share the story of their own life and learn about how the Good News of Jesus touches them. Over a long process, the catechumens are welcomed more deeply into the life of the community and gradually realize what it means to live in the Spirit of Jesus.

For young persons who were baptized as infants, the period of preparing for confirmation serves as a stage similar to the catechumenate. Lasting for one or two years, a confirmation preparation program is meant to give young persons the chance to learn about and grow in the faith they are consciously embracing.

The Gifts of the Spirit Unfolding

In the opening story, Emily had a special gift that was not being fully expressed; it was lying dormant until it was recognized and nurtured. Likewise, at the time of confirmation, seven special gifts are called forth in those being confirmed. These **gifts of the Holy Spirit** are actually virtues or abilities that were given at baptism and that gradually unfold in a person as she or he matures. Thus, the time of confirmation, when the young person has already reached a certain level of maturity, is an ideal time to accept these gifts wholeheartedly and try to develop them.

The Seven Gifts

In the Rite of Confirmation, the bishop or priest prays that these seven special gifts will grow in the candidates:

- wisdom
- understanding
- right judgment
- courage
- knowledge
- reverence
- wonder and awe in God's presence

By presenting these seven gifts in the form of questions, we can see more clearly the opportunities they offer to grow in Christian maturity.

Wisdom: Am I a seeker of wisdom? Do I thoughtfully explore the wisdom of Jesus and of other great teachers of the past? Do I step back to see the whole truth hidden behind the obvious facts at hand? Do I attempt to look at life from many different perspectives besides my own?

Understanding: Do I try to understand what I have learned? Do I look closely at underlying causes and not just at results? Am I understanding toward others—especially those who rub me the wrong way? Can I admit my faults?

Right judgment: Am I developing my conscience? Do I consult the teachings of the church in trying to make judgments? Do I seek guidance from informed and conscientious people?

Courage: Can I freely act on my decisions, remaining faithful to my conscience? Do I act rightly and justly even when risking ridicule or going against the crowd?

Knowledge: Am I challenged but not overwhelmed by the vast amount of information that I can still learn? Am I trying to keep informed about life and its workings? Do I follow the debates on important current issues so that I can make intelligent decisions?

Reverence: Do I treat myself and the people and things of the world with reverence? Do I recognize fellow human beings and other creatures of the earth as my brothers and sisters? Is compassion for others an important measuring stick for my choices?

Wonder and awe in God's presence: Do I take time to pray and worship so that I can more deeply appreciate God's presence in my life? Do I reject boredom as a condition of life and instead seek to live with the joy and enthusiasm of a child of God?

Naturally, the development of these gifts cannot happen instantly at the time of confirmation. These gifts are the fruits of maturing in God's life. Let's examine the notion of what it means to mature.

Maturity: A Journey, Not a Destination

How do you see yourself ten years from now? Will you be settled down? Will you be working in your lifelong profession? Will you be married? Will you have children? maybe a dog? a house with a TV set and a great sound system? Will you have "arrived"? Will you be an "adult"? Will you be settled and secure until the next stage—retirement?

Many people have an image of maturity that might be called the "destination" model, as the previous questions imply. According to that model, we travel through adolescence until one day we arrive at our destination—maturity as an adult. After that, our life remains much the same.

Another image of maturity might be called the "journey" model. This alternative image understands life as a continuing process of growth, filled from start to finish with peaks and valleys, rough roads and straight paths, dyings and risings. It is thus filled with paschal-like events. There is never any set destination we reach that allows us to claim

4. Next to a list of the seven gifts of the Holy Spirit, indicate which two you would most like to grow in. Then, for each of the two, reflect in writing on possible opportunities for growth in those gifts—opportunities that might come up in the next week or month that would give you the chance to grow in those gifts.

5. Imagine yourself ten years from now. What do you think you will be doing? Name four things you can imagine yourself being involved in or committed to.

fulfillment in maturity, as in, "Now I've got it made; I've reached maturity; I'm an adult. All I have to do is continue along this same path for the next thirty years and I will have lived my life."

Much in our culture endorses a destination model of maturity. Adolescence is portrayed merely as the trip that one must take to arrive at a destination—maturity as an adult. Yet the journey model, which is really more consistent with the Christian vision of how we grow, suggests that maturing is a process that takes a lifetime.

The story of Emily, recounted earlier in this chapter, offers an unwitting but almost perfect parallel to the journey model of maturity and to the sacrament of confirmation. Emily had a gift at work in her, but she herself was only dimly aware of it until Mrs. Daly gave her recognition for it. When Mrs. Daly "confirmed" Emily's gift for speech, she did not say that Emily had reached her highest point or that Emily had no more room for growth and improvement. Rather, Mrs. Daly recognized and encouraged Emily for her gift and her desire to develop that gift. In a similar way, confirmation does not *confer* maturity, just as getting married or entering a profession does not confer maturity. Instead, confirmation recognizes and encourages developing maturity.

In the Christian vision, the process of growing, changing, and maturing goes on in us as long as we are alive.

Taking on the Ministry of Jesus

To be confirmed in Catholic Christian faith is to consciously accept the gift of Jesus' Spirit given in baptism—with everything that gift implies. The phrase "with everything that gift implies" is crucial. For implied in the gift of Jesus' Spirit is the call to become more like Jesus, to take on as one's own ministry Jesus' mission of healing, reconciling, and conveying God's love to all persons.

As seen in chapter 7 on baptism, sharing in the mission of Jesus is an important dimension of being initiated as a Christian. But for an infant or small child being baptized, sharing in Jesus' ministry is a remote reality; it cannot be realized until much later. Young people often experience sharing in Jesus' ministry in a conscious way around the time of their confirmation.

Most programs that prepare young people for confirmation emphasize that the candidates be involved in service of some kind. The value of such service gets lost if it is viewed as an obligation to be gotten over, as in, "You did your twenty hours; now you can be confirmed." Instead, service experiences are emphasized for two primary reasons: first, to give

6. If you were in preparation for confirmation this year and were expected to do some service activity, what service would you choose? Explain your choice in writing.

candidates a taste of living Jesus' life of ministry, and second, to enable them to try out their own gifts for service as a way to discern how they might serve in the future.

Many teenagers give themselves generously to a certain kind of service in preparing for confirmation. Those who do are often rewarded with personal growth that they never imagined for themselves. They discover (and are often surprised by) the skills they have. They discover self-worth. And they discover that in sharing their time and talents with other people, life becomes fuller and richer. Jesus' call to join in his ministry comes with this promise: "'I came that they may have life, and have it abundantly'" (John 10:10).

Other world religions acknowledge and support the developing growth of young people through their own initiation programs.
Photo: In a Hindu ceremony in Calcutta, India, boys of ages ten to twelve are initiated into a period of apprenticeship under a swami—a spiritual and practical guide.

For Review

- When does confirmation typically take place for people baptized as infants in the Roman Catholic church? When does it take place for those baptized as older children or adults?
- What is the purpose of a confirmation preparation program?
- Name the seven gifts of the Holy Spirit.
- Explain the two models of maturity. Which one is more consistent with the Christian vision?
- How does the opening story about Emily provide a parallel to the sacrament of confirmation?
- Why do most confirmation preparation programs emphasize service experiences?

Confirmation's Symbols and Rituals

Ideally, candidates for confirmation go through a process similar to what catechumens go through for baptism. And like the baptismal process, certain rituals are celebrated with the whole community during the process of confirmation. The culmination point, the Rite of Confirmation itself, usually takes place in the context of celebrating the Eucharist.

The symbols and rituals used at confirmation are not unique to that sacrament. They are used in other church sacraments, no doubt because they are powerful communicators of meaning. The two rituals central to confirmation are the laying on of hands and the anointing with chrism.

The Laying On of Hands: A Powerful Connector

Hands are a symbol of power. Specifically, "the laying on of hands" refers to an ancient practice of conferring power onto a person by placing both hands on that person's head. In Genesis, old Isaac lays his hands on his son Jacob to give him authority over the tribe. Kings and knights traditionally received their official power through a laying on of hands. The practice was also common in the early church to symbolize passing on the power of the Holy Spirit, which the Apostles had received at Pentecost.

Blessing, Creating, Comforting, Supporting

Hands are a particularly apt symbol for the Holy Spirit working in people. We bless with our hands. The priest at Mass gives the sign of the cross with his hand over the assembly. Friends pat each other on the back to offer encouragement or congratulations. Artists often depict the hand of God creating the world or giving life.

Similarly, we work with our hands, create things with our hands, and "give each other a hand." Hands greet, comfort, and console. Hands touch other people and can help heal simply by their touch. Hands can support and lift others up. They can help to guide. They can be used to reach out and make connections with people.

Spirit Touching Spirit

In the Rite of Confirmation, the bishop initially "lays hands on" all the candidates together by extending his hands over the whole group. Meanwhile, he prays for the

7. Recall a personal experience in which hands—yours or someone else's—communicated strength, power, healing, or support. If the hands could have talked, what would they have said? Write an imaginary monolog given by the hands.

Spirit to help and guide the candidates with the seven gifts of the Holy Spirit. A few moments later, when the candidates individually come up to the bishop to be anointed with chrism (the special consecrated oil also used in baptism), he places a hand on each person's head, which is symbolically the place of wisdom. The feeling of a hand on the head also gives a person the feeling of being strengthened by another's touch. A bond is made; the spirit of one touches the spirit of the other.

Hands can communicate blessing, symbolizing the Holy Spirit at work in people.

Anointing with Chrism: A Commissioning to Service

Have you ever watched public officials take oaths of office? They raise their hands and vow to carry out the duties and responsibilities of their offices. In ancient times, anointing with oil served that function. Kings and priests were anointed to symbolize their commission to those roles. Jesus himself is called *Christ,* which means "the Anointed One." In the Rite of Confirmation, Christians are anointed by the bishop

Confirmation in Words and Symbols

Renewal of Baptismal Promises

Do you reject Satan and all his works and all his empty promises?
   I do.
Do you believe in God, the Father almighty, creator of heaven and earth?
   I do.

The Laying On of Hands

All-powerful God, Father of our Lord Jesus
   Christ,
by water and the Holy Spirit
you freed your sons and daughters from sin

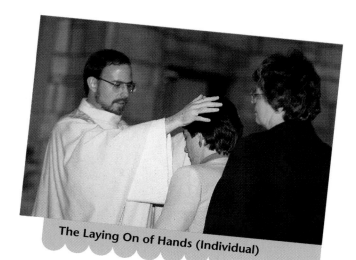

The Laying On of Hands (Individual)

Renewal of Baptismal Promises

The Laying On of Hands (Group)

and gave them new life.
Send your Holy Spirit upon them
to be their Helper and Guide.
Give them the spirit of wisdom and under-
    standing,
the spirit of right judgment and courage,
the spirit of knowledge and reverence.
Fill them with the spirit of wonder and awe
    in your presence.
We ask this through Christ our Lord.
    Amen.

The Anointing with Chrism

[Name], be sealed with the Gift of the Holy
Spirit.
    Amen.
Peace be with you.
    And also with you.

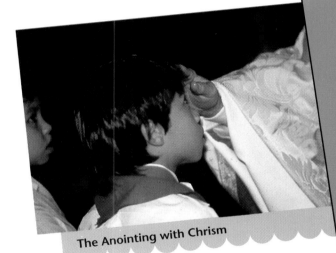

The Anointing with Chrism

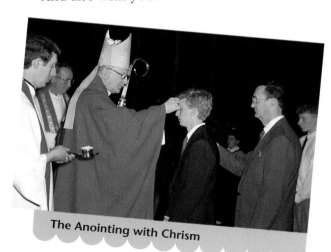

The Anointing with Chrism

General Intercessions

For these sons and daughters of God,
confirmed by the gift of the Spirit,
that they give witness to Christ
by lives built on faith and love:
let us pray to the Lord.
    Lord, hear our prayer.

Blessing

The Holy Spirit
came down upon the disciples
and set their hearts on fire with love:
may he bless you,
keep you one in faith and love,
and bring you to the joy of God's kingdom.
    Amen.

8. List all the modern uses of oil and oil-based products that you can think of. Does oil seem like an effective symbol in confirmation today? Write your opinion in a paragraph.

with chrism and thus are symbolically commissioned to be Christ for others. This action also recalls their anointing with chrism at baptism.

A "Reconfirming" of Baptism

The anointing at confirmation is more a "reconfirming" of the baptismal anointing than an entirely new symbolic act. In the Roman Catholic church, the bishop usually does the anointing, as well as the laying on of hands, to link the person symbolically to the universal church, the church of the Apostles. Where adults or older children are being initiated in a ceremony that includes the sacraments of baptism, confirmation, and the Eucharist, a priest, not a bishop, is usually the one presiding.

A Sign of the Cross

To be anointed, the candidates come forward one by one. As each one approaches the bishop, that candidate's sponsor places his or her right hand on the candidate's shoulder and gives the bishop the candidate's name. The bishop dips his right thumb in the chrism, puts his hand on the person's head, and makes the sign of the cross on the forehead, saying, "Be sealed with the gift of the Holy Spirit." The bishop then gives the person the sign of peace.

In addition to including the central rituals of the laying on of hands and the anointing with chrism, confirmation—when it is not celebrated with baptism—includes other actions that echo the baptismal rituals. These actions remind the candidates and the whole community of the essential connection between being baptized and being confirmed. The renewal of baptismal promises by the candidates includes the renunciation of sin as well as the profession of faith. These promises were a part of the candidates' baptismal ceremony long ago, when they were actually made by their parents and godparents.

9. If you were to affirm your original baptismal promises today, what particular false values would you think of in rejecting all of Satan's "empty promises"? Jot down these false values on paper, ranking them from "most harmful" to "least harmful."

For Review

- To what ancient practice does "the laying on of hands" refer? How does the bishop first perform this action in the Rite of Confirmation?
- What is the significance of anointing with chrism in the Rite of Confirmation? How is the anointing carried out in the rite?

Confirmation's History

As discussed in chapter 7 on baptism, confirmation cannot be considered apart from baptism. In the early church, confirmation was not a separate sacrament. Instead, as the act of anointing with chrism, it was part of the initiation rite for catechumens at the Easter Vigil, which also included baptism and the celebration of the Eucharist.

In confirmation, the anointing and the laying on of hands are usually done by a bishop, who, as a successor to the Apostles, symbolically links the person being confirmed with the universal church.

A Separate Ritual

In the Western (Roman Catholic) church, the anointing with chrism by the bishop after the water ritual of baptism eventually had to take place long after the water ritual. Membership growth had led to more baptisms being performed (by priests) in widespread communities than there were bishops available to perform the anointing with chrism at baptism. Delaying the anointing by the bishop allowed priests to continue performing the water ritual and allowed bishops to get around to their communities to "confirm" all the baptisms that priests had performed over the past months or years. In this manner, confirmation in the Roman church took on its own distinct ritual status by the third century. However, this separate anointing became a "regular" practice only after the fifth century, especially with the popularity of infant baptism.

In the Eastern Catholic and Orthodox churches, confirmation was never separated from baptism. Throughout their history, the Eastern churches have baptized, confirmed, and given the Eucharist to infant newcomers in one ceremony, presided over by a priest.

10. List the pros and cons of using the "soldiers of Christ" image to describe what Christians should be. Briefly state and explain your own opinion on the use of the term.

"Soldiers of Christ"?

In the fifth century, when many people were neglecting the separate anointing of confirmation, a certain abbot preached that confirmation was related to preparedness for spiritual combat, to preparing people for their life's battles with the devil. This idea that the sacrament would make an individual a "soldier of Christ" and a "witness for Christ" caught on in the wider church. For the next fifteen centuries, this perspective would influence people's understanding of confirmation.

As strange as it may seem, the sign of peace, which the bishop traditionally gave the person in the anointing ceremony, was administered more and more quickly, until it became a slap on the cheek rather than an embrace. Gradually, the slap on the cheek came to be standard practice, symbolic of becoming a soldier of Christ. Only in the past thirty years has this symbol been dropped from the practice of confirmation and the sign of peace restored.

Coming of Age Versus Lifelong Growth in the Spirit

In recent decades, a great deal of discussion has taken place in the Catholic church about the meaning of confirmation. For a time, the sacrament was thought to represent a kind of "coming of age," a reaching of spiritual maturity. This explanation had some appeal, especially because young people were being confirmed more frequently around the time of adolescence. However, along with this notion came the mistaken idea that confirmation would *complete and finish* one's learning and formation as a Christian. Nothing could be further from the intent of this sacrament.

The current understanding is that confirmation does not represent an arrival point, a destination, or a "graduation" from childhood to adulthood. Instead, it celebrates and deepens the ongoing initiation into a new life with Jesus, which began at baptism. Thus, confirmation readies a person for all the conscious growing and ministering that is ahead in life. It is part of the beginning, not the end, of a person's faith journey.

A Current Debate

Connected with the Catholic church's discussion about the meaning of confirmation is a debate about the order in which the sacraments of initiation should be celebrated in a person's life, as well as the age that is most appropriate for

Confirmation is part of the beginning, not the end, of a person's faith journey.

confirmation. Some theologians argue that the "original sequence" should be restored—that is, baptism, confirmation, and the Eucharist should be celebrated in that order. Others claim that with the present practice of infant baptism, it makes sense to delay confirmation until the young person is old enough to be truly conscious of the Spirit at work in him or her. Roman Catholic law states that the sacrament should be conferred at the "age of discretion"—but there are a variety of opinions on when discretion is possible in the life of a young person. The practice in recent decades in the United States has been to confirm young persons anywhere between the ages of seven and eighteen. However, debate and clarification continue in the church regarding the sequence and administering of these sacraments; the situation is still in flux.

11. The appropriate age for confirmation has been debated widely; people in the church variously propose anywhere from infancy to young adulthood. What do you think is the best age for confirmation? Explain your position in writing.

For Review

- Why did confirmation become a separate sacrament in the Western church?
- Describe two positions in the Catholic debate about the order in which the sacraments of initiation should be celebrated.

Toward Full Initiation

The Rites of Baptism and Confirmation are well-defined, identifiable moments that only happen once in a Christian's life. However, these two sacraments of initiation celebrate a reality that is not limited to a certain date or age: the ongoing birth of the Christian into new life. The third sacrament of initiation, the Eucharist, is different in that it is celebrated not once but often in a Christian's life.

Receiving the Eucharist for the first time is a great personal event, and it plunges the Christian more deeply into the paschal mystery, Christ's dying and rising. The Eucharist can then become a frequent event for the Christian, a source of strength and nourishment that can sustain him or her for a lifetime. Let us now turn to this sacrament, which represents the fullness of Christian initiation.

Bread of Life,
    we meet you while sitting around a table—
    laughing, singing, listening,
    sharing bread and wine
    and companionship.
Heaven, we know, is like this.
For this we give you our thanks,
    our Eucharist.
Amen.

9

The Eucharist:
Celebrating Christ's Presence
in Our Midst

The first two sacraments of initiation—baptism and confirmation—celebrate the realities of belonging to Christ, being identified with him, and being gifted by his Spirit in the community of his followers, the church. Like all the sacraments, baptism and confirmation are signs that Christ is truly present in the world today, through the church.

But in the sacrament of the Eucharist, Catholics have the foremost, ultimate sign of Christ's presence in their midst: the sharing of bread and wine as Jesus' own body and blood. Receiving the Eucharist for the first time represents the fullness of Christian initiation by most closely uniting the person with the mystery of Jesus. After that first reception, frequently celebrating the Eucharist becomes a way for Catholics to deepen their lifelong initiation into Christ's life, death, and Resurrection.

All the other sacraments and dimensions of Christian living can be viewed as leading up to or flowing from the Eucharist. For Catholics, the Eucharist is central.

Let's look at two stories that shed some light on the meaning of the Eucharist.

Having completed the Creation, God looked it over and saw that it was good. Of all the creating, bringing forth man and woman had given God the most delight, for they were made in the image of freedom and love. And so it was that God wanted them, most of all, to remember that their Creator would always be with them.

So God called together representatives of all of Creation besides human beings. Delegations from rock and from fire, from sky and from earth—all were present. Flowers and trees also sent their representatives. And every kind of animal—wild and tame, crawling and swimming, walking and flying—was notified of its right to attend the assembly.

God ushered all the representatives into a huge hall and told them about wanting to give people a sign of love—a sign of God's own continued presence among them. The question God placed before them was, "Who should I send?"

A loud roar at once shook the assembly hall as all the representatives shouted: "Send me! Send me!" So God sent to humans many messengers—gushing waters and mighty winds, the bright sun and protective clouds, the stars and moon of the sky, and the living things of the earth. All of these were powerful reminders indeed, and as long as people looked at them—really looked at them—people remembered God.

Yet eventually, some people forgot how to look, and others got too busy, so they no longer saw the reminders. And as brightly as the great sun shone, and as high or low as the cool clouds

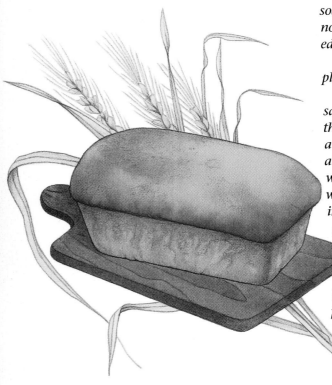

soared, and as swiftly as the gushing waters flowed, these things no longer reminded people of God's love for them. Everyone ended up confused.

God felt sad and lonely, wanting very much to remind people, but who else could be sent?

Then, in the quiet of one evening, bread came to God and said, "Your people are crying out in hunger, O God. They cry out that you have forgotten them, for they have no food. Send me as a sign that you love them and are with them. They will not be able to forget me, for they will be in need of me every day. Nor will they be alone when they eat me, for I beg to be shared. So I will bring them together. And when they come together to share in me, your bread, then they will remember that you love them and are with them. I am the sign for which you have searched so long."

Of course, thought God, I can send bread! So bread went among God's people. The people shared the gift of bread, and they shared in their God's love. And that is why from that day until this, when people come together to share bread, they know that God loves them and is with them.
(Adapted from Juknialis, "Send Me")

* * *

Long ago a family lived in a clearing in the woods. The family was well fed and happy because of the father's prowess as a hunter. But there came a time when game was scarce and the family began to go hungry. When it looked as if they would all starve to death, the woman said to her husband, "This is what you must do. You must kill me and then drag my body in a circle around the clearing." The man refused for several days, though she continued to urge him to do as she had said, until starvation was upon them. Then in desperation he consented to his wife's demand. That night corn grew up wherever the woman's blood had soaked the soil. By morning this new food had grown to maturity and was ready to eat. Ever since, people have eaten corn and remembered Corn Mother's gift to them. (Tinker, "Native Americans")

1. Imagine that you are "bread" called upon to report to God after your two thousand years of use in eucharistic celebrations. Write up a one-page report.

What Does the Eucharist Celebrate?

Remembering Love Shared, Life Poured Out

The first of the two previous stories has a simple message familiar to Christians: Bread has been sent to us, to nourish us, as a daily reminder of God's love. In the Gospels, we read that at the Last Supper, the night before he was put to death,

> [Jesus] took a loaf of bread, and when he had given thanks, he broke it and gave it to [the disciples], saying, "This is my body, which is given for you. Do this in remembrance of me." (Luke 22:19)

The Native American story about Corn Mother also contains a theme familiar to Christians: Love poured out as the giving of one's life brings forth new life. The Gospel account of the Last Supper recalls this truth:

> And [Jesus] did the same with the cup after supper, saying, "This cup that is poured out for you is the new covenant in my blood." (Luke 22:20)

A Ritual Meal

Jesus placed the meaning of his life and death in the context of an ancient, deeply human action—the sharing of a meal. The Gospels indicate that it was probably not just any meal, but a special Jewish ritual meal called the Passover seder. Held yearly in the Israelites' homes since the time of Moses, the Passover seder remembered and celebrated God's saving action of freeing their people from slavery in Egypt. It was essentially a meal of thanksgiving.

A Transformed Meaning

At the Last Supper, Jesus transformed the meaning of that ritual Passover meal by identifying the bread and wine, which were customarily blessed and shared at the seder, with his own body and blood. From that time on, then, the simple gestures of breaking bread together and sharing a cup of wine have been related to Jesus' being broken and shared as nourishment and to Jesus' pouring out his life to give people new life.

The name given to this sacrament, **Eucharist**, is derived from a Greek word that means "thanksgiving." So when Christians celebrate the Eucharist, they are thanking and praising God, in the context of a sacred meal, for all the good God has done for them, through Jesus.

God's Banquet

It is not surprising that Jesus would have chosen a special meal as the setting for giving himself to his friends. In the stories he told that are recounted in the Gospels, Jesus often used the symbol of a banquet to describe sharing in the Kingdom of God. In one story, he refers to a wedding

2. Think back on a particular meal that was also a celebration for you. What rituals were involved? Write about the experience.

3. The word *Eucharist* is derived from a word that means "thanksgiving." We give thanks by appreciating and enjoying gifts. Name five gifts you have received from God. Write a paragraph explaining what you do to enjoy one of them.

feast. In another, he describes a great banquet that the invited guests are too busy to attend; upon learning that the invited guests are not coming, the lord of the house shares the meal with street people instead.

On several occasions, Jesus shocked his companions by eating dinner with tax collectors, prostitutes, and other outcasts of his day. God's love takes in everyone, especially those thought to be of little value by society, and a meal was one significant setting for Jesus to use in communicating what God's love is like.

It was quite appropriate, then, for Jesus to offer himself to his followers and say, "Do this in memory of me," while sharing food and drink with them. For Jesus, the Last Supper was a banquet whose meaning would be made clearer by his death and Resurrection shortly thereafter. In other words, by giving of himself, both symbolically through bread and wine and in deed through his death, Jesus brought about a truly human community worth celebrating in the Eucharist.

The Eucharist thus symbolizes how life and human relationships ought to be: All persons are reconciled. All individuals are invited to gather around the table, forgive one another and make peace, encourage one another, sing songs, and share their life with one another—even going so far as to lay down their life for one another.

Sacrifice: Giving Life to Bring Life

The Last Supper that Jesus shared with his friends cannot be separated from his death on the cross the next day and his being raised from the dead on Easter. At the Eucharist today, Christians remember and thank God for those saving actions of Jesus' life, death, and Resurrection. The sacrament thus recalls Jesus' sacrifice, his pouring out of life in love for all humankind, to bring life to all persons.

4. On the surface, the expression "life-giving sacrifice" sounds self-contradictory—gaining something by giving something up. Using three examples, illustrate how this expression is not self-contradictory but is actually true.

But the Eucharist celebrates more than past deeds; it is more than a meal that is a memorial service. It calls to mind and brings about a *present* reality—that Jesus gives of himself to us in the here and now, bringing new life to us in the process. Although Jesus' death is over once and for all, his self-gift to us goes on today.

By being united to Jesus in the Eucharist, we join our own life struggles and "deaths" (small and large) to his. Our dreams, disappointments, joys, and hurts become one with those of Jesus' own life and death.

Those who gather at the Eucharist are called not simply to remember and be grateful for Jesus' sacrifice; they are invited to bring their everyday life to the table of the Lord and unite that life with Jesus' sacrifice. Thus, their own life is transformed with new meaning; they are "risen" with Jesus. The paschal mystery is not simply a historical event but becomes a present reality in their own life, and the Eucharist celebrates this truth.

The Real Presence

Central to Christians' understanding of the Eucharist is their belief in the real presence of the Risen Jesus among them, not just in memory but in the present moment, nourishing them and enabling them to give their own energy and life to others, to be "bread for the world."

Having "Presence"

What is meant by the real presence of Jesus? Let's first consider what we mean when we say that someone has "presence." It is a hard quality to define, but we usually recognize presence when we experience it. A story taken from the Jewish Hasidic tradition may help.

> Every evening the disciples of Rabbi Baal Shem Tov (the Hasidic founder) gathered to learn. After the evening prayers, the master would go to his room "where the candles would be lit and 'the mysterious Book of Creation' lay open on the table." Those who sought advice were then allowed in as a group to hear the teacher. "One evening as the students left the room, one apologized to the others for monopolizing so much of the Baal Shem's attention. Throughout the entire audience, the master had spoken to him personally. His friend told him not to talk such nonsense. They had all entered the room together and, from the very beginning, the master had spoken only to him. A third, hearing this, laughed and said that they both were mistaken, for their teacher had carried on an intimate conversation with him alone for the entire evening. A fourth and a fifth made the same claim—that the Baal Shem had spoken to them personally, to the exclusion of everyone else. Only then did they realize what had happened, and all fell silent." (Kushner, quoted in *Context*)

To say that someone has presence is to say that the person is fully *there*, with all his or her resources gathered to attend to others, to self, and to whatever the situation requires.

Think of the difference between driving a car "absently" versus driving a car "presently." When we drive absently, we do not pay attention to the road, the traffic, or the pedestrians. Our mind is a million miles away; in a sense, we are just

Presence as a personal quality can be seen in those who give full attention to others and to whatever a situation requires.

driving on automatic pilot. Driving presently, however, means that we are fully alert to conditions on the road; we are engaged and attentive, ready to respond to whatever situation arises.

To be fully present to another person is to be completely there for her or him, like the Baal Shem Tov, who was so present that each of his disciples felt personally cared for and responded to.

Jesus' Presence in the Eucharist—and Ours

In light of the previous examples, consider the meaning of the **real presence** of Jesus in the Eucharist. Catholic faith holds that Jesus is truly present in the Eucharist—in the people gathered for the celebration, in the word of God being proclaimed and preached, and especially in the bread and wine given as Jesus himself, as his own body and blood. Jesus is present, *all there* for us, without holding back. The Eucharist can thus be the ultimate grace-filled experience for a Christian.

However, Jesus' presence in the Eucharist is not experienced fully by participants unless they are truly present also. Here is an example of how you might be truly present in a different kind of group event:

Imagine that your school's basketball team is playing in the championship game of the state tournament. You are there in the audience, cheering and stomping, your entire being alive to what is happening in that game, to every basket made or missed, to every time the ball changes hands. You are tuned in to the emotional lifts and falls in your team, in your friends among the crowd, and in yourself. You are all one, present to one another and to the drama of the event.

That kind of peak experience of being present does not happen often in groups. Similarly, most celebrations of the Eucharist are not marked by such intense presence on the part of the participants, and we cannot expect them to be. But imagine what being truly present, tuned in and attentive, to the mystery of the Eucharist would be like. Through the Eucharist, Christians proclaim that Christ—Most Intimate Friend, Savior of the World—is actually in their midst. If we could fully experience Christ's presence, then surely any other kind of transforming experience, such as a worldly success, would pale by comparison.

Life and Eucharist as One

At one time or another, you may have been involved in a liturgy that so intensely brought together people's lives, concerns, struggles, dreams, and sorrows that the meaning of the Eucharist came alive in a way it never had before. Consider the experience of the young people at one Catholic high school:

Everybody knew Jim was the best rock guitar player in his high school. He had steadily improved since grade school. By his junior year, he had his own group that played at school dances and occasionally at local clubs. He had even played with some professional musicians from the area who recognized his talent. In September of his senior year, however, Jim complained of severe back pain. By December, he was in a hospital, barely able to move his lower body. By April, he was dead. Cancer had eaten away at Jim's spinal column, ending the life of a promising musician and beloved human being.

What were his friends to do? Practically the entire senior class and many others attended the funeral Mass. Jim was prayed for during school. He was given special mention in the yearbook. Still, everyone wanted to do more. Then someone found out that the family was struggling to pay off the heavy debt incurred by Jim's long hospitalization. So the students decided to have a benefit dance. A musical celebration and gathering of friends seemed like an especially appropriate way to remember Jim, and two bands gladly volunteered their time.

Held at the local parish hall, the benefit dance was jammed. To a stranger, the dance probably would not have seemed different from any other high school dance—vibrant music and much excitement. Given a closer look, however, it would have been obvious that this was not an ordinary dance. The police were present

5. On paper, make two columns, headed "Present" and "Absent." In the appropriate column, list the behaviors, attitudes, and thoughts that you have in a situation where you are truly present versus in a situation where you are truly absent.

as usual, but they weren't needed and merely strolled around the parking lot, enjoying the music. Inside, the mood seemed to be a mixture of cheer and sadness. More people than usual smiled at one another. Lots of little groups were dancing together. A special spirit was present—a spirit of friendliness, of togetherness. The promise of a great guitar player had become the reality of a closer, warmer community.

At the end of the evening, around midnight, someone suggested to the campus minister that they close the event with a Mass for anyone who wanted to stay. Almost everyone stayed, even those who didn't usually get into that sort of thing. It just felt *right* to be there.

Jim's best friend from his band played piano, and the parish hall rang with heartfelt singing that expressed hope and fear, love and longing, joy and trust in the midst of hardship and sorrow. The lyrics that most people were only faintly aware of in church now sank in and hit home. Some people had tears in their eyes.

At Communion, friends of Jim came forward to offer the bread and wine to their fellow students. Looking into the faces of those giving and receiving Communion, an observer might have said what the pagans used to say about the early Christians: "See how they love one another!" For those participating in the Mass that night, life and Eucharist had become one.

The people privileged to be part of that celebration had experienced the real presence of Jesus, fully alive in their midst, in one another and in the sharing of bread and wine. It was almost as if Jim, like Jesus, had been there with them too, giving them a gift to treasure even in his death. Many of those people would later carry that memory of a transforming Eucharist to the other, more ordinary celebrations of the Mass they were accustomed to. The Eucharist could never quite be just a routine to them again, but a ritual full of meaning—at some times experienced more deeply than at other times.

The Challenge of the Eucharist: *Be* the Body of Christ

The incident about Jim, his death, and his classmates' caring response to Jim's family points to the crucial challenge that the Eucharist poses to us. We are challenged in every eucharistic celebration not only to *receive* the body of Christ, under the forms of bread and wine, but to *be* the body of Christ in our everyday life. This transformation is possible

6. The experience of community is essential to celebrating the Eucharist. Identify a community to which you belong. What shared values and purposes sustain it? How important is this community to you? Write about what you bring to this community and what you get from it.

only because of the grace of being nourished and strengthened by Jesus himself in the sacrament of the Eucharist.

Becoming What You Receive

The students at Jim's high school discovered the link between the Eucharist and the rest of life when they experienced themselves that night as a welcoming, inclusive community whose members shared one another's concerns. They ached at losing Jim, but they also realized that even in their loss—or perhaps because of it—a new spirit was being born among them as a community. At a level that most of them were only beginning to comprehend, they were uniting their experience with Jesus' death and Resurrection. They were *becoming* the risen body of Christ that they were also receiving.

A Mirror of Everyday Life

The members of the early church recognized that the Eucharist was meant to mirror the way they lived their lives. This is how the Acts of the Apostles describes the Eucharist fitting into the lives of the first Christians:

> All who believed were together and had all things in common; they would sell their possessions and goods and distribute the proceeds to all, as any had need. Day by day, as they spent much time together in the temple, they broke bread at home and ate their food with glad and generous hearts, praising God and having the goodwill of all the people. And day by day the Lord added to their number those who were being saved. (2:44–47)

The Eucharist is meant to be a mirror of what happens outside the Mass itself. It is a reality to be lived out among people who not only receive the body of Christ but become his body as a community.

Looking at Reality

The Eucharist challenges us to be a welcoming community that offers peace, reconciliation, and sharing to all persons, not just to those we want to associate with as friends. But think about the reality of our church, school, family, and neighborhood communities.

- We can proclaim in the Eucharist that we are open to everyone. But strangers or outsiders may still feel unwelcome in our communities. It is easier to talk about the ideals of unity and inclusiveness than to live them.

- Part of the ritual of the Mass is to offer one another a sign of peace. It is relatively easy to reach over and shake hands with the person next to us in the pew and say, "Peace be with you." It is much harder, however, to reach out to people in our life with whom we have a conflict and create genuine peace with them.

- We can eat of the same bread and drink wine from the same cup in the Eucharist, and thereby believe that we share the body and blood of Jesus. Yet we may not be "breaking the bread of our life" outside of Mass—sharing what we have, nurturing one another, and sacrificing for one another. The act of sharing Jesus in the bread and wine becomes an empty gesture unless it is lived out in the rest of life.

The more that Christians share a sense of community, the more they want to celebrate the Eucharist together. If even a small number of people share something of their lives during the week, then for them, participating in the Eucharist on Sunday will be much more meaningful. A handsome church building, good music, and trained readers will always enhance genuine liturgies, but the most important element in really *celebrating* the Eucharist is a sense of belonging, sharing, and community.

Bread for a Hungry World

The challenge of the Eucharist extends beyond the limits of our own communities and into the wider world, where Christians can respond to many forms of hunger and thus become "bread for the world":

- Millions in our own society and around the world, especially children, go hungry every day. There are complex reasons for this, but chief among them is a gravely unjust worldwide economic system that continues to widen the gap between rich people and poor people, rich nations and poor nations.

- In addition to enduring obvious and glaring deprivation from physical hunger and poverty, some people also experience hunger for hope, for freedom to make decisions

7. In the text column on this page, which one of the descriptions (about the difficulty of living out the Eucharist) seems most challenging to you? Write your reflections in a paragraph.

8. Hunger can take many forms besides physical hunger. Write a one-page essay about a particular hunger that you see in your community.

Just as wheat, nourished by sun and soil, can become bread for the world, Christians, nourished by the Eucharist, can give themselves to fill the many kinds of hunger in the world.

that affect their own destiny, for companionship and a sense of community, and for the opportunity to be creative with their lives.

• The whole of creation is threatened by unwise human practices that are destroying many of the earth's resources and delicate ecosystems. The earth is hungry to be treated with justice and to have its health restored.

When Jesus walked the earth, the world was hungry for love, justice, peace, and freedom. Jesus gave himself as nourishment to fill that hunger. Today the world is still hungry. Christians now live on a planet that is desperate for hope in the future. The Eucharist, celebrated with conviction, challenges participants. It remains a hopeful sign that Jesus is still nourishing the world through Christians who give themselves to fill the hunger of the world.

For Review

• How does receiving the Eucharist for the first time represent the fullness of Christian initiation?

• Why is the word *Eucharist* an appropriate name for this sacrament?

• Why was a sacred meal or banquet significant as a setting for the Eucharist in Jesus' day?

• In terms of Jesus' sacrifice, what are Christians who gather at the Eucharist invited to do?

• What does Catholic faith hold about the real presence of Jesus in the Eucharist?

• What is the crucial challenge that the Eucharist poses to Christians?

• Give three examples from the text to show how the reality of our communities may contradict the meaning of the Eucharist.

"They'll Feed You"

The following account illustrates how one child saw the connection between the Eucharist and hunger in the human family.

Margaret, seven years old, had recently made her First Communion. Her mother, her brother Joe, 14, and she were traveling from Norfolk, Virginia, to New York state to visit relatives. They traveled by bus overnight and arrived in Manhattan very early in the morning.

When they got to Port Authority, New York's huge bus station, they saw many homeless people sleeping there, washing in the bathrooms, getting ready for the day. Joe and Margaret had never seen homeless people before, and their mom had to explain who they were and why they were there.

Since it was so early, and their bus to upstate New York didn't leave until later, they went into the city to sightsee. At that hour, the only thing open was St. Patrick's Cathedral. At altars all around St. Patrick's, they saw priests celebrating Mass. They also saw people sleeping in the pews. "More people without homes," Joe said softly.

Margaret, still excited over being able to receive Communion, began to ask her mother if she could go to Communion now. "Not now," said her mother. "We don't have time for Mass. We're sightseeing."

"Please," begged Margaret until her mother relented. She told Margaret, however, that if she was going to go to Communion, she had to sit quietly for a while and pray first.

So Margaret chose to sit and prepare for Eucharist while her mother and brother continued to tour St. Patrick's. As they came back down the aisle, the two saw that seven-year-old Margaret was speaking to one of the men who had been sleeping in the pew in front of her.

As her mother hurried back she caught the conversation that her daughter was having with the scruffy man: "I know you must be hungry. They have some bread and wine at those altars. I'm sure if you ask them, they'll feed you."

Margaret, at seven, may not have been able to explain about how we are all the Body of Christ, but she knew in her heart that we have to act like brothers and sisters, no matter who we are. She saw clearly that food for hungry people was part of what Jesus meant by "Take and eat." (Northup, "Why Is the World Hungry?")

The Eucharist's Symbols and Rituals

On the day before he died, Jesus blessed and shared bread and wine with his disciples, identifying the meal with his own body and blood. Referring to his actions, he said to the disciples, "'Do this in remembrance of me'" (Luke 22:19). Thus, Christians have always felt the Eucharist to be their central sacrament, a holy ritual filled with great meaning, to be done in memory of Jesus until the end of time.

The people who gather together for the Eucharist are its primary symbol, for they are the body of Christ at the local level, and they represent the whole worldwide body of

Christ. The people perform simple gestures such as greeting one another, listening to the words of the Scriptures, praying together, singing, eating, and drinking. As a community, they celebrate the presence of Christ in the Eucharist.

The Eucharist as the Whole Celebration

Catholics use the term *Eucharist* in a variety of ways, all of which are "correct" but have slightly different meanings:
- The whole celebration of the Mass is referred to as the Eucharist. (The word *Mass* comes from the Latin word *missa,* meaning "dismissed." The Eucharist was called the Mass from the parting words of the priest: "Go, you are dismissed," or "*Ite, missa est,*" in Latin.)
- The second part of the Mass, the part that follows the liturgy of the word, is called the liturgy of the Eucharist. This includes the consecration of the bread and wine and the Communion ritual.
- Communion—consuming the body and blood of Christ under the forms of bread and wine, or only of bread—is the way that an individual receives the sacrament of the Eucharist.
- Catholics believe that the Blessed Sacrament, the consecrated bread not consumed during the Mass but reserved in the tabernacle, is Jesus—really present, to be honored and adored. The Blessed Sacrament itself is called the Eucharist.

In this discussion of the Eucharist's symbols and rituals, we will use the term *Eucharist* to mean the whole Mass. The entire Eucharist consists of these two main parts:
1. the **liturgy of the word**—that is, the proclaiming of the word of God in the Scriptures
2. the **liturgy of the Eucharist**—that is, the outpouring of thanks to God that includes the consecration and sharing of the bread and wine in which Jesus is present

Over the centuries, many secondary rituals were added to the ceremony, and today some of these secondary rituals are standard practice. Within the Mass, however, three rituals remain primary: proclaiming the word of God (in the liturgy of the word), breaking the bread, and sharing the cup of wine (in the liturgy of the Eucharist).

Proclaiming the Word of God

The ceremony that surrounds the proclamation of the word of God indicates that the reading of the Scriptures is not simply for getting information. It is an opportunity for encountering God.

Bread and wine are consecrated in the Eucharist to be given and shared as the body and blood of Jesus Christ.

9. One major purpose of a Benediction service is simply to gaze at the Eucharist and remember how wonderful it is that Christ is present. Name some ways that you could keep alive the memory of someone dear to you who is physically gone but present with you nonetheless.

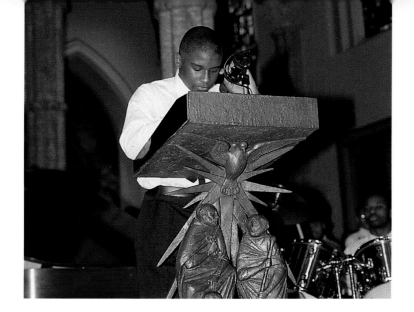

The word of God is proclaimed during Mass in readings from the Scriptures. On Sundays there are three readings, with a lector reading the first two.

As befits its status, the book of readings is carried and raised high in the liturgical procession, kissed, and generally treated with a great deal of reverence. The readings are understood to be God's revelation just as Jesus is God's revelation. On Sundays, three readings are usually given: one from the Hebrew Scriptures, one from the Christian Testament besides the Gospels, and one from the Gospels. Often, the people sing a response to the reading as a way of taking the words to heart. The people sing "Alleluia!" before the Gospel reading and stand during that reading to show their joy at hearing of Jesus, the living Word of God. All these rituals symbolize that the proclamation of the word is special and sacred. The priest's homily after the readings is intended to help the people discover the meaning of the word for their own life.

Just as the memory of Jesus remains alive for Christians in the breaking of the bread and the sharing of the cup, so too is Jesus alive for Christians, present to them, in their hearing the words and stories of Jesus' life and community.

10. The readings at Mass are sacred stories meant to inspire and affirm the faith of the listeners. Ask an older member of your family to tell you a story from the past that she or he found inspiring. Record the story in writing or on tape.

Breaking the Bread

When the early Christians talked about the Eucharist, they said that they gathered for the breaking of the bread. As the most basic and essential food of the people in Jesus' culture, bread often represented life and was thus an appropriate symbol for the Eucharist. The act of giving thanks over the bread, breaking it, and distributing it remains the core ritual of the Mass.

Gift of God and Work of Human Hands

Bread is a basic food for many people and is closely associated with God's and nature's bountifulness. Images of vast wheat fields swaying in the wind or stalks of wheat beside a plate evoke a sense of gratitude for God's gifts to us, especially for our "daily bread." At the same time, bread is the product of human work. It is wheat that has been ground, kneaded, and baked. Bread is both a gift of God and a work of human hands.

11. Compare homemade bread with factory-made bread. Which seems to better symbolize the meaning of the Eucharist and why?

Blessed, Broken, Given for Others

In the ritual of the Eucharist, bread is transformed. It becomes Christ offered up, broken, and given to his people. The gathered people are reminded that they too are Christ—meant to be bread that is offered up, broken, and given for others.

Consider the example of parents. Fathers and mothers offer up themselves, the "bread of their own lives," to nourish their children. By working to support the children with food, clothing, and shelter, they provide physical nourishment. In addition, they give their love and energy to surround their children with an emotionally and spiritually nourishing home. In a similar way, you have probably had experiences of giving yourself, "breaking the bread of your own life," for the sake of others.

Bread is a powerful symbol; *breaking* bread is an action that adds to its symbolism, and *sharing* bread adds another dimension of meaning. However, *eating* bread most clearly brings out its natural significance. Eating the bread implies gaining life from it. Similarly, receiving the body of Christ in Communion means sharing life in the body of Christ—the church.

Sharing the Cup

We can survive for about forty days without food but for very few days—perhaps five—without water. Consequently, drink is just as essential to life as food, as basic a "staff of life" as bread. Like bread, wine is both a natural gift of God and the work of human hands. It is the part of nature's bounty that has been harvested and worked on until it becomes a pleasing drink.

A Sign of Celebration

Wine is not a *necessary* type of drink, as water is. Wine adds a hint of celebration to the basic symbolism of drink as necessary for survival. As a sign of celebration, wine is an appropriate, awesome symbol for the blood that Christ willingly shed in freeing humanity from sin and death. Christians sharing the cup of wine at the Eucharist celebrate the life-giving sacrifice of Christ while committing themselves to pour out their lives for others. And that is a joyful act.

The Liturgy of the Word

First Reading

A reading from the book of the prophet Isaiah.

Rise up in splendor, Jerusalem! Your light has come,
the glory of the LORD shines upon you. . . .
(60:1)

The Word of the Lord.
Thanks be to God.

First Reading

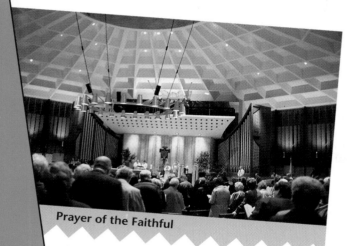
Prayer of the Faithful

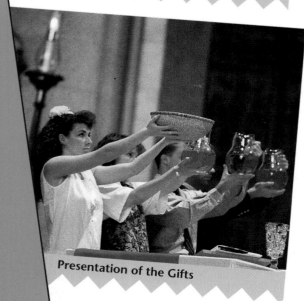
Presentation of the Gifts

Gospel Reading

A reading from the holy gospel according to Matthew.

After Jesus' birth in Bethlehem of Judea during the reign of King Herod, astrologers from the east arrived one day in Jerusalem. . . . (2:1)

The gospel of the Lord.
Praise to you, Lord Jesus Christ.

Prayer of the Faithful

For peace in our families, community, and world, we pray,
Lord, hear our prayer.

The Liturgy of the Eucharist

Presentation of the Gifts

Blessed are you, Lord, God of all creation.
Through your goodness we have this bread to offer,
which earth has given and human hands have made.
It will become for us the bread of life.
Blessed be God for ever.

Eucharistic Prayer

We come to you, Father,
with praise and thanksgiving,
through Jesus Christ your Son.
Through him we ask you to accept and bless
these gifts we offer you in sacrifice. . . .

The day before he suffered
he took bread in his sacred hands
and looking up to heaven,
to you, his almighty Father,
he gave you thanks and praise.
He broke the bread,
gave it to his disciples, and said:
Take this, all of you, and eat it:
this is my body which will be given up for you.

When supper was ended,
he took the cup.
Again he gave you thanks and praise,
gave the cup to his disciples, and said:
Take this, all of you, and drink from it:
this is the cup of my blood,
the blood of the new and everlasting covenant.
It will be shed for you and for all
so that sins may be forgiven.
Do this in memory of me.

Let us proclaim the mystery of faith:
  Christ has died,
  Christ is risen,
  Christ will come again.

Eucharistic Prayer

Communion Rite

Communion Rite

Communion Rite

The peace of the Lord be with you always.
  And also with you.
Let us offer each other the sign of peace. . . .

The body of Christ.
  Amen.
The blood of Christ.
  Amen.

Concluding Rite

Go in peace to love and serve the Lord.
  Thanks be to God.

A Common Cup, Not Individual Cups

Sharing the cup of wine was ritually as significant for the early Christians as *drinking* the wine itself. They knew that Jesus' blood was shed for all men and women, so they shared joyfully in receiving his life. Thus, in the present Catholic eucharistic celebration, each person does not receive an individual cup; rather, everyone drinks from a common cup. Realizing the commitment implied by receiving the Eucharist can bring people to desire the community support symbolized by sharing the cup.

For many centuries before the Second Vatican Council, the Catholic practice was that only the priest who presided at a Mass drank from the cup. This was not the original intent of the Eucharist, however. The cup, as well as the bread, was meant to be shared by all the believers. Now, in most parishes on Sundays, people are invited to partake from the cup after receiving the bread.

For Review

- What are the two main parts of the Mass?
- Why is bread an appropriate symbol for the Eucharist?
- In the Eucharist, into what is the bread transformed? What does this transformation remind the gathered people of?
- Why is wine an appropriate symbol for the Eucharist?

The Eucharist's History

Its Jewish Roots

More than any other sacrament, the Eucharist reveals the Jewish roots of Christianity. That is to say, both major parts of the Mass—the liturgy of the Eucharist and the liturgy of the word—began as Jewish rituals.

A Jewish Meal: Roots of the Liturgy of the Eucharist

At the Last Supper, Jesus celebrated a Jewish community meal, very likely the Passover seder, with his friends. Meals, especially family meals, are a very important form of worship for Jews. Meals can be steeped in ritual; the Passover meal, which celebrates God's liberation of the Israelites from

The liturgy of the Eucharist began at the Last Supper, which was most likely a Passover meal.
Photo: A table is set today for the ritual of the Jewish Passover seder.

slavery in Egypt, is a notable example. Often, bread and wine play a central role in the ritual of family meals. And "giving thanks" is generally the theme of a meal. So when Jesus gathered his friends to share bread and wine, he was not doing anything strange or uncommon.

Jesus' actions and words at the Last Supper *were* unique. First, he identified the bread and wine with himself and with his impending death on the cross, implying that the body and blood he was soon to give up would be the source of liberation for humankind. Second, Jesus commanded the Apostles to continue to share bread and wine in his memory.

In the early years of the Christian church, on Sunday, the day on which Jesus was resurrected, believers gathered for a meal, which included breaking the bread and sharing the cup in Jesus' memory. In this ritual, believers commemorated the Resurrection and experienced the presence of the Risen Jesus with them. This shared, ritual meal was the origin of the liturgy of the Eucharist as we know it today.

12. Interview a Jewish person who is familiar with the Passover seder about how this ritual meal is celebrated today. Write down any similarities you note between the seder and the Eucharist.

A Synagogue Service: Roots of the Liturgy of the Word

A Jewish synagogue service traditionally centers around hearing the word of God in the Hebrew Scriptures or the Torah. The people's prayers, the various songs and chants, and the teaching by the rabbi support that central action. For the Jews, the Lord is present in the written word.

The earliest Christians, who were also Jews, naturally attended the synagogue services on Saturday, the Sabbath. But eventually, when the Christians began admitting Gentile converts who were not obligated to keep the Jewish Law, the non-Christian Jews regarded the Christians as a threat to needed Jewish unity. (The Jews had just been crushed by the

Romans and fostered an intense nationalistic unity in order to survive.) So the Christians were no longer allowed to attend synagogue services.

The Christians then went their own way, devising their own service of the word, which probably incorporated the letters of Saint Paul, and eventually the Gospel stories, with readings from the Hebrew Scriptures. The early Christians soon combined this service with the eucharistic meal and celebrated it as one service on Sunday: the liturgy of the word and the liturgy of the Eucharist. Thus, the basic elements of the Mass as we know it today were established.

From Supper to Sacrifice

A "Love Feast"

In the beginning of the church's history, the Eucharist was celebrated as a fellowship meal or "love feast," called an **agape.** Christians shared the food that each person brought to the Sunday assembly, and they referred to this meal as the Lord's Supper. As the number of members increased, the meal was gradually reduced to a simpler fare of bread and wine, the essential elements of the Eucharist.

For many years after the full meal ceased being common practice, however, Christians still brought food to their services to share with poor people. Today, the offertory collection echoes that early spirit of giving at the Eucharist.

A Ritual Meal of Sacrifice

Over the first three centuries of Christianity, the Eucharist evolved from a fellowship meal to a ritual meal. Some variations in its celebration existed from community to community, but the basic pattern was the same. The eucharistic part of the ritual consisted of an offering (gifts of bread and wine), a thanksgiving prayer over the offered gifts in the earlier Jewish style, a breaking of the bread, and a receiving of the bread and wine by all the participants.

More and more, Christians realized that by participating in this ritual meal, they were entering into the mystery of Christ's sacrifice, death, and Resurrection. They were doing more than sharing a love feast; they were participating in their own redemption.

From Participants to Silent Spectators

An Elaborate Ceremony

After Christianity was declared a legal religion in the fourth century, the church's rituals went public. That change set the stage, by the end of the sixth century, for the devel-

13. How could church communities share their resources with poor people today? List at least five suggestions.

opment of a highly elaborate, almost regal ceremony around what had once been a simple sharing of food and drink. Prayers that had once been offered spontaneously by the presiding bishop were written down and standardized. The place of worship moved from homes, where rituals were carried out secretly during times of persecution, to magnificent church buildings that Christians were proud to build and to celebrate Mass in.

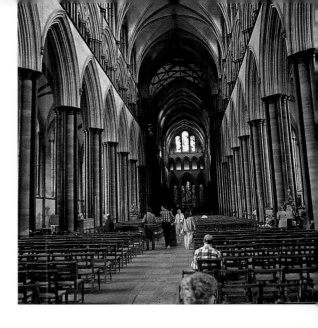

Churches of the Middle Ages were constructed to emphasize the awesomeness of the eucharistic mystery and thus encouraged worship from a distance.

Less and Less of a Role for the People

The shift in emphasis from the Eucharist as a community meal to the Eucharist as a highly elaborate and dramatic ceremony of sacrifice naturally affected participation in the ritual. Specifically, the priest-presider did more and more of the action while the people in attendance participated less and less. By the Middle Ages, priests were "saying" Mass while the people watched in silence. In fact, priests often said Mass privately on weekdays, or with only a single server present, for the special intention of some member of the congregation. The community dimension of the Eucharist had all but disappeared.

Worship from a Distance

At the same time that people's participation in the Eucharist was lessening, the significance of the wine was being de-emphasized, and the bread became more important as a symbol. In fact, the awesomeness of the presence of Christ in the bread was so strongly stressed that people hesitated to receive Communion. They contented themselves with viewing the bread elevated at the Consecration. People received Communion so infrequently that the church had to require that the faithful receive it at least once a year.

Also, with the emphasis on devotion from a distance, the idea of "gathering around the table" faded. As a result, the table became an ornate altar that was set against a decorated wall. The priest, with his back to the people, faced the altar and led the people in the holy sacrifice. Everyone faced the same direction, but the people were unable to see what was going on at the altar.

14. The Mass re-enacts a great story, but we can find any story boring if we do not really "hear" it. Rewrite the story of the Last Supper in the first person—as if you were actually there. Make the story as real and as interesting as possible.

An Unfamiliar Language

At one time in the early church, the language of the Mass in the West had been changed from Greek to Latin because Latin was the language of the people. But in the Middle Ages, Latin continued to be used, even though fewer and fewer of the common people were able to understand it. (The use of Latin in the Mass was standard up until the 1960s.)

The Presence of God Revealed

As chapter 6 explained, the Council of Trent further solidified the Eucharist as an intricate, standardized sacrament filled with many secondary symbols, prayers, and gestures. In short, the original, central rituals had become much-added-onto. The dramatic nature of the eucharistic celebration made attendance at Mass seem more like watching a performance than like sharing a meal. Nevertheless, the awe-inspiring ritual of the Eucharist revealed God's presence through Jesus to millions of faithful Christians of those times, just as the Eucharist continues to reveal God today, but in a simpler, more participatory way.

A Return to Participation and Table Companionship

To restore the original, communal spirit of the Eucharist, the Second Vatican Council of the 1960s called for vast reforms.

Changes in the Liturgy

These quite-noticeable changes in the Mass came in the aftermath of Vatican Council II:

- The altar facing the wall became once again a table set in the midst of or close to the congregation, with the priest facing the people.
- The Latin language, used for centuries to celebrate the Mass, was replaced by the common, spoken languages of the cultures in which the Mass was being celebrated.
- Prayers and responses were spoken by the entire assembly, not just by the altar servers.
- The altar rail that separated the congregation from the sanctuary was removed.
- Kneeling for Communion at the altar rail was replaced by the earlier custom of standing while receiving Communion to express joy and thanksgiving.
- People were invited to take the Communion bread in their hands and to chew the bread, whereas it had once been considered proper to receive Communion only on the tongue.
- Communion wine as well as bread was offered to the whole congregation.
- Singing by the whole congregation was encouraged.
- Prayers of petition addressing the immediate concerns and needs of the people and the wider world were added.
- Laypeople were invited to participate in special roles as lectors (readers), members of the offertory procession, and eucharistic ministers (distributors of Communion).

15. Imagine that you were a Catholic in the 1960s and early 1970s when many changes in the Mass, such as the changes listed on this page, came about. Which changes would you have found most striking or noticeable? Would you have welcomed the changes? Why or why not? Write down your reflections.

Why Sunday Mass?

The topic of Sunday Mass often brings up the following comments by teenagers:

- "Mass is so boring; it's the same old thing every week."
- "I don't get anything out of going to Mass."
- "I don't need Mass; I worship God in my own way."
- "I don't think Mass should be forced on people."

Why Mass at All?

All of these statements point to a question that has been expressed by many young people: "Why should I go to Mass on Sunday?" In several ways, the broader question about simply *going* to Mass—"Why celebrate the Eucharist *at all?*"—has already been answered in this chapter. Mass is a way to welcome God's presence in our life and a reminder of Jesus' loving sacrifice for us. Catholics also proclaim their faith at Mass, are nourished in that faith, and gain the encouragement of other Christians in living out their faith. In Christians' commitment to celebrate and *be* the body of Christ, the Eucharist is not an optional part of being Catholic.

Why Should I go to Mass on *Sunday?*

Behind the question "Why should I go to Mass on *Sunday?*" lies an issue worth reflecting on—why *has* the church traditionally placed such great emphasis on *Sunday* worship and made it an obligation for Catholics to attend Mass on Sunday or on the evening before?

The early Christians celebrated the Eucharist on Sunday because it was the day of the Resurrection. Once Christianity became legitimate, Sunday became the Christian Sabbath, or day of rest. (And the Sabbath was considered to begin on the Saturday evening before.) An early Christian writer taught that anyone not in the assembly at Sunday Eucharist weakened the church. This suggests that Christians recognized very early on that all the church members together make up the unified body of Christ. Every Eucharist clearly symbolizes that unified body. In the earliest reference to the Eucharist in the Christian Testament, Paul writes, "We who are many are one body, for we all partake of the one bread" (1 Corinthians 10:17). But celebrating the Eucharist on Sunday, when all Catholics are called to participate, most strongly signifies the total, worldwide nature of the body of Christ.

Receiving the Eucharist at Sunday Mass is unique because it reminds us that the body of Christ is not only the bread that is eaten but also the entire, worldwide church. Presence at the Sunday Eucharist strengthens the message of support and nourishment for oneself and for others; absence weakens that message. As a symbolically rich day, then, Sunday is a fitting time to celebrate as a community the most pivotal of the seven sacraments.

Christ Present in the People

The changes brought about by Vatican Council II re-affirmed a simple truth that had become obscured over the centuries: Those who celebrate the Eucharist together are a symbol, with the bread and wine, of Christ's presence. People are to enter actively into the Eucharist, be transformed by it, and live it out. The homily, or sermon, following the readings is intended to bring the word of God alive in people's experiences. Presenting the bread and wine at the offertory symbolizes bringing the everyday work and experiences of life to God.

The Eucharist: At the Heart of the Church's Life

In most Catholic parishes throughout the world, the Eucharist is celebrated in a special way on Sundays, and many parishes have daily Mass as well. Even in places where a priest is not present every week, communities of Catholic Christians gather regularly for a worship service centering on receiving the Eucharist. A number of Catholics attend Mass daily for much of their life, finding in the Eucharist the spiritual nourishment that sustains them. In many Catholic schools, when a major occasion or event like a graduation is celebrated, the Eucharist is typically a central part of the festivities. More than any other sacrament, the Eucharist celebrates Christ's real presence and is thus at the heart of the church's life.

Through the Eucharist, Jesus continues to be present to us today as he was to the Apostles at the Last Supper: at the table with his friends, in the bread and the wine, and in the sharing of life, sacrificing, and finding of new life by his body and blood. And through the Eucharist, those who receive the body of Christ are strengthened to *be* the body of Christ for others in their life.

For Review

- What are the Jewish roots of the liturgy of the Eucharist and the liturgy of the word?
- What effect on people's participation in the Eucharist was caused by the shift in emphasis from its celebration as a community meal to its celebration as a highly elaborate ceremony of sacrifice?
- Name five changes in the Mass that came about from the reforms of Vatican Council II.

16. Plan a Sunday for you and your friends that would reflect a spirit of worship, recreation, thanksgiving, and enjoyment. Present in writing an outline of your Sunday of worship and rest.

The Eucharist:
Linking Past, Present, and Future

By now it is probably apparent why full initiation into the Catholic faith comes only with the third sacrament of initiation, the Eucharist. The life of the whole church centers on the Eucharist, in which the past, present, and future are brought together in a powerful ritual. To be a full member of the church is to enter into that mystery.

At the Last Supper, Jesus said of his actions, "Do this in remembrance of me." Thus, in the Mass, the church ritually re-enacts the closing events of his life on earth. Through the church's symbolic action, Jesus is not relegated to the dead past but instead remains a living presence in the members of his body, the church. The Eucharist expresses the present condition of the church community, which must receive in order to give the nourishment that will make the world whole again. And the Eucharist anticipates the future Reign of God, the "heavenly banquet" promised by Jesus, while it helps to make that longed-for future a reality even in the present.

In the Mass, Catholics unite with all other Christians throughout the world and down through the ages in celebrating Jesus. Because of him, Catholics can gather around the table and be one family, at least for a few moments. The Eucharist becomes a constant reminder—all the more powerful because it is a ritual—of the words of the Lord's Prayer: "Thy Kingdom come . . . on earth as it is in heaven."

Like the Eucharist, rituals of remembrance from other religions are intended not only to keep alive the memory of those who have died but to point to a hoped-for future that is different because of the sacrifices of those who have died.

Photo: In Hiroshima, Japan, a pathway of candles marks the anniversary of the dropping of the atomic bomb on that city on 6 August 1945. Public rituals of remembrance recall the deaths of many thousands of Japanese people and express longing for a world without war and destruction.

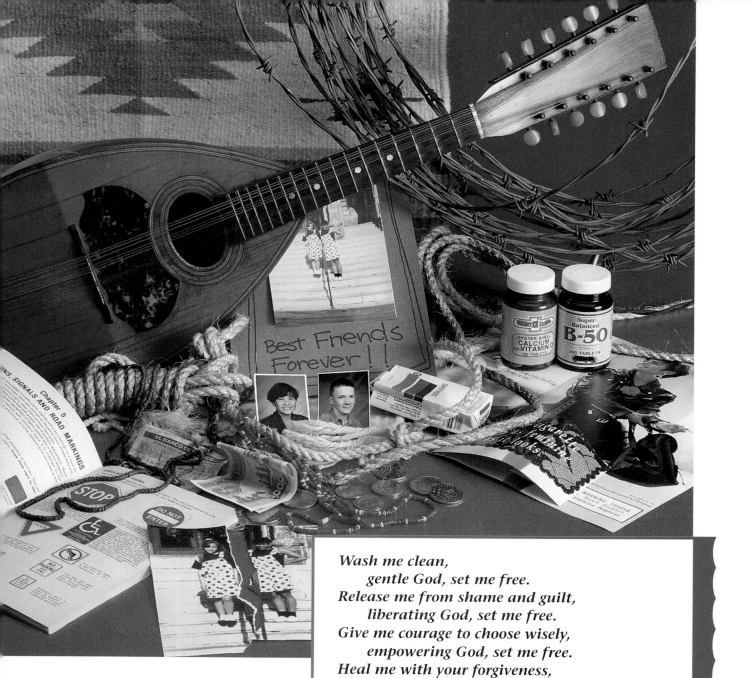

Wash me clean,
   gentle God, set me free.
Release me from shame and guilt,
   liberating God, set me free.
Give me courage to choose wisely,
   empowering God, set me free.
Heal me with your forgiveness,
   compassionate God, set me free.
Amen.

10

Reconciliation: Celebrating Forgiveness

Two of the Catholic church's seven sacraments recall and bring into our midst the healing ministry of Jesus: the sacraments of reconciliation and anointing. We will consider reconciliation in this chapter and anointing in chapter 11.

The sacrament of reconciliation, also called the sacrament of penance, celebrates the unfailing forgiveness that God extends to us. In his public ministry, Jesus communicated that forgiveness of God over and over to those who approached him with sincere faith: "Your sins are forgiven."

The Catholic church has ritualized into a sacrament the deeply human need to experience the forgiveness of both God and community when we have sinned. The sacrament of reconciliation also provides a way for us to heal our spirit by telling the story of our own brokenness and failings.

The following Scandinavian folktale gives us a way to understand the intent behind the sacrament of reconciliation.

Once there was a man from Iceland, a great poet and storyteller named Ivar. He won fame for his storytelling in the court of Istine, the king of Norway. King Istine thought much of Ivar and bestowed many favors upon him and even upon his brother Thorfin, who also lived in the court.

One day, Ivar's brother decided to return to his native Iceland. Before Thorfin left, however, Ivar asked him to bear a message to Adney, a young woman whom Ivar had loved and who had loved him since childhood. Ivar asked his brother to tell Adney that he would return in the spring to marry her.

When Thorfin arrived in Iceland, he himself fell in love with Adney and she with him. And so they married. Thus, when spring came and Ivar arrived in Iceland to marry Adney, he was heartbroken at what he found. Filled with sadness and bitterness, he returned to the court of King Istine in Norway.

Everyone at court noticed a change in Ivar, especially the king. The joy in Ivar's singing was gone. The beautiful truths in his stories were replaced by ugly witticisms. Ivar was a sad man, and his bitterness cast a cold shadow over the entire court.

Wanting to help his friend, the king called Ivar to his throne one night after the evening banquet. Ivar approached the throne, and the king quietly asked the young man what was upsetting him. Ivar merely said, "I am sorry, my lord, but I am not free to disclose what is troubling me."

Guessing that the problem might concern a woman, the king asked, "Is there a woman, Ivar—someone back home, perhaps?" Ivar remained silent. The king knew that he had asked the crucial question. Ivar finally nodded yes.

The king smiled and said: "Ivar, there's no difficulty with that. I am the mightiest king in this part of the world. No one would dare to interfere with my wishes. The next boat that leaves for Iceland will have you on board. You will take a letter from me to this young woman's family, saying that it is my wish that she shall become your bride."

Ivar said, "That is impossible, my lord."

The king looked at him and said, "Do you mean that she is already married?" Ivar nodded.

The king fell silent in thought. Yet, after a few moments, he spoke again: "Well, then, Ivar, we must think of something else. The next time I make my rounds of the countryside and visit the villages and towns, I will take you with me. As I take you from place to place, you will meet many beautiful women. Perhaps you will find one of them to satisfy your deepest needs."

Ivar shook his head and said, "No, my lord, for every time I see a beautiful woman I am reminded of Adney, and my grief is deepened."

The king then said: "Well, then, Ivar, I will give you land and estates—large estates so that you might devote your energies to taking care of the farming and the livestock and all other business matters that will keep you preoccupied and busy for the entire year. With your hands full of work that has to be done, you will soon forget the woman. Then happiness will return to you."

But Ivar said, "No, my lord, I have no wish, no desire, and no ability to do such work."

The king, who cared deeply for Ivar, thought some more and then ventured another idea: "Ivar, I know. I will give you money. I'll give you enough money to travel wherever your heart seeks to go, to the farthest corner of Europe. In your travels, you will see many things and experience many adventures. Then you may forget the woman in Iceland!" Once again Ivar refused, saying he had no desire, no wish, and no ability to travel anywhere.

The king thought and thought and thought. Finally, he offered his last idea: "Ivar, there is one last thing I can think of. I know that this suggestion might seem weak compared to the others. Yet perhaps it may be of some help to you, so I will make it anyway. Ivar, after supper every night, I invite you to stay here with me and to spend as much time as you need to tell me of your feelings for this woman, Adney. You may do that for as long as you need. I will be here."

Reluctantly, Ivar agreed. So every night, when the meal was over and the tables were cleared, Ivar sat next to the throne of King Istine and told him his story. He told his story for days, weeks, and even months. And at the close of each evening, the king never let Ivar leave without some token of his friendship. At the end of each evening, the king gave Ivar a small but meaningful gift.

Finally, after several months, Ivar found that he no longer needed to tell his story. His old joy returned to him, and once again Ivar began to sing and to tell the ancient stories that Scandinavians love so dearly. In the following year, he met a young woman whom he fell in love with and who loved him. Ivar was once again a happy man, but he was now also a wiser person. Thus, Ivar soon gained even greater fame as a storyteller whose tales had wise and happy endings.

Ivar was lucky to have King Istine as a friend. Istine genuinely cared for Ivar and was willing to help him any way he could. Ivar, however, wanted no bandages to cover up his pain, no matter how fancy the bandage. He felt his pain too deeply to try to hide it. Ivar needed to forgive Thorfin and Adney for the pain they had caused him, even though they had not intended to hurt him by falling in love. Ivar himself also needed forgiveness for the bitter conduct he had shown to the court. The king finally offered the simplest gift he possessed—himself, his presence in listening to Ivar's story, as long and as often as Ivar needed. That simple gift turned out to be very powerful: Istine gave Ivar the chance to lay his burden down.

1. Imagine that after one year in Adney and Thorfin's marriage, Adney deeply regrets that she did not marry Ivar. She becomes very sullen, and she constantly treats her husband in a nasty manner. Suppose that she comes to you for help. What would you offer her? Would your approach resemble the king's response to Ivar? Describe your response in writing.

What Does Reconciliation Celebrate?

The forgiveness of God celebrated in the sacrament of reconciliation happens in many ways, but common to all is the chance to lay our burdens down. We can take up this chance by telling our stories, "turning ourselves around," and restoring our wounded relationships.

Telling Our Stories

Life *can* present heavy burdens sometimes. And unfortunately, like Ivar, we often react in ways that add to life's burdens. Acknowledging and then examining our own human weaknesses is one step in laying our burdens down.

Sin: Passing On the Hurt

Sometimes our response to the hurt in our life is to pass it on to others, causing even further hurt. This is how **sin**—the condition of being alienated from oneself, other persons, and God—gets perpetuated in the world. Sin often results from carrying around a legacy of hurt that we refuse to lay down. The burden of that legacy manages to disrupt even our best intentions. Saint Paul understood this dynamic well: "I do not understand my own actions. For I do not do what I want, but I do the very thing I hate" (Romans 7:15).

So out of our own complex history of hurts, we may say words that cut deeply into the hearts of people we love. We may make promises and break them. We may see a weakness in another person and never cease to mention it. We may hide the truth about something we did so that people will think well of us. Like Ivar, we need to lay down our burden of cutting words, forgotten courtesies, and mistaken actions so that we can be free to love again with a whole heart.

Healing: Bringing the Darkness into the Light

We all have our dark side—weaknesses that cause us to do things we would rather not do or things we *know* we should not do. We have stories that we can barely acknowledge to ourselves, let alone share with other people. So we conceal our hurts and our faults. All of us, then, are in need of healing. The story of Ivar points to the truth that our healing comes from bringing our dark side into the light. Maturity is marked by the ability to admit that we have a dark side, and by the determination to bring that dark side into the light.

We often seek healing through some kind of story-telling. Isn't the chance to share the story of our own self one of the special things about having a best friend? A best friend is usually someone who knows our whole story—our dark side as well as our bright side—and still accepts us. A best friend is someone with whom we can be ourselves and even make mistakes—without fear of embarrassment or rejection.

Healing comes from bringing our dark side into the light.

The Gift of a Good Listener

Some persons, like King Istine, are better listeners than others. Often these are people who know their own faults well enough to be able to accept the weak spots in others. They are also able to ask the right questions or are just genuinely interested in people and their problems. Good listeners make it clear through their smiles or warm tones of voice that they accept and care for us.

During your own childhood, who were your favorite teachers, priests or ministers, relatives, and other adults? Chances are that they had at least one of two traits: Either they gladly listened to your stories, or they shared their own stories with you. All through our life, we need persons with whom we can share our stories.

Scenes of Sharing Our Stories

Here are some examples of what the sacrament of reconciliation celebrates—people sharing the stories of their own weakness, laying down the burdens that have kept them from loving with a whole heart:

- Mike can tell his close friend Jeff things about himself that he cannot admit to anyone else: "You know, after I broke up with Ellie, it hit me that the only reason I'd had the guts to break up was that I thought maybe Cheryl was interested in me again. Which made me feel kind of phony about why I'd been going with Ellie in the first place—I wasn't that crazy about her, but I felt like I had to be going out with *some* girl."

- Megan is in treatment for alcohol addiction, and she is required to go to Alcoholics Anonymous meetings. At her fourth meeting, she admits: "When I first came here, I thought I really wasn't alcoholic, that I wasn't like the rest of you, that I was better. And I was just playing along with this whole AA routine to keep my counselor happy. But I'm starting to see that I have a real problem, like everybody else here. Whenever I'm feeling the least bit anxious or uncomfortable, all I can think of is, 'I gotta have a drink.' I have to admit, I'm not on top of it, and it scares me."

- Joan is alarmed at how enraged she has been getting at her two-year-old son for his almost-constant misbehavior. She confides to her friend Rita: "You know, when I'm spanking him, sometimes I really get carried away—I just feel crazy, like I have to let all this rage and frustration out of me, and I forget about what I'm doing to *him.* After I calm down, he clings to me and acts so sweet, like he's scared I'm going to get mad and start hitting him again. And then I feel like such a *terrible* mother."

2. Recall an instance when storytelling was a healing experience for you. Tell about the incident in writing.

Good listeners make it easy for us to tell our stories, because they let us know that they accept us and care for us.

Confession as a Ritual of Telling Our Stories

In the sacrament of reconciliation, the sharing that happens in everyday life, the sharing of one's weakness and woundedness, is ritualized in a process called **confession.** In order to make a good confession, a person must first of all honestly face the sin that is within him or her. Only then can the person share the story of his or her weakness with a priest, who represents both God and the whole Christian community. In confession, the priest listens and offers acceptance, guidance, and forgiveness on their behalf.

The telling of specific sins keeps the process of reconciliation from becoming too abstract. In the sacrament, people do not seek forgiveness "in general" or resolve to change "in general." Rather, they name specific attitudes and behaviors that they find to be trouble spots in their relationships with God and others.

Although church teaching states that Catholics should confess their most serious sins (called *mortal sins* because they represent a total turning away from God and goodness) at least once a year, confession of lesser (or *venial*) sins is recommended as well. Acknowledging our sins to a confessor in the context of a reconciliation service can be a profound experience of healing and a great help to growth in Christian maturity and love.

Turning Around

One of the most beloved of Jesus' stories in the Gospels is the parable of the prodigal son (Luke 15:11–32). Recall that in the story, the younger son turns his back on his parents, taking his inheritance and going off to spend it in reckless living. But when his money runs out, he is left with feeding pigs as his only means of survival. Finally, he realizes how foolish and shortsighted he has been. He decides to go home and beg forgiveness, hoping to live even as a servant in his parents' house.

Coming to Our Senses

We know that the father in the story welcomes his son back with open arms, so delighted is he that the young man has returned. He throws a big party for his son, insisting that he be treated specially. The point of the story is to demonstrate God's unconditional, all-embracing forgiveness of those who wander away. But note how the young man opened himself to *experiencing* forgiveness. In a journey that was both spiritual and physical, he came to his senses, acknowledged his mistakes, made a turnaround, and traveled back to his parents' home in order to make things right with

3. Suppose that you are in charge of designing a reconciliation service for your high school. From the questions on page 209, select ten that seem most meaningful to include in a reflection time for an examination of conscience.

An Examination of Conscience

Here are some questions that might be used to make an examination of conscience before confession or at any time. They are divided into three areas: relationship with God, relationships with others, and relationship with self.

Relationship with God

- Have I developed ways to make God's presence active in my life?
- Do I take time for God by participating in Sunday Eucharist or setting aside moments to pray or read the Scriptures?
- Do I bring Jesus' perspective to bear on my decisions about my relationships with others, my use of money and other materials, and my view of myself?
- Do I speak of God and my faith with reverence?

Relationships with Others

- Do I love and respect my parents and other family members and try to resolve my differences with them peacefully?
- Do I treat other people with respect, not with abuse, prejudice, or manipulation?

- Do I share what I have with those in need and reach out to suffering persons with support?
- Do I reverence all human life, do whatever I can to help life thrive, and avoid actions that harm life?
- Am I truthful, fair, and genuine in my dealings with others?
- Do I work honestly at my job or studies?
- Have I hurt others' reputation by speaking falsely about them or spreading gossip?
- Do I try to become informed on issues affecting society and the whole world?
- Do I treat all of creation with respect and justice?
- Have I honored the sacredness of sexuality by not using another person sexually and by reserving full sexual expression for marriage?
- Am I a faithful friend?
- Do I deal with conflict in a constructive way?
- Do I drive with care and safety?
- Do I waste resources?

Relationship with Self

- Do I try to develop myself as a person, making full use of my strengths and talents?
- Do I explore my own motivations and attitudes about things to become more honest with myself?
- Do I put myself down?
- Do I try to put destructive attitudes into perspective so they do not control me?
- Do I let fear stand in the way of doing what I think is right?
- Do I take care of my health—eat well, exercise, and get enough rest and relaxation?
- Have I been respectful of my own sexuality and not mistreated who I am as a sexual person?
- Do I seek the help of other, wiser persons when emotions or problems are causing me a lot of distress?
- Do I abuse alcohol, other drugs, or leisure activities such as watching television?

4. Read the story of the prodigal son (Luke 15:11–32). Write a one-page reflection on the story as it relates to situations you have experienced or known about.

his father. Only after this journey is the young man himself, in his own heart, ready to be received into his father's arms.

Every time we "come to our senses" about an attitude or pattern of behavior we have been engaging in that is hurting our relationship with God, with others, or with self, we begin a conversion of heart. God's loving forgiveness is always present, always offered; but to experience God's forgiveness, *we* must make a turnaround, acknowledging that we have sinned and want to change. It is this conversion that is celebrated in the sacrament of reconciliation.

To get in touch with where we need both forgiveness and renewal, we can periodically make an *examination of conscience,* a review of recent personal events using a series of questions about how well we have responded to God's call to love. This kind of self-examination is also a good way to prepare for the sacrament of reconciliation.

Experiencing Penance as Conversion

Another name for the sacrament of reconciliation, as mentioned at the beginning of this chapter, is *penance,* a word derived from the same roots as *repent,* which means "to be sorry." *Penance* refers to a conversion of heart, a turnaround. Such a conversion is shown externally in changed behavior, which indicates the sincerity of the change of heart. That is why as part of the sacrament, the priest advises the person in confession (the penitent) to take some action that will indicate genuine repentance. Usually, this action includes prayer, deeds of kindness, or sacrifices. The action itself is called a *penance.*

With genuine conversion, new life springs up even in the midst of our faults and limitations.

Restoring Wounded Relationships

Sin always involves a break in a relationship or harm done to a relationship with others, with self, or with God. When we undergo conversion, we "come to our senses" about how a relationship has been torn apart. This enables us to turn away from the misguided steps we have taken. Then we are freed to seek restoration of the relationship that was broken or strained.

Living the Paschal Mystery

The process of conversion and the restoration of broken relationships are a part of everyday life. Although we may experience death or woundedness in relationships, by responding to God's grace, we can find new life in them at an even deeper level. This is the paschal mystery lying at the heart of our existence and at the heart of the sacraments—the movement from death to resurrection.

Here is a story of such a movement:

Lisa and Michelle, best friends through grade school, began to grow apart in ninth grade. Michelle threw herself into the challenges of schoolwork and into participating in school-sponsored activities. Lisa got swept up in the excitement of spending time with a new group of classmates from across town. This group seemed so different from the classmates Lisa had known since the first grade. It was a "faster" crowd, more daring than Lisa was used to. She found the change exciting and fun.

Michelle and Lisa gradually saw less and less of each other, and they found they no longer had much to talk about together. Michelle ran for class president and won; Lisa started going out with a junior boy who was popular in her new group of friends. Throughout ninth grade and into tenth, the girls went their separate ways.

Then came Christmas of their sophomore year. Just before the holidays, Lisa and her mother were called into school to meet with the vice-principal. Apparently, Lisa had been cutting her last class every day and hanging out with her boyfriend at a nearby park. The vice-principal said that Lisa would not be suspended this time, but change needed to occur.

Lisa's mother was furious. "I forbid you to spend time with that crowd ever again."

"But Mom, they're my only friends!" Lisa protested.

"Whatever happened to Michelle?" her mother asked. "Why don't you see her anymore?"

"She's a snob now, Mom," Lisa answered tersely.

Nonetheless, that evening, Lisa called Michelle. Michelle already knew about Lisa's trouble, and the conversation was brief and somewhat strained. But after speaking with Lisa, Michelle went to her room and rummaged through her treasures from grade school. There she found a booklet that Lisa had made her for her twelfth birthday. The last page contained a photograph of the two friends smiling and hugging, with the caption "Best Friends Forever!" written underneath it.

Michelle thought about all the times she and Lisa had spent talking together and playing together. To her, they were special moments, and she missed her friend. She decided to pull out the last page of her old birthday booklet and send it to Lisa. Beneath the caption "Best Friends Forever!" Michelle added "Still!" followed by "I miss you," and "Merry Christmas."

Lisa received this gift in the Christmas Eve mail. She cried when she first read the caption and again as she walked over to Michelle's house. When Michelle came to the door, the two girls smiled nervously. But then they began talking about Christmases shared in the past and finally about all the changes that high school had brought for them. By evening, they felt their friendship rejuvenated. In fact, they found the bond between them stronger than ever, because they knew now they were more than just fair-weather friends. Lisa discovered that she had a friend she could always turn to, and Michelle found out that Lisa would not let pride stand in the way of making up with her friends.

Reconciliation as Coming Back Together

The word *reconciliation* literally means "coming back together." **Reconciliation** among people involves the restoring of relationships that have been broken or wounded. It is the fruit of the process of conversion; it is the new life that comes when we are freed from what has held us back from loving. With conversion, we are enabled to embrace others, self, and God with a whole heart. Reconciliations like Lisa and Michelle's are celebrated in the sacrament of reconciliation.

Ideally, before celebrating the sacrament, we would go to anyone with whom we needed to patch things up or from whom we needed to ask forgiveness, and we would rebuild that relationship. Then we would be ready to celebrate that restoring of life in the sacrament itself. Or perhaps as a result of the sacrament, we might approach those whom we have hurt to be reconciled.

5. Think about someone you feel you need to forgive, or someone from whom you would like to receive forgiveness. Write that person a letter expressing your feelings. When you are finished, respond to your own letter as you imagine the person receiving it would respond. Would you consider actually mailing your original letter? Why or why not?

The Ripple Effects of Our Actions

The pain we cause by our wrongdoing goes beyond those whom we have hurt directly. For instance, when we make prejudiced remarks or hold hurtful attitudes about particular individuals because of their race or class or social group, we hurt those individuals. We also add to the climate of negative expectations or cruelty that surrounds all persons in that group. And that creates more barriers for everyone to overcome—more tension, mistrust, and hostility.

Nor is sin against ourselves a totally "private" issue. Whenever we harm ourselves, whenever we reject God, God's love for us, and our worthiness to be loved, we damage our own ability to love and care for others. We damage our ability to *live* freely and fully. And because we as human beings live in community, harm to us will also affect others.

Thus, sin is not just a matter between "me and God" or "me and one other person." Its scope is much wider than what we immediately see. Just as a pebble tossed into a pond disturbs the entire pool of water, so our actions both for good and for ill have far-reaching effects.

The following story from the tradition of Hasidic Judaism gives a sense of how widespread are the ripple effects of one person's sin and how great is the need for forgiveness:

A wealthy merchant happened to share a compartment on a train with a poorly dressed old man whom he treated rudely and disdainfully. When they arrived at their common destination, the merchant saw in the railroad station a throng of people waiting in ecstatic joy to greet the arrival of one of the holiest and wisest rabbis in all of Europe. To the merchant's chagrin, he then discovered that the old man who had traveled in the compartment with him was himself the great rabbi.

Embarrassed at his own disgraceful behavior and distraught that he had missed a golden opportunity to speak privately with a wise and holy man, the merchant pushed his way through the crowd to the old man. When he reached him, he begged the rabbi's forgiveness and requested his blessing.

The old rabbi looked at him and replied, "I cannot forgive you. To receive forgiveness, you must go out and beg it from every poor, old person in the world." (Adapted from Cavanaugh, *The Sower's Seeds,* page 11)

When we sin, we need to ask forgiveness not just from the person or persons we have harmed directly but, in a sense, from the whole community and even the whole world that is worse off because of our sin. But of course, as in

A sinful action or attitude has ripple effects that extend far beyond the persons who are obviously or directly affected. In a certain sense, an individual's sin reaches the whole world.

6. Draw four concentric circles, with the circle in the center representing a stone hitting the water, and the other, surrounding circles representing the ripples that go out from the stone across the water. On the "stone," write something you have done that you know was wrong. In each circle surrounding the "stone," write the effects of your actions. Begin with the most direct or closest effects in the nearest circle, and end with the most indirect or remote effects in the farthest.

Why Tell a Priest?

One author who works with teenagers describes here how she answers a question frequently asked about confession:

> I often hear the question, "Why do I have to confess to a priest? Can't God forgive me himself if I tell him I'm sorry?" I argued these points with an experienced pastor several years ago. He explained that Jesus gave us the sacrament because *we need it.* Although God can and does forgive us whenever we repent, we need to *hear* his forgiveness for ourselves. It's our humanness that demands visible, audible, tangible signs. We need a time and space when we can put our sin behind us and *know* that God "remembers not the sins of the past" (see Psalm 79:8). When we commit serious sin, or actually choose to be "outside" the Church, it's all the more vital to present ourselves for "reentry," a welcome back. That's why we as Catholics are required to

> confess all serious sins to a priest. It is an obligation that is, in reality, an opportunity— an opportunity to start over and an opportunity to grow. (Paiva, "Bless me, Father")

the wealthy merchant's situation, it is impossible to find everyone who has been touched by the ripple effects of our sin and ask their forgiveness.

Forgiven by God and the Whole Community

The sacrament of reconciliation provides for our need to be forgiven, not only at the one-to-one level but also at the community level. Reconciliation gives us an opportunity to confess our wrongdoing before someone who represents God and the entire community—a priest—and to hear the words of forgiveness given on their behalf. After experiencing this powerful, community-wide forgiveness, many people discover they have an answer to the questions that previously concerned them: "Why should I confess my sins to a *priest?* Why not just tell the person I hurt or a friend who is a good listener?"

The name given to this sacrament, *reconciliation*, highlights its community focus. If sin can be understood as things or actions that break a community apart, then reconciliation can be understood as the processes or actions that rebuild community. In the sacrament of reconciliation, community members come together to admit their weakness and celebrate their return to God and one another.

The sacrament of reconciliation is meant to be a celebration of the experiences of forgiveness already present in our everyday life. In other words, it is meant to be the peak moment of a broader healing process that takes place around kitchen tables, in cafeterias, during visits to chapel, in classrooms, in workplaces, or on late-night walks.

For Review

- What was King Istine's gift to Ivar? How did it help Ivar?
- What is sin?
- What does the word *penance* refer to? What is the penance that the priest advises for the penitent in confession meant to indicate?
- What does the word *reconciliation* mean? What does reconciliation among people involve?
- Explain why sin is not just a matter between "me and God" or "me and one other person."

Reconciliation's Symbols and Rituals

Perhaps you have experienced the Rite of Reconciliation at your school or parish in a way that truly felt like a celebration of forgiveness. At a communal service, you may have had the opportunity to look back over your recent past for attitudes and actions that needed to be forgiven. Along with the other people present, you may have acknowledged your sorrow and asked God's help in transforming your life. As part of the ritual, you may have spoken with a priest in confession, who reminded you personally of God's enduring love for you. Leaving the ceremony, maybe you felt refreshed and renewed—walking forward as a more courageous and capable person because you knew that you did not walk alone.

As we will see in the section on the history of this sacrament, reconciliation evolved from a highly community-focused ritual to a highly individualized, private one. In the aftermath of Vatican Council II, the Rite of Reconciliation was revised to integrate both the communal dimension and the emphasis on individual repentance and forgiveness. A scriptural focus was also added to connect the sacrament with its biblical roots.

Reconciliation in Words and Symbols

Greeting

Grace, mercy, and peace
from God the Father and Jesus Christ his Son
be with you in truth and love.
  Amen.

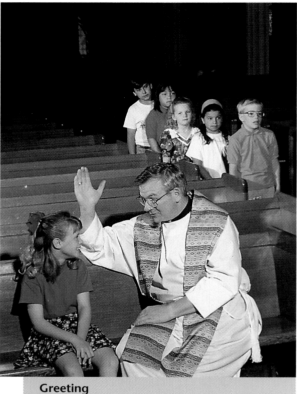
Greeting

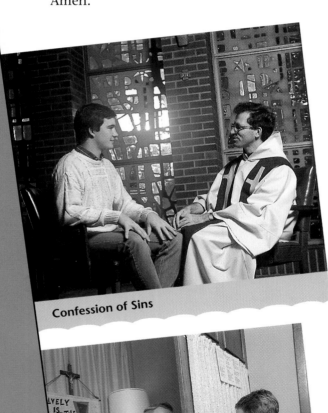
Confession of Sins

Prayer of the Penitent

The Word of God

Let us listen to the Lord as he speaks to us:

> I will give them a new heart, and put a new
> spirit within them; I will remove the heart of
> stone from their flesh and give them a heart
> of flesh, so that they may follow my statutes
> and keep my ordinances and obey them.
> Then they shall be my people, and I will be
> their God. (Ezekiel 11:19–20)

Confession of Sins

I confess to almighty God,
and to you, my brothers and sisters,
that I have sinned through my own fault. . . .

Prayer of the Penitent

My God,
I am sorry for my sins with all my heart. . . .

Absolution

God, the Father of mercies,
through the death and resurrection of his Son
has reconciled the world to himself
and sent the Holy Spirit among us
for the forgiveness of sins;
through the ministry of the Church
may God give you pardon and peace,
and I absolve you from your sins
in the name of the Father, and of the Son,
and of the Holy Spirit.
 Amen.

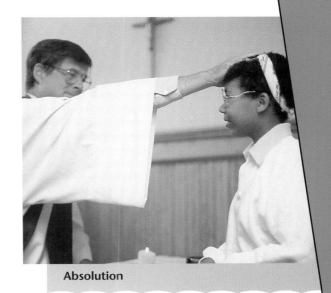

Absolution

Praise of God and Dismissal

Give thanks to the Lord, for he is good.
 His mercy endures for ever.
The Lord has freed you from your sins. Go in
 peace.

Praise of God and Dismissal

Three Forms of the Rite

At present, three different forms of the Rite of Reconciliation can be celebrated:

1. a celebration for an individual penitent
2. a communal celebration for several penitents with individual confession and absolution
3. a communal celebration for several penitents with general confession and absolution

Celebration for an Individual

A person can choose to celebrate the sacrament of reconciliation with a priest on an individual, one-to-one basis. A parish or school may have times set aside when a priest is available for this purpose. Or an individual might ask for an appointment with a priest, especially when he or she wishes to have ample time for talk and discussion without the pressure of knowing that other people are waiting for their turn.

Still a community focus: Even when the sacrament is celebrated for an individual, reconciliation is still considered a community celebration. Thus, the community itself and the priest as its representative are primary symbols in reconciliation. As a representative of God and the whole church, the priest is a reminder of the loving community that welcomes the person and desires reconciliation for him or her. The instructions for celebrating the rite explain the importance of the priest's greeting the penitent warmly, conveying the love of God and the community. The guidelines for building parish reconciliation rooms (where individual confession takes place) state that the room should reflect a spirit of welcome and warmth. In other words, the very physical space where reconciliation is celebrated individually should mirror the church community as a home where people can experience God's loving forgiveness.

Face-to-face or separated: Spaces set aside for confession usually allow for two possible methods of communicating with the priest—either face-to-face, with the priest and penitent seated in chairs, or separated visually, with a screen between the priest and penitent. This second option is preferred by some persons, especially those more comfortable with the anonymous style of confession that was customary before Vatican Council II. But a face-to-face, personal confession is more in the spirit of the revised rite.

A personal exchange: Whether confession takes place in an anonymous or a face-to-face setting, a genuine, spontaneous exchange is meant to happen between priest and

7. Design a room to be used as a reconciliation room for confession. Draw a floor plan and describe in writing the furnishings, decorations, lighting, and so on. Describe your reasons for designing as you did.

penitent. Individuals celebrating reconciliation should try to explore not only their actions but also their attitudes and motivations. The priest is to listen in an accepting, non-judgmental way and offer words of advice and encouragement, along with a suggested penance and the words of absolution, or forgiveness of sins. The common but misguided image of confession as a fearful, judgmental event ought to be a thing of the past. Individual confession today, when done as the church intends it, can be a rich, healing, and comforting experience.

Communal Celebration
with Individual Confession and Absolution

The communal celebration of this sacrament was introduced as an option after the Second Vatican Council. This form highlights the communal dimension of reconciliation in a more obvious way than does individual celebration. The community members gather, sing songs and hear the word of God together, collectively focus on how they need to be reconciled with one another and with God, and join in praising God for forgiving them. Part of the rite is the opportunity for individuals to confess privately to a priest and receive individual counsel and absolution.

Communal Celebration
with General Confession and Absolution

The communal rite with general confession and absolution is reserved only for emergency situations, when there may be neither time nor enough priests to hear confessions individually. So persons would express their confession of sins in a general way as a community and receive absolution together. However, church rules state that once the emergency situation passes, these individuals should confess their serious (mortal) sins to a priest individually.

Common Elements of the Three Forms

All three forms of the Rite of Reconciliation have these elements in common:
1. a warm greeting by the priest
2. the reading of the word of God (optional or usually abbreviated in the individual form of the rite), recited by the priest
3. the confession of sins by the penitent and offering of counsel by the priest
4. the reciting of the prayer of the penitent, expressing sorrow for sins

Today, celebrations of the Rite of Reconciliation highlight the community dimension of the sacrament.

8. As practiced today, the sacrament of reconciliation emphasizes community and the need for the whole community to seek forgiveness. If our society today were personified—imagined as one person—and that person had the opportunity to go to confession, for what five "sins" should the person most ask forgiveness?

5. the absolution (words of forgiveness) given by the priest, communicated with the laying on of hands

   (If the penitent and the priest are face-to-face, the priest can place a hand on the person's head, symbolizing God's reaching out to the individual with healing, reconciling love. If a screen separates them, the priest can simply raise his hand in blessing over the penitent.)

6. a prayer of thanksgiving for God's forgiveness, spoken by the priest

At some point before the confession of sins, the penitent makes an examination of conscience. In a communal celebration, this usually takes place after hearing the word of God. In an individual celebration, self-examination takes place before the person enters the reconciliation room for confession.

In recent years, communal reconciliation services that are less formal and that differ from the official rite have become popular. Your school or class may at times hold such a service. The reconciliation service may have many of the elements that are part of the official rite. Although individual confession and absolution of sins are not included, this kind of service gives people an opportunity as a community to become aware of what areas of their life need healing, to express sorrow for their sins, to experience a special kind of "community spirit," and to be reconciled with God and one another. These communal services are wonderful expressions of the spirit of the sacrament of reconciliation.

For Review

- What are the three forms of the Rite of Reconciliation?
- How does the individual form of the rite incorporate a community focus?
- What elements do all three forms of the rite have?

Reconciliation's History

Jesus was a healer. He drew all kinds of people to him—children, women, lepers, outcasts, foreigners, sinners, saints. He healed people's bodies, calmed their minds, and forgave their sins. Belief in Jesus seemed to carry with it a healing of body, mind, and soul all at once. Throughout its history, the church has tried in various ways to be a sacrament of healing forgiveness, in imitation of Jesus the healer.

The Early Experience: Community Healing and Forgiveness

For the most part, in the earliest years of the church, the healing process for minor sins took place informally within the community. Members of the community listened to one another's stories in the kind of healing-storytelling process described earlier. This process involved two elements: discernment and thanksgiving. That is, Christians usually tried to determine (discern) just what an individual's problem was—why the person was falling into a certain weakness. Then, as a community, they praised God in thanksgiving for forgiveness.

In the spirit of the early church, the present church teaches that Christians should become reconcilers and healers for one another. The role of reconciling is not solely the priest's; it belongs to all the members of the community.

Reconciliation for Major Sins: Available Only Once

Although celebration of God's forgiveness happened informally and person-to-person in the early church, baptism was thought to be the primary means of reconciliation between God and a sinner. When converts renounced the life of sin in baptism, they were considered reconciled with God once and for all. The earliest Christians did not imagine that anyone would actually fall into serious, scandalous sin after the overwhelming liberation of being baptized. In addition, the Eucharist was always there to sustain Christians in their efforts to overcome sin.

Excommunication as a Break from the Community

Despite the powerful experience of baptism and the vitality of the early church community, some members occasionally slipped back into their former pagan ways and thus cut themselves off from the community. When members clearly renounced the faith or practice of the church, they were *excommunicated*—that is, no longer allowed to share the Eucharist with the assembly. They were, in effect, thrown out. This was considered a permanent, irrevocable break with the community.

But the church faced a dilemma: What was the community to do if an excommunicated person sincerely repented and wished to come back and rejoin the church? The answer to this dilemma emerged in the second century with the development of a lengthy process of re-entry into the church.

In the early church, when members renounced Christian faith or practice, they were excommunicated, or "locked out" of communion with the church. At first, this excommunication was considered permanent, but later a lengthy process for re-entry was developed.

A "Second Baptism" for Re-entry

The process for re-entry into the church was modeled after the process of preparing for baptism. Actually, re-entry was considered something of a second baptism. As a kind of "second chance" after baptism, it was available to a person only once in a lifetime. The excommunicated person joined the Order of Penitents, which was similar to the Order of Catechumens that prepared for baptism. Penitents could remain in this order for years, until they were judged worthy to re-enter the church. During celebrations of the Eucharist, the penitents sat in the back of the place of worship, left after the homily, and looked forward to the time when they would again share Communion with their friends.

Other members of the community "took on" the sins of the public penitents; they prayed for and with them, and they did penances with them. Lent was a time of intense prayer and fasting to demonstrate a genuine change of heart, not only in the public penitents but in the entire community. The ceremony in which the public penitents returned to Communion took place on Holy Thursday and was presided over by a bishop.

This official, public process of reconciliation continued for about a thousand years. However, few people took advantage of it, because the process was extremely difficult and long, with severe penances required. Some excommunicated persons preferred to wait until they were on their deathbed to be reconciled; in such an emergency, absolution could be given without requiring penances. Gradually, the serious sins requiring the lengthy process of public reconciliation were narrowed down to three actions—murder, apostasy (denial of the faith), and adultery.

Private Confession: Reconciliation with a Personal Touch

As was just stated, most early Christians never went through the official, public process of penance. Instead, they found forgiveness for their less-serious sins by sharing in the Mass, giving alms to the poor, seeking forgiveness from others, and doing other common reconciling actions. Then, in the fifth century, a new practice—private confession—began among Irish monks.

The Irish Monks as Confessors

Dedicated to spiritual perfection, the Irish monks would regularly confess their faults to each other. The monk hearing the confession would pray with the other and prescribe

10. In a paragraph, describe how you might support a friend who is trying to get back on track after a period of serious moral problems.

Within Irish monasteries in the fifth century, monks began the practice of private confession with each other. Before long, the monks made confession available to help people outside the monasteries as well.

actions to help him overcome the fault. Certain monks came to be renowned for their assistance to the other monks, so they became popular confessors. People outside the monasteries began to take advantage of the help of these monks. Gradually, the practice of private, individual confession spread to the rest of Europe.

From Public Penance to Private Confession

For a time, two major forms of reconciliation existed in the church. The official system of penance was public, community-centered, available only once, and administered by a bishop. The unofficial system of confession, which grew up alongside the official form, was private, available whenever desired, and administered by a priest. By the ninth century, the public system of penance was nearly gone. Finally, in the thirteenth century, private confession was decreed the one official form of reconciliation, and it remained so until the post–Vatican II changes of the 1970s allowed for communal celebrations.

Current Practices: Combining the Personal and the Communal

As was mentioned in the section on the rituals and symbols of reconciliation, the three forms of the Rite of Reconciliation in use today integrate the communal dimension of the early church with the individual focus of later developments. Since Vatican Council II, the changes in the celebration of this sacrament have been remarkable—although perhaps not yet well-adjusted-to, as evidenced by a drop-off in the use of the sacrament in recent years.

Why a Drop-off?

A few decades ago, most Catholics would not have thought of receiving Communion without first going to confession. The lines for confession on Saturday afternoons were long, and priests were kept busy listening attentively in the "confessional box." Now the pendulum seems to have swung in the opposite direction, with the sacrament being celebrated much less often and by many fewer Catholics. Perhaps to some people, even the word *confession* (as the sacrament was formerly called) may carry negative associations with an earlier age, when an emphasis on guilt and judgment was more prominent. Other people may remember how they used to simply reel off their sins to the priest like reading a shopping list. Although they rightly reject such an unthinking approach, they may be unaware of the post–Vatican II changes and mistakenly assume that reconciliation is supposed to be rote and mechanical.

On the other hand, some Catholics who are aware of the personal tone that is part of the revised rite can feel uncomfortable with that change. They may prefer the more rote, impersonal approach they grew up with. Some people do not wish to talk about themselves and their faults with a priest, reasoning that if they tell God or another person they are sorry, that is enough. They may figure that because reconciliation comes to them through the Eucharist, why bother with another sacrament?

A Needed Symbol of God's Forgiveness

There are other sacraments in which forgiveness takes place—baptism and the Eucharist, for instance. And as we know, reconciliation does happen in everyday life, apart from the official rite. Nonetheless, the official sacrament is a specific, tangible symbol of the forgiving power of God in our life. It offers an opportunity to celebrate forgiveness in a

way that is personal as well as communal, private as well as public, focused as well as all-embracing. Many Catholics who regularly take advantage of this sacrament find it a profound experience of Christ's healing forgiveness.

The Catholic sacrament of reconciliation is a sign to the world of the need for reconciliation not only among individuals but also among nations, religions, and racial and ethnic groups.
Photo: Leaders of the world's major religions, called together by Pope John Paul II, gathered at Assisi, Italy, in 1986 to pray for global peace and reconciliation. Assisi is the birthplace of Saint Francis, known and respected across religious lines today for his role as a peacemaker.

For Review

- In the early church, what was thought to be the primary means of reconciliation between God and a sinner?
- Briefly describe the process in the early church by which an excommunicated person could re-enter the church.
- When and how did private confession originate?

Toward Healing the Whole Person

The health of a person's spirit is intimately connected with the health of the whole person. The body and soul are not really separate. Thus, many physical illnesses can be traced to spiritual ills—to grudges held onto tightly, for example, or to guilt not relieved. The sacrament of reconciliation, in providing experiences of healing forgiveness, helps the church to care for the spiritual ills of its members and to carry out the healing ministry of Jesus.

In addition to addressing people's spiritual health, the healing ministry of Jesus also focused on people's physical suffering and sickness. In another sacrament of healing, the sacrament of anointing, the church turns its concern to the needs of those who suffer from physical ills. That sacrament is the focus of chapter 11.

Healing God,
    comfort the sick,
    caress those in pain,
    and bring peace to the dying.
Restoring God,
    make the lives of all of us
    healthy, holy, and wholesome.
Amen.

11

Anointing: Celebrating God's Healing Love

Both the sacrament of reconciliation and the sacrament of anointing offer Catholic Christians a way to celebrate and carry out the healing ministry of Jesus. Reconciliation deals with the harm caused to a person's relationships by sin. The sacrament of anointing, however, focuses on healing the damaging effects that pain, suffering, and death can have on a person's (and community's) spirit. The sacrament celebrates the meaning that Jesus' own suffering, death, and Resurrection can bring to human experiences of suffering. The mental anguish that often accompanies illness, for example, can be greatly relieved by partaking in the grace-filled love offered through the sacrament of anointing—as the following story illustrates.

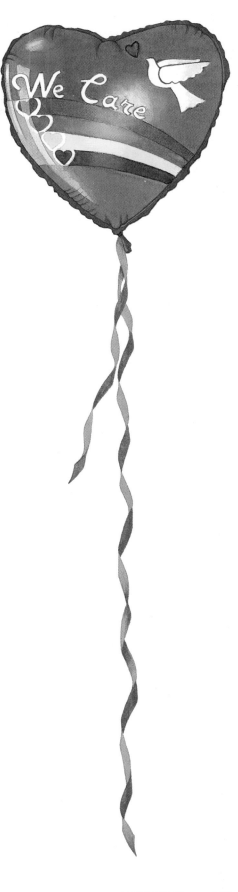

Mrs. Beck has spent the last forty years of her life taking care of her home and family. A devoted Catholic of her time, she attended daily Mass whenever she could and was very active in church and community service projects. To both her neighbors and her family, Mrs. Beck has been a joyful, faith-filled person, always patient and willing to lend a kind word and a helping hand.

Five months ago, however, sickness changed things radically. Just as she once took care of her children, they now take care of her. Previously, she kept busy with many projects. Now she must spend most of her time in bed or in her special chair in the living room. Prior to her illness, Mrs. Beck was seldom concerned about her needs. Presently, her body, racked with constant pain, cries out for attention. And whereas once she would drop in to visit friends occasionally, they now have to come to see her.

Ever since becoming ill, Mrs. Beck has had to wrestle with a whole new image of herself. No longer is she the strong, independent woman whom family and friends once relied on. Many things taken for granted in the past have become matters of great concern for her. Who will help her dress? Should she venture downstairs or wait until she is more rested? Will this be her last Christmas with her family?

Even her prayers have changed. She was used to saying, "Thank you, Lord, for my family and friends, and for all the gifts you have given to me." Now she finds herself praying, "Jesus, into your hands I commend my spirit."

Mrs. Beck is fortunate compared to many seriously sick people; she has a loving family, friends, her faith, and the memories of a lifetime well spent. Yet she still needs all the help she can get. Her doctors do what they can, but the help that she needs in her present illness cannot be found in pills, shots, and bed rest. She needs, more than pills, the touch of loving concern. She needs to hear again the words of Jesus about God's healing *and forgiveness and compassion. She needs to hear her family say, "I love you," and her friends say, "We're with you." Loving touches from her children, warm smiles and hellos from her friends, and simple handshakes from parish visitors never meant so much as they do now.*

Thus, to Mrs. Beck, the sacrament of anointing offered by the priest seems to follow naturally from the support she has felt from her family, neighbors, and friends at the parish. The sacrament makes a big difference in how she understands her illness. The anxieties and fears that accompany her discomfort and confinement are eased. Although she is still physically impaired, Mrs. Beck feels healed, somehow more whole. She also feels that she belongs, that she is not alone in her time of suffering. In addition, celebrating the sacrament of anointing reaffirms her belief in Jesus, who suffered so much himself, and in Jesus' healing touch.

What Does Anointing Celebrate?

The fears and anxieties felt by Mrs. Beck due to her illness and the drastic changes that illness has brought to her life are not uncommon experiences for persons suffering from ill health, whether physical or psychological. When people are

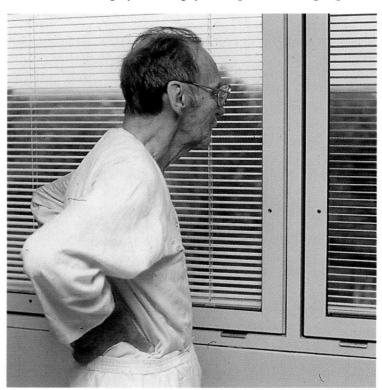

People who are seriously ill often experience a great sense of loneliness, isolation, and emptiness.

sick or close to death, they often talk about a great sense of loneliness and isolation. They describe their feelings with words like *fear, anxiety, frustration, depression,* and *helplessness.* Some speak of a strong desire to pray, to get more in touch with God. Others, however, report a sense of abandonment by God. To many people, times of illness and suffering seem senseless and devoid of meaning, permeated by an overwhelming emptiness.

The Catholic sacrament of anointing offers what might be called a "spiritual antidote" to the damaging effects of illness. Pain, suffering, and coming face-to-face with one's mortality can greatly undermine a person's sense of well-being, especially one's spirit. Anointing is a statement by the whole Christian community that God's gracious concern does not leave us in times of suffering, illness, and even death. Christian faith asserts that experiences that try the human spirit need not be seen as hopeless and meaningless. In the midst of suffering, we need to hear most forcefully the healing words of the Christian message.

God's Loving Concern: A Gift to the Whole Person

God's loving concern for sick, suffering, or dying people is, in fact, the first and foremost truth celebrated in the sacrament of anointing. In this sacrament, the people of God seek not only to remind sick, suffering individuals among them of God's unconditional love and forgiveness, but also to reassure them that God cares about their total well-being.

Knowing that God cares about us when we are hurting can have a powerfully healing effect on us. As we read in the opening story of this chapter, Mrs. Beck experienced firsthand the restoring grace that comes by way of anointing:

- Her fears were relieved and her discomfort eased.
- Her sense of inner wholeness was built up even in the face of her physical decline.
- Her feelings of isolation were dispelled.
- Her faith was renewed and strengthened.
- She was enabled to see her suffering in a new, meaning-filled light.

Healing the Whole Person

If either you or people close to you have ever been seriously injured or sick, you know that being sick affects all of you—your body, mind, and soul. In other words, physical illnesses do not just affect our body. They often have damaging effects on our state of mind and our spiritual well-being.

1. If you were seriously sick, what would you want your friends to do for you? Reflect in writing on how they could support you through the illness.

2. Write about a time in your life when you were sick enough to stay home at least several days. How did being sick affect your spirit and emotions?

3. Interview a person from one of the medical professions. Ask the person what he or she has observed about the spiritual or psychological dimensions of illness and healing. Take notes or tape-record the interview.

Even something as simple as a headache affects our emotions and our outlook. Likewise, emotional difficulties, such as depression or stress, usually have some sort of negative impact on our physical health. Depression, even in a mild form, often results in a lack of energy. Stress has been firmly linked with ulcers, some forms of arthritis, and other kinds of ailments.

An illness that has both physical and emotional causes is termed *psychosomatic* illness (from the Greek words *psyche,* meaning "spirit," and *soma,* meaning "body"). Some sickness is clearly psychosomatic. However, most illnesses—and most healthy states—are psychosomatic in the sense that they are more than just physical conditions. Modern medicine acknowledges the relationship between emotional and physical health, and many health-care professionals are giving increasing regard to the emotional and spiritual needs of their patients. Indeed, doctors and other health-care workers who care about more than just physical ailments receive high praise for their healing skills from their patients.

The Catholic sacrament of anointing acknowledges and celebrates the wholeness of the human person, and in doing so recognizes the need to address the person's physical and spiritual well-being. However, although the sacrament does attend to the physical, bodily conditions of illness, the primary emphasis of anointing is to bring spiritual strength and healing to sick and dying people. In the words of one Christian teacher,

> The meaning of the sacrament is that God is offering the anointed person the grace to overcome anxiety and despair, to find comfort in an uncomfortable situation, to be healed and whole even if their body is diseased or broken. (Martos, *Doors to the Sacred,* page 339)

How Do We Know God Really Cares?

How do Christians know that God cares about people in their experiences of physical, emotional, and psychological pain? Two elements lie beneath the Christian belief in God's compassion. Both come to us from the Gospels, and both involve actions and undertakings by Jesus:

1. Jesus cast out demons, relieved the suffering of people afflicted with many kinds of physical ailments, and actually restored people to life.
2. Jesus himself experienced suffering, death, and Resurrection.

The significance of Jesus' suffering, death, and Resurrection for the sacrament of anointing will be addressed later in this chapter. For now, let's focus on Jesus the Healer.

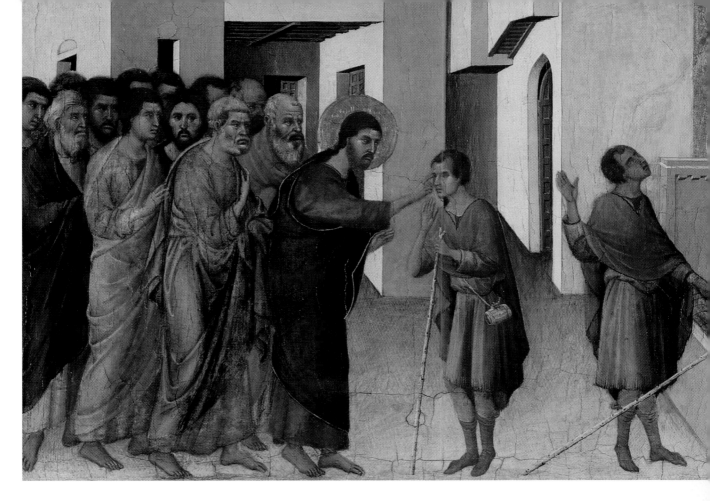

Jesus' Healing Actions

The accounts in the following Gospel passages exemplify Jesus' concern for and healing of people:

- In Mark 5:21–43, Jesus brings the daughter of Jairus back to life and cures the woman with a hemorrhage.
- In Matthew 15:21–28, Jesus cures a Canaanite woman's daughter. Jesus also shows compassion for the Canaanite woman, who in Jesus' day was a "marginalized" (rejected or outcast) person in society.
- In Matthew 15:29–39, Jesus heals many people—lame, maimed, blind, mute—who have been brought to him by the crowds. Jesus also speaks of his compassion for the crowds and feeds them before sending them away.
- In John 9:1–12, Jesus heals a man born blind. While healing the man, Jesus also refutes the then-common belief expressed by the disciples that the man's physical deformity must have been a direct consequence of personal sin.

From these accounts and from many others found in the Gospels, the message about Jesus' healing actions comes through loud and clear: Jesus healed because he felt compassion for hurting people. He wanted to show people firsthand the power and depth of God's compassion. In fact, it was the uncompromising and compassionate love of God working

In his ministry of healing, Jesus relieved people's suffering and expressed God's love and care for all persons who are ill. *Photo:* "Jesus Healing the Blind Man," by thirteenth-century artist Duccio

4. Choose one of the Gospel stories in which Jesus heals somebody. Read the story and then rewrite it from the point of view of the person being cured. How would that person tell the story?

through him that enabled Jesus to heal people and to work so many wonders. Jesus in action was God in action through him. As a sacrament of God, Jesus concretely witnessed the power of God to touch people's lives even at their most painful moments and to restore people to the fullness of life.

The Healing Power of the Faith Community

When the Christian community brings God's compassion and love to its members who are in pain or near death, as it does through the sacrament of anointing, the community is acting as an instrument of God's healing grace. Thus, the role of the Christian community in carrying on the healing ministry of Jesus is a second truth celebrated in the sacrament of anointing.

The Personal and Social Sides of Sickness

In many ways, illness is a deeply personal experience. Although others can empathize with our condition, only we as individual persons feel our pain, discomfort, and anxiety. Illness usually causes us to spend a lot of time asking ourselves why we are sick, what is truly important to us, what our life means, what we have accomplished, and many other soul-searching questions.

Because human beings are profoundly social creatures who live in community, however, illness is never completely personal; it always has a social or communal side to it. Alcoholism, for instance, is a disease that causes much physical and emotional damage in many societies today. The development of alcoholism is often influenced by physical, genetic factors, but alcoholism can also result in part from unhealthy social situations in which people struggle to be accepted, to escape or cope with difficulties, and so on. In other words, while an individual's illness can affect a community or society, unhealthy conditions or "sicknesses" in society can likewise affect individuals. The effects of illness are interactive at many levels.

The Personal and Social Sides of Healing

Just as illness has both its personal and social dimensions, so too does healing. Persons who are ill in any way rarely find healing by isolating themselves from others. In fact, much recent scientific research suggests that physical touch and the presence of others are critical to the recovery of sick persons. In the same way, social illnesses like alcoholism call for social solutions and communal efforts.

5. Within your community, what are three priorities, attitudes, or customary behaviors that foster sickness? What are three priorities, attitudes, or customary behaviors in your community that foster wellness? Describe these in writing.

The communal aspects of healing can be seen in everyday occurrences. Mrs. Beck, in the chapter's opening story, certainly experienced loving concern and healing from her community. Common, everyday healing actions might include sending cards of sympathy and prayers to people who are sick or to families in mourning; visiting sick friends and bringing them gifts or food; or uniting with family members when a relative has died or is seriously ill. Sometimes, people even find themselves offering a consoling touch or words of comfort to a sick person with whom they have never communicated before.

Sharing the burden of an illness is the first step in helping to bring about a cure, whether that "cure" involves actual physical healing or healing the person's spirit. Anointing challenges Catholics to not let their ailing sisters and brothers be cut off from the community, even though illness may prevent these sisters and brothers from full participation in the everyday rhythms and interactions of the community. As Mrs. Beck realized, the support from her family, neighbors, and friends at her parish greatly aided her own sense of inner healing. She knew she did not bear her suffering alone.

The Christian Community as "Wounded Healers"

In the Christian tradition, experiences of suffering and healing are linked to service to others. The sacrament of anointing both celebrates and affirms this reality. To understand the connection between suffering, healing, and service to others, consider the following Chinese tale:

A woman's only son died. In her grief, she went to a holy man and said, "What prayers, what magical incantations do you have to bring my son back to life?"

Instead of sending her away or reasoning with her, he said to her, "Fetch me a mustard seed from a home that has never known sorrow. We will use it to drive the sorrow out of your life." The woman went off at once in search of that magical mustard seed.

She came first to a splendid mansion, knocked at the door, and said, "I am looking for a home that has never known sorrow. Is this such a place? It is very important to me."

They told her, "You've certainly come to the wrong place," and began to describe all the tragic things that recently had befallen them.

The woman said to herself, "Who is better able to help these poor, unfortunate people than I, who have had misfortune of my own?" She stayed to comfort them, then went on in search of a home that had never

A simple, heartfelt gesture of concern from someone who cares can have a healing effect on a person who is sick.

6. How can sick or dying persons play a significant role in the Christian community? What advice might they offer to the physically healthy members? In a one-page essay, discuss three ways that ill people can aid physically healthy members of a community.

known sorrow. But wherever she turned, in hovels and in other places, she found one tale after another of sadness and misfortune. She became so involved in ministering to other people's grief that ultimately she forgot about her quest for the magical mustard seed, never realizing that it had, in fact, driven the sorrow out of her life. (Cavanaugh, *The Sower's Seeds,* page 5)

The lesson of this parable, and the linking of suffering and healing with service to others, is simple yet meaningful. Although experiences of sickness and suffering are not good or to be sought after in themselves, they can be "healing" if they lead to compassion for others. For instance, the best counselors for drug-dependent people are often former addicted persons. And former addicted persons can find great healing for themselves in helping others.

The examples of Jesus and his first followers clearly indicate that Christians are not immune from suffering. But rather than let their sufferings overwhelm and depress them, Jesus and his followers challenge all who profess Christian faith to transform their suffering into healing for themselves and for those around them. In that sense, the Christian community is meant to serve as "wounded healers"—people touched by pain who nonetheless offer healing to one another.

Anointing: A Profession of Resurrection Faith

Meeting Jesus' challenge to us by transforming our own suffering into opportunities of healing for ourselves and others is indeed a mark of deep faith. This caring response points to yet another truth celebrated in the sacrament of anointing: Participation in the sacrament of anointing is a profession of faith in the hope-filled, life-giving message of Jesus' own suffering, death, and Resurrection.

Life, Not Death, Has the Final Word

Along with recounting stories of Jesus' healing of many sick persons, the Gospels also tell us that Jesus himself suffered much mental and physical pain and was finally put to death by the terribly painful method of crucifixion. Significantly, however, the story of Jesus does not end with his Passion and death. As Christians profess in the Nicene Creed, "On the third day, he rose again. . . ." Although Jesus' Resurrection did not eliminate suffering and death from human experience, it did make clear that they are not the end of life but steps on the way to new life.

Healing and the Parable of the Lost Sheep

Jesus' parable of the lost sheep (Luke 15:4–7) vividly portrays the communal dimension of illness and healing. The shepherd has one hundred sheep—that is, a large, complete flock. When one sheep is realized to be missing, the shepherd leaves the ninety-nine to go off in search of the one that is lost. At first, this course of action seems impulsive and impractical— wouldn't it be better to guard the ninety-nine? Jesus explains, however, that no community is truly whole unless all of its members are caring for one another. The whole community is affected by the well-being of each member. Likewise, curing one member helps bring about the healing of all.

This is the powerful, hopeful message of the paschal mystery: The God of Jesus is the God of life. And life, not death, will always have the last word. When an entire community takes part in the sacrament of anointing, all the members of the community can reaffirm their Resurrection faith. Anointing provides a special opportunity for persons who are sick or dying to reaffirm their faith in the Risen Jesus.

A Sacrament of Hope

Christians are called to struggle against suffering in all its forms, just as Jesus did. They are to pray for healing and do all that they can to bring health and wholeness to themselves and others. Yet, Jesus' own suffering and death also challenge his believers to recognize that suffering, illness, and death—and life itself—are not totally understandable and controllable realities.

In other words, although in the Gospels Jesus is identified as a healer, he and his early followers experienced great suffering and pain. Today, the mystery of human suffering continues to baffle us, to disturb us, and to call forth Christian hope.

Despite our best hopes and intentions, however, all of our prayers, anointings with oil, invokings of the power of God's Spirit, support, and best medical treatments may leave a person still sick or dying. In such instances, Jesus' suffering, death, and Resurrection, as well as the sacrament of anointing, take on special significance. They stand as testimony to God's loving presence in the midst of human suffering. They give Christians hope that their care and deep concern for the sick person will make her or him feel "whole" in spite of physical suffering. And even though the sick person may die, the sacrament of anointing enables Catholic Christians to express the hope that their loved one will die healed in the Spirit.

For Review

- What is the foremost truth celebrated in the sacrament of anointing?
- What is the primary emphasis of the sacrament of anointing?
- Give two examples of Gospel passages that show Jesus healing people. What enabled Jesus to heal people?
- What are three everyday healing actions that people can do for sick persons or for families in mourning?
- Describe what it means to say that Christians themselves can be "wounded healers."
- What is the hopeful message of the paschal mystery with respect to illness and death?

Anointing's Symbols and Rituals

Different Rites for Different Circumstances

Several slightly different rites are available for celebrating the sacrament of anointing. The differences allow for the varying circumstances and situations that naturally come up in the community. (There are even directives for baptizing and confirming sick or dying people, if they wish to receive those sacraments and have not done so before.)

Offered to the whole faith community: The sacrament of anointing can be celebrated by a whole faith community, either as a part of a Mass or in a separate, special healing service.

For instance, every year for Grandparent's Day, one Catholic school in Iowa has a special Mass that includes the sacrament of anointing. The students, their families, and any members of the parish who wish to celebrate this sacrament are invited to participate in the Mass. The invitation makes it clear that the sacrament of anointing will be offered to all those whose health is greatly impaired in some way—whether from physical injury or illness, from emotional or psychological turmoil, or simply from the process of aging.

Offered to nonterminally ill persons: The sacrament of anointing can also be celebrated by individuals who are seriously, but not terminally, ill—for instance, by people about to undergo major surgery for an illness that is serious but not life-threatening. In situations like this, the celebration of the sacrament usually takes place outside the context of a Mass, in the home of the ill person, in a hospital, or in some other institution such as a nursing home.

Offered to dying persons: Finally, the sacrament of anointing is also available to bring a special comfort and peace to those persons who suffer from a terminal illness or are close to death. Again, the celebration of the sacrament in these circumstances usually happens apart from a Mass. If death is close at hand, special prayers of "commendation," or entrusting the dying person over to Christ, are part of the sacrament. Also included in this situation is a special rite in which the dying person receives his or her last Communion. Holy Communion offered to a dying person is officially called *viaticum,* a Latin term meaning "a farewell meal" or "provisions for a journey."

Not Just for Dying Persons

Like reconciliation and the Eucharist, anointing is a sacrament that may be received more than once. Although the circumstances must be serious to warrant celebrating the sacrament, persons can find themselves in serious situations more than once in a lifetime.

8. If you were giving a farewell dinner for a very close friend who was moving far away, how would you make the meal and the occasion special? Describe what you would do in a paragraph.

For those persons whose health is impaired, the sacrament of anointing can be celebrated in a parish communal healing service or a Mass.

Over the course of a lifetime, a person might well experience traumatic injury from a car accident, undergo major surgery, grow weak from old age, and inevitably reach his or her deathbed. For persons in each of these situations, receiving the sacrament of anointing would certainly be appropriate. Anointing is not just for members of the Catholic community who are dying.

Common Elements in Anointing

Among the many forms and circumstances under which the sacrament of anointing is celebrated, a number of key elements are common to all of them:
1. prayers
2. a penitential rite
3. readings from the Scriptures
4. the laying on of hands
5. anointing with oil on the forehead and hands
6. Holy Communion

Shared Symbols

We have already encountered these six actions, or key elements, in discussing other sacraments. In fact, the sacrament of anointing makes use of many symbols and symbolic actions from other sacraments: anointing with oil, from baptism and confirmation; the laying on of hands, from confirmation and reconciliation; and Holy Communion and readings from the Scriptures, from the Eucharist. The opportunity for confession of sin and reconciliation is also offered. In short, in the sacrament of anointing, the Catholic faith community employs many of its resources to help its ailing members.

Attending to the Whole Person

As discussed earlier in this chapter, the Catholic church recognizes the need to attend to hurting persons in their entirety—to their body, mind, and spirit as well as to their social being. This attention to healing the whole person is fully integrated into the anointing rituals:
- The penitential component of the sacrament seeks to restore our harmony with other persons and with God. During our illness, we naturally tend to reflect on past experiences and the state of our relationships with God and our friends. Sacramental reconciliation is provided in order to assist healing in those relationships.
- Both the forehead, as a symbol of mental powers, and the hands, as a symbol of physical strength, are anointed with oil.

When we are sick or infirm, receiving Holy Communion from a member of our faith community can be a strengthening experience. Holy Communion is an integral part of the sacrament of anointing.

9. If you were creating a sacrament for sick or dying people, what would you include as symbols, rituals, or activities? What would you want to do for or say to a person you loved who was dying? Explain your recommendations in writing.

- Prayers and readings from the Scriptures focus our heart and mind on healing as the action of Jesus.
- The laying on of hands and receiving of Communion emphasize that healing occurs in the context of a caring community.

For Review

- Describe three different options for celebrating the sacrament of anointing.
- Name the six elements common to all forms of the sacrament of anointing.
- What do the laying on of hands and receiving of Communion emphasize in anointing, and in what other sacraments are these rituals used?

Anointing's History

Healing in the Early Church

Earlier in this chapter, healing was presented as an integral part of Jesus' life and ministry. As faithful followers of Christ, the Apostles and the first Christian communities felt compelled to continue his healing mission. The following well-known quote, from the Letter of James, suggests that prayer, the laying on of hands, and the use of blessed oil were all common healing practices within the early church:

> Are any among you sick? They should call for the elders of the church and have them pray over them, anointing them with oil in the name of the Lord. The prayer of faith will save the sick, and the Lord will raise them up; and anyone who has committed sins will be forgiven. Therefore confess your sins to one another, so that you may be healed. The prayer of the righteous is powerful and effective. (5:14–16)

During the early period of the sacrament's history, evidence suggests that any Christian could pray for sick people or anoint them with oil or lay hands on them, calling on the Spirit to heal them. The oil, blessed by the bishop, was used as an ointment on the injured part of the body or as a balm that covered the entire body. Sometimes, it was even drunk. In many instances, ill Christians were anointed with the blessed oil on a regular basis.

10. Do you agree or disagree with the following statement? Explain your reasons in a paragraph.
- Praying for someone who is ill is a significant act with great value and purpose. I would want to be prayed for if I were ill.

Anointing in Words and Symbols

Opening Prayer
(Anointing within Mass)

God of compassion,
you take every family under your care
and you know our physical and spiritual needs.

Transform our weakness by the strength of your
    grace
and confirm us in your covenant
so that we may grow in faith and love.

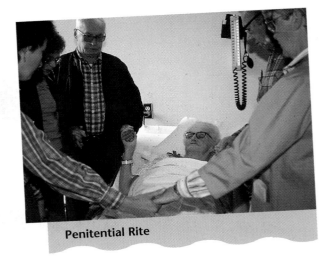

Penitential Rite

Penitential Rite
(Anointing outside of Mass)

My brothers and sisters, to prepare ourselves for
this holy anointing, let us call to mind our sins.

Liturgy of the Word
(Anointing outside of Mass)

A reading from the holy gospel of Luke:

> Once, when [Jesus] was in one of the cities,
> there was a man covered with leprosy. When
> he saw Jesus, he bowed with his face to
> the ground and begged him, "Lord, if you
> choose, you can make me clean." Then Jesus
> stretched out his hand, touched him, and
> said, "I do choose. Be made clean." Imme-
> diately the leprosy left him. (5:12–13)

Liturgy of Anointing

Laying on of hands: [In silence, the priest lays
his hands on the head of the sick person.]

Anointing of the forehead:
Through this holy anointing
may the Lord in his love and mercy help you
with the grace of the Holy Spirit.
    Amen.

Liturgy of the Word

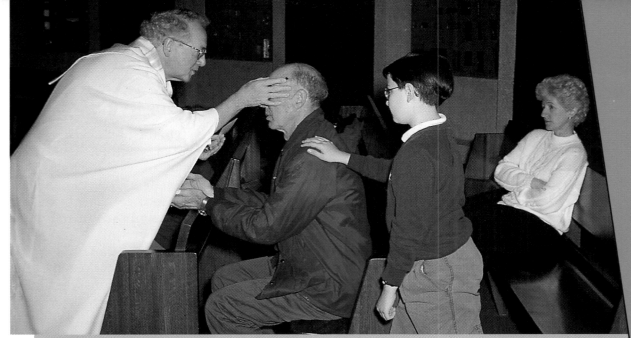

Liturgy of Anointing (of the Forehead)

Anointing of the hands:
May the Lord who frees you from sin
save you and raise you up.
    Amen.

Liturgy of Communion
(Anointing outside of Mass)

All-powerful and ever-living God,
may the body and blood of Christ your Son
be for our brother/sister . . .
a lasting remedy for body and soul.
We ask this through Christ our Lord.
    Amen.

Liturgy of Anointing (of the Hands)

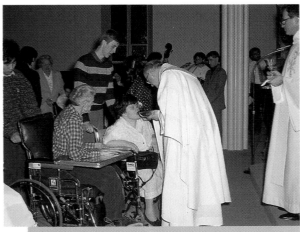

Liturgy of Communion

Blessing

May the God of all consolation
bless you in every way and
grant you hope all the days of your life.
    Amen.
May God restore you to health
and grant you salvation.
    Amen.
May God fill your heart with peace
and lead you to eternal life.
    Amen.

Anointing
Becomes a Preparation for Dying

Gradually, from about the eighth to the twelfth century, significant changes in the sacrament of anointing occurred. By this time, some people had begun treating the blessed oil like a magic potion. This exaggerated regard for the oil, along with a general increase in priests' sacramental duties, accounts in part for the fact that the ministry of anointing became reserved for priests.

During this period, anointing also became associated with penance, which, as chapter 10 noted, was generally administered to excommunicated persons only when they were near death. The sacrament of anointing therefore came to be seen as a preparation for death rather than as an act of healing. By the twelfth century, the sacrament was officially called *Extreme Unction*—a term meaning "last anointing" or "last rites." For the most part, the association of anointing with impending death prevailed until changes were made in the sacrament by the Second Vatican Council.

The Original Purpose Is Re-emphasized

Today, anointing's original purpose—healing—is once again emphasized. The official designation of anointing as part of the Catholic church's overall pastoral care and concern for sick and dying people strongly indicates this fact.

Anointing, as it is celebrated today, highlights Jesus' healing presence in the church. Although the priest has a specific role in the sacrament, all the members of the faith community are called to participate in the church's healing ministry. Here are just a few suggestions for how you could actively take part in this sacramental healing to others:

- By taking time out during school to pray for a classmate who is in the hospital, you would be participating in the pastoral care of the sick.
- By sending a card or visiting the person in the hospital, you would be participating in a more personal way.
- By praying with the person, or actually laying hands on the person, you would be tangibly adding to your personal participation.
- And by performing volunteer service in a hospital or nursing home, or by becoming a member of one of the healing professions, you would clearly be giving witness to the healing that the church celebrates in its sacrament.

The actual Rite of Anointing is, of course, only a moment in the healing process. Ideally, however, it symbolizes and culminates all the pastoral care performed by the caring

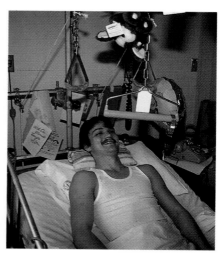

When we send a card to someone who is sick, or visit the person in the hospital, we are participating in Jesus' healing presence and ministry.

community in praying for sick people, visiting them, helping their families, and taking on other activities in the service of healing.

In summary, then, the Catholic church's sacrament of anointing celebrates the following realities:
1. the loving compassion and strengthening grace that God gives to all who suffer
2. the healing power of Jesus that keeps flowing through the Christian community, the church
3. the wholeness of the human person
4. the transformation of human suffering into an avenue of spiritual growth and service to others
5. the mysterious truth that—as in Jesus' own life—suffering, sickness, and even death can be part of the healing journey toward resurrected life and wholeness

11. From your own experience or from history or the news, recall an individual for whom suffering, sickness, or even death was not a defeat but a path toward victory, toward a new, richer life. Write an account of what happend to that individual.

For Review

- In the early church, how did Christians carry out the healing mission of Jesus?
- What does the term *Extreme Unction* mean? Why was this term used for the sacrament of anointing until recent decades?
- Summarize the realities celebrated in the sacrament of anointing.

From the Healing Sacraments to the Sacraments of Vocation

Reconciliation and anointing, as the two sacraments that celebrate God's healing in our life, minister to the physical, emotional, and spiritual well-being of church members. Like the other sacraments, they inevitably focus on a person's relationships in community—on forgiving one another, caring for one another, and surrounding one another with God's love, especially at times of hurt or suffering.

Christians who experience the healing ministry of other Christians, in the sacraments of healing and in everyday life, are thereby strengthened to respond generously to the life call that God offers them. The last two sacraments, of marriage and holy orders, are concerned with specific life callings, or vocations.

God bless our home.

Compassionate God,
   when two become one in marriage,
   we are reminded that you became one
   with us through your Son, Jesus.
God of people,
   give strength to couples
   and to all those who seek
   a life of love and generosity.
Amen.

12

Marriage: Celebrating the Covenant of Love

Every person, as an adult, is invited by God to follow a certain vocation, or life calling. The vocations that people choose are the paths that seem the best way for them to live happily in the world and contribute to building the Kingdom of God. The Catholic church celebrates the living out of two particular vocations in its sacraments of marriage and holy orders. This chapter focuses on marriage, also known as matrimony; chapter 13 considers holy orders.

The following abbreviated version of "The Gift of the Magi," a classic short story by O. Henry, offers a tender portrait of what marriage is all about.

One dollar and eighty-seven cents. Despite the cheer of the Christmas season, Della was heartsick. With all her careful saving of pennies, she had only a pittance with which to buy her beloved husband, Jim, a nice present. Times were hard, and after the rent on their apartment was paid, there was barely enough from their twenty-dollar-a-week income to take care of essentials, let alone buy extras like gifts.

Despite their poverty, Della and Jim had two possessions in which they took great pride: Jim's gold watch, which was a family heirloom, and Della's long, beautiful hair. Della's hair, unpinned, fell around her like a cloak and reached below her knees, like a shining waterfall of brown. These two treasures were all the couple had of any material worth.

In the midst of her Christmas Eve sadness, while gazing into a mirror, Della suddenly realized how she could afford to buy Jim a present. There were shops that bought hair for wigs—why not get her hair cut off and sell it? The sum it would bring would be enough to buy a gift worthy of Jim!

An hour later, twenty dollars richer, and sporting a short, new, chorus-girl haircut, Della went shopping gleefully for Jim's present. She found the perfect gift: a simple but elegant platinum chain that Jim could use with his precious watch, to replace the old leather strap he now used with some embarrassment. The chain cost twenty-one dollars; Della paid gladly and hurried home.

By the time Jim came home, Della had curled her short, boyish hair. Jim reacted strangely to seeing her this way, and Della, thinking he might be overly shocked, assured him that she would not miss the hair, that it would grow back, and that it had gone for a good cause—him.

Jim then showed her the present he had gotten for her: a set of beautiful, expensive, tortoiseshell combs, combs that Della had seen in a shop window and yearned over for weeks, knowing she could never own them. And now her beautiful hair, in which

1. Do you think that Della and Jim were better off or worse off after their exchange of Christmas gifts? Explain your answer in writing.

the combs could have been worn so perfectly, was gone. Her tears and sad laughter soon passed, and Della quickly presented Jim eagerly with his present—the watch chain.

"Isn't it a dandy, Jim? I hunted all over town to find it. You'll have to look at the time a hundred times a day now. Give me your watch. I want to see how it looks on it."

Instead of obeying, Jim tumbled down on the couch and put his hands under the back of his head and smiled.

"Dell," said he, "let's put our Christmas presents away and keep 'em a while. They're too nice to use just at present. I sold the watch to get the money to buy your combs."

What Does Marriage Celebrate?

As a sacrament, marriage represents an encounter with God. Specifically, the sacrament of marriage celebrates a couple's commitment to share the whole of their life together and to reveal God's love to themselves and others through their marriage relationship. Della and Jim's story warmly portrays the essence of the meaning of marriage. In this chapter, we explore four concepts that underscore the rich, sacramental quality of marriage: **mutual self-giving, covenantal faithfulness, the becoming of one's real self,** and **creativity.**

Mutual Self-giving

Wherever there is human love and friendship, God is revealed. The First Letter of John expresses this reality with a beautiful simplicity: "God is love, and those who abide in love abide in God, and God abides in them" (4:16).

A husband and wife reveal God's love to each other and those around them through their own mutual gift of self.

Because of the unique aspects of the friendship that is the marriage relationship, marriage has always had a special place in the Judeo-Christian vision as a way of revealing God's love in human terms. Of all human relationships, the marriage relationship represents in the most vivid way how God relates to us. In a real sense, a husband and wife reveal God to themselves and those around them through their own love for each other.

Of course, no marriage is perfect. However imperfect a particular marriage may be, though, it is sacramental insofar as it is the place where wife and husband, children, family, and family friends meet the living God. Recognizing marriage as a sacrament serves as a reminder that in all of our attempts to give and to love, God is the principal actor.

A Symbol of God's Gift of Self, Freely Bestowed

From the beginning years of the church, marriage has been regarded as a symbol of God's total gift of self to human beings. For Christians in particular, the mutual giving and love between a husband and wife helps us understand Jesus' loving gift of self in his death and Resurrection. Like the sacrifices that Della and Jim made for each other in the opening story, Jesus' sacrifice for humankind transforms, heals, and nurtures human existence.

Relating marriage to Jesus' love for us points to what the sacrament ideally can be. The gift of self in marriage, like Jesus' gift of self, must be freely given or it is not love at all. Freedom in giving ourselves to another person implies that we feel good about ourselves, that we recognize we have much to offer another person and deserve that person's respect in return. Freedom makes possible the move from "I" to "we" that is married love. When we can love someone genuinely for his or her own sake and as a free and confident person ourselves, we reveal God's way of loving.

A Countercultural Vision

The act of giving oneself freely runs counter to an acquisitive, possessive impulse in society that affects many contemporary attitudes and behaviors, including those toward marriage. One Christian couple, writers Mitch and Kathy Finley, offer this critique of the way marriage is handled in our society:

> The prevailing belief is that a happy marriage depends upon all kinds of material and economic realities, realities which end up taking first place in the life of the couple. This is an attitude toward marriage that is encouraged by a consumer culture, even from the moment

Couples thinking about getting married can fall under the illusion that the happiness of their marriage will depend on how well off they are financially—whether they have a beautiful house, a new car, all the best things for their children, and so on.

2. Interview two couples who have been married for at least five years. Ask the partners what sacrifices they made for each other in the early years of their marriage, what motivated those sacrifices, and whether those sacrifices still seem like "losses." Write up the results of your interview.

the engagement is first announced. The message broadcast in many ways to engaged couples is that the future success of their marriage depends on how much money they spend on the engagement ring. Then their future happiness depends on how elaborate the wedding and reception can be. Next, the more money the couple spends on their honeymoon, the more likely that their marriage will be a good one. And we're off and running: Your marriage will be all it can be if only you have a big beautiful house filled with new furniture and appliances (even if you find it necessary to go into great debt for this to be possible); and of course you really do need a brand-new car before you will feel really married. . . .

Of course, once the couple is married the same set of materialistic and commercial values begin to take other forms. . . . Your effectiveness as parents is determined by the *things* you buy for your child: That's the message.

. . . Husband and wife may continue to say that their marriage is most important for them, but . . . the marital relationship is neglected in the pursuit of greater affluence. (*Christian Families in the Real World,* pages 52–54)

A Christian vision of marriage counteracts the trap of consumerism by putting the emphasis for partners on the free gift of self to each other rather than on the relentless quest for the "perfect" household. The sacrament of marriage affirms that no amount of possessions will ever bring the hope and joy that two people can feel when they love each other freely and generously.

"A Communion of the Whole of Life"

When we think about what marriage involves, we often focus on the sexual intimacy that ideally accompanies marriage. Actually, the mutual physical gift of self that happens in sexual intercourse is meant to express a man and woman's sharing of their most intimate selves at every level of life—talking and laughing, struggling over finances, expressing hopes and dreams, raising children, working out conflicts, settling on a common lifestyle, clarifying values, going on family vacations, suffering loss or grief, and learning, changing, and growing together.

Sexual intercourse is intended for marriage because it embodies the total sharing of a whole committed life together. In the words of a 1978 church document, marriage is "a communion of the whole of life." A loving sexual relationship can joyfully and pleasurably express that communion.

The Faithfulness of a Covenant

Legally, marriage is a contract, and traditionally it has been thought of in contractual terms. That is, marriage is thought of as holding the man and woman to certain obligations and conferring on them certain rights.

Contract Versus Covenant

In the Judeo-Christian tradition, alongside the notion of marriage as a legal contract grew the idea of marriage as a covenant, modeled on the covenant between Yahweh and the Chosen People (the Jews), or between Christ and the church. **Covenant** is a key biblical concept, perhaps *the* central concept of the Hebrew Scriptures. It refers to a promise made between two parties that flows from their deeply personal relationship. It is not a law-based agreement like a contract; rather, it is a relationship grounded in love. Whereas a contract attempts to stipulate conditions and put limits on a relationship, a covenant is unconditional.

Between Yahweh and the Chosen People

In the Hebrew Scriptures, we learn that Yahweh established a covenant with Abraham and his descendants, and later renewed it by giving the Israelites the Law on Mount Sinai. The essence of that covenant was the promise between God and the people that they would be faithful to each other. From the history told in the Hebrew Scriptures, we know that the people often broke that covenant; they were repeatedly unfaithful to God through idolatry and injustice. But God never abandoned the promise of the Sinai covenant, remaining faithful to the people in good times and in bad.

Over time, the prophets helped the people to understand that God's love for them was like the absolute, undying love of a person who has been hurt by a spouse's infidelity but nonetheless remains faithful and constant.

3. Write about someone who has stood by you faithfully, in good times and in bad. Detail the ways this person supported you and kept faith with you in a bad time. Do you think this person could choose you as someone to write about who has been faithful to her or him? Why or why not?

Between Christ and the Church

The early Christians saw the Sinai covenant as applying to the relationship between Christ and the church. The marriage bond was also interpreted as a covenant, in terms of the love between Christ and the church. Thus, Saint Paul urged the Ephesians:

Husbands, love your wives, just as Christ loved the church and gave himself up for her. . . . In the same way, husbands should love their wives as they do their own bodies. He who loves his wife loves himself. For no one ever hates his own body, but he nourishes and tenderly cares for it, just as Christ does for the church, because we are members of his body. "For this reason a man will leave his father and mother and be joined to his wife, and the two will become one flesh." This is a great mystery, and I am applying it to Christ and the church. Each of you, however, should love his wife as himself, and a wife should respect her husband. (Ephesians 5:25–33)

In speaking of the mystery of marriage, both Jesus and Paul referred to a well-known passage from Genesis: "Therefore a man leaves his father and mother and clings to his

In the Christian tradition, marriage is understood as a sacred covenant between a woman and a man, like the relationship between Christ and the church.

wife" (2:24). But to further clarify the unbreakable and sacred nature of the relationship between husband and wife, Jesus added, "'So they are no longer two, but one flesh. Therefore what God has joined together, let no one separate'" (Mark 10:8–9).

Paul's message that husbands should love their wives as Christ loves the church stood in stark contrast to the assumptions of a culture that saw women as basically inferior and as having few rights. Now, of course, we take it for granted that there should be deep, mutual love and respect between spouses, but this was a radical notion in the first-century Mediterranean world. Today, too, we would not draw quite the same analogy that Paul drew in equating the husband with Christ and the wife with the church. Rather, we would see *both* the husband and the wife as called to love their partner as Christ loves the church (or, in the terms of the Hebrew Scriptures, as Yahweh loves the Chosen People).

Covenantal Faithfulness: Images for Today

We receive from our culture many messages about what love, married life, and family life should be like. Movies, television shows, and romance novels often offer unrealistic portraits of intense and passionate relationships that real-life marriages seldom achieve. Comparing marriage to God's covenant is not meant to place a heavy burden on couples—presenting a divine ideal not humanly achievable. The challenges of living together and sharing a lifetime are great enough. However, referring to marriage as a covenant places before couples a model of fidelity that can help them build up their relationship and make it more loving.

Faithfulness implies more than just sexual fidelity, which means that the spouses reserve their sexual intimacy exclusively for each other. True marital faithfulness goes beyond only sexual exclusivity to encompass these three characteristics:

Constancy: Fidelity implies the ability to love through all the ups and downs of life, in times of crisis and hardship. In the traditional words of the marriage vows, the partners promise to be true to each other "for better, for worse, for richer, for poorer, in sickness and in health, until death do us part." Such faithfulness requires a constant concern for each other's well-being, not only during the romantic times but during the day-in and day-out, year-in and year-out routines that develop in a life spent together. This fidelity is not a couple's simply resigning themselves to being "stuck" with each other, no matter what. Instead, it is their commitment to *grow together* in supporting and caring for each other.

4. Of the three characteristics of fidelity discussed—constancy, loving confrontation, and lived values—which one do you think would be the most difficult for you in a marriage? Explain your answer in writing.

Loving confrontation: Fidelity includes caring enough about the relationship to confront problems honestly and struggle through them together. The ability to confront lovingly assumes that the spouses believe in each other's inherent goodness and lovableness, even when certain behaviors or personality traits are annoying or even hurtful.

Lived values: Fidelity includes actively living out values and priorities. Do the spouses choose to put a priority on their relationship by giving it the time and nurturance that it needs to grow? In this connection, a wise saying applies:

> Where you spend your time
>   is where you spend your life.
> And where you spend your life
>   is where you spend your love.

Becoming One's Real Self

Obviously, a marriage covenant implies a lot more than does a marriage contract. A marriage covenant is commitment freely and gladly given, a sign to the world of the love that sustains life. This special covenantal relationship does not leave untouched those who enter it; it will cause tears and scars. However, insofar as the couple give themselves to each other in the marriage relationship, that relationship in turn marks them with deeper sensitivity and a stronger identity. This process is part of the paschal mystery, which moves from death and suffering to risen life. As we have seen throughout this course, that mystery is a central reality celebrated in all of the church's sacraments.

Over a lifetime together, married partners become persons they never would have become if it were not for their marriage to each other. Blessed by the grace of the sacrament of marriage, a couple can believe, even in the hardest times, that God has given them each other as the means to their own salvation, to their own individual, ultimate destiny as a "real" person.

5. Using the passage from *The Velveteen Rabbit* as a starting point, write a one-page reflection entitled "Romance Versus Love: What's the Difference?"

Creativity

The mutual self-giving, the faithfulness, and the personal development of partners in marriage all manifest God's love and grace in the world. Yet the loving relationship of the spouses is not the only purpose of marriage. Just as God's love is creative and always brings forth goodness and new life, the couple's love is meant to lead to something wonderful beyond itself.

What Is "Real"?

A beloved children's story, *The Velveteen Rabbit,* by Margery Williams, tells of the wondrous, almost miraculous developments that the love of one person can cause to happen in another. In a conversation between two children's toys, one of them, the Skin Horse, tells the Rabbit about becoming "Real." As you read the passage, try to connect the conversation with the paschal-like mystery of marriage.

"What is REAL?" asked the Rabbit one day. . . . "Does it mean having things that buzz inside you and a stick-out handle?"

"Real isn't how you are made," said the Skin Horse. "It's a thing that happens to you. When a child loves you for a long, long time, not just to play with, but REALLY loves you, then you become Real."

"Does it hurt?" asked the Rabbit.

"Sometimes," said the Skin Horse, for he was always truthful. "When you are Real, you don't mind being hurt."

"Does it happen all at once, like being wound up," he asked, "or bit by bit?"

"It doesn't happen all at once," said the Skin Horse. "You become. It takes a long time. That's why it doesn't often happen to people who break easily, or have sharp edges, or who have to be carefully kept. Generally, by the time you are Real, most of your hair has been loved off, and your eyes drop out and you get loose in the joints and very shabby. But these things don't matter at all, because once you are Real you can't be ugly, except to people who don't understand." (Pages 16–17)

To become "Real" is to become the person one is meant to be by God. Through God's grace, which sustains a couple's love over a lifetime, husband and wife help each other become "Real."

Certainly, a marriage goes through phases in turning inward versus turning outward. Particularly in the beginning, the couple may be intensely absorbed in each other and in the relationship itself. At times, partners will need to renew that focus on themselves and their own bond.

The point of marriage, however, is not to begin and end with the couple. Love not eventually shared with others becomes stagnant, resulting not in genuine love but in mutual self-absorption. In other words, the assured and enthusiastic statement "We care for each other" needs to become "We care for others as well," in order for love to be creative.

There are many ways for couples to be creative and fruitful. The most obvious and natural way is for couples to bring children into the world and raise them.

Children as a Blessing, Not a Burden

Vital to the sacrament of marriage is the couple's willingness to welcome any children that may come from their union. This intention is so central to marriage's meaning that the church does not permit a sacramental marriage between a man and a woman if they as individuals or as a couple are not open to having children, provided they are physically able. If they are incapable of having children, or decide not to adopt children, there are many other ways they can share their love with those around them. Their marriage can be just as fruitful as one that brings forth children, but in different ways.

Of greater importance than the number of children brought into the world by a couple is the couple's generosity and spirit of welcoming new life, treating each child as a blessing to the family, not a burden. Babies and children *inevitably* change a childless marriage or lifestyle, and they can require immense sacrifices from parents. But raising children brings growth, joy, and love as well, and in a loving marriage, the sense of welcome and gratitude for a new life supersedes the awareness of the changes that are sure to come.

Here is an account of how one couple lived the spirit of openness that characterizes families where children truly feel like blessings:

> Susan was into her eighth month of pregnancy, but vacation plans had been made the year before. "The children will be disappointed if we don't go on holiday," she told her husband, Joe. "I'll be fine." So off the family went to the seashore, their station wagon bulging with bicycles, beach chairs, and children.
>
> Susan set up her base of operations in the enclosed porch of the beach house, where she could oversee the comings and goings of all family members. No one came or went without checking in with Mom.
>
> Four days into the vacation, Susan began having labor contractions regularly. "It's time to go to the hospital," she told Joe. She gave last-minute instructions to all the children, and then she and Joe sped off to the hospital, which was over two hours away. Halfway into the ride, both driver and passenger had visions of a child being born at a highway rest stop, but with only minutes to spare, they made it to the hospital.
>
> A baby boy was born that night into a boisterous but loving family. Susan still orchestrates family activities, and although family outings are busier, livelier, and more complicated with the addition of a new little one, they are also more loving than ever.

In a loving family, children feel like they are blessings, not burdens.

6. React to this statement in writing:
- Intending to have and raise children is central to the meaning of a marriage.

Being Creative for the Reign of God

Creativity and fruitfulness in marriage are not limited to raising children. A husband and wife are called to bring new life into the world, but this new life can take many forms. The spirit of welcome and hospitality with which the couple anticipate children often leads to involvement in the wider community, in making their local or global environment better for *all* people.

Thus, couples seeking ways to be creative as a family might become involved in improving their community's schools, working against racial discrimination in their neighborhood, or helping to develop a recycling system for their city. They may take on a special family-oriented service, like welcoming people who are poor or considered different or strange in their community. In these ways, marriage partners share in building the Reign of God as a couple, not merely as individuals. The creative intent of marriage is oriented ultimately toward just that—making God's love, justice, and peace a reality in the world.

For Review

- From the beginning years of the church, what has marriage been regarded as a symbol of?
- In what sense does the Christian vision of marriage counteract the trap of consumerism?
- What is sexual intercourse meant to express in marriage?
- What is a covenant? How does a covenant differ from a contract in regard to a relationship?
- In addition to sexual fidelity, what are three characteristics that are included in marital faithfulness? Briefly describe them.
- What is the creativity of marriage ultimately oriented toward?

Marriage's Symbols and Rituals

Living Out the Sacrament

The sacrament of marriage, as you might guess by now, is not just the ceremony that takes place on the wedding day. Rather, the sacrament is the couple's sharing of the whole of their life together. The wedding ceremony itself is a one-time

Marriage is celebrated with beautiful rituals and ceremonies in every culture.
Photo, top: A royal bride at a wedding in Morocco, a country in northwest Africa
Photo, bottom: A wedding in Kazakhstan, a former Soviet republic in Central Asia

event that celebrates and affirms the sacrament that encompasses a lifetime. As mentioned earlier, marriage is "a communion of the whole of life."

We have already talked about other sacraments as lifetime endeavors. Baptism, it has been said, is not just a ceremony that happens once and then is ignored. Nor is the Eucharist just a Sunday morning event with no connection to the rest of the week. In an even more obvious way, the sacrament of marriage is not simply the wedding ceremony; it is the living out of the meaning of that ritual.

The Husband and Wife as the Primary Symbols

The husband and wife themselves are the primary symbols in the sacrament of marriage. They, not the priest or deacon, are the ministers of the sacrament. All the acts of love that the couple perform in their married life are "rituals" of a sort. When a husband and wife linger over an evening meal and share stories about their day, they are celebrating their marriage. When they support each other in a volunteer project for the community, they are witnessing the sacrament's bearing of fruit. The most powerful love ritual, of course, is sexual intercourse, which symbolizes and brings about physical and spiritual union in marriage. Children born from this union or welcomed into the couple's relationship are the clearest statement that a marriage is greater than the joining of the couple themselves. So the sacrament is not a one-time-only event but an ongoing shared life.

The Community as a Symbol

When people decide to marry, they are making a choice that will affect their whole community and that will require the support of that community—relatives, friends, and the wider church they belong to. To marry "in the church" means much more than simply having a "church wedding"—that is, a wedding that happens to take place in a church building. Marriage in the church means the couple make their promises to each other with the support and presence of the faith community, so that the community can celebrate the man and woman's love and let them know that they will help the couple be faithful to the commitment they are making. The community itself is one of the symbols in a marriage; the priest or deacon at the wedding of a Catholic is a witness of the marriage, a representative of the whole church community.

The Ritual Itself: Adaptable to Various Needs

Within or Outside the Mass

Normally and ideally, the marriage ritual for Catholics takes place within the celebration of a Mass. This is particularly appropriate because the Eucharist both symbolizes and brings about oneness in God.

In a marriage between a Catholic and a non-Catholic, however, frequently the couple will choose not to have their wedding during Mass. This is generally a matter of courtesy to persons attending who are not Catholic, because Catholic church practice is that only Catholics may receive Communion. To exclude from receiving Communion one member of the couple and potentially half of the congregation at a wedding—which is intended to celebrate the couple's unity—would not be in the spirit of the celebration.

The Location

Since Vatican Council II, much greater flexibility is possible for the wedding of a Catholic and a non-Catholic than previously existed. Although the ideal place for the wedding is in the Catholic parish church, permission can be obtained in most dioceses from the bishop or the parish priest to hold

7. Suppose that a woman has written to an advice column with these questions:
- My boyfriend and I love each other deeply and plan to be together always. We've made our commitment to each other. So why should we get married? Why not just live together? And what difference would getting married in the church make?

Answer the questions with some wise advice.

the wedding in another Christian church, whose minister might officiate rather than the Catholic priest. Sometimes, a bishop may give permission for the wedding to be held in a suitable place other than a church. Before this flexibility was built into the church's rules, the location and form of the wedding was often a major stumbling block (and a cause of hurt and division) for couples when one of them was not Catholic.

Common Elements of Marriage Rituals

There are three possible rites for marriage in the Catholic church:

- the rite for celebrating marriage during Mass
- the rite for celebrating marriage outside Mass (which can be used for the marriage of a Catholic and a baptized non-Catholic)
- the rite for celebrating marriage between a Catholic and an unbaptized person

Regardless of which rite is used, the ceremony itself combines a focus on the couple with a recognition that marriage is an event greater and more encompassing than what happens between two individuals alone. Common to the three possible rites are these elements:

1. the liturgy of the word
2. the consent (traditionally known as the vows)
3. the blessing and exchange of rings
4. the nuptial blessing
5. the final blessing

The liturgy of the word, as learned in chapter 9, is the proclaiming of the word of God in the Scriptures. And the final blessing is simply that—a final blessing and prayer for the couple spoken by the minister or priest on behalf of the gathered community. Let's examine the other three elements of the Rite of Marriage a bit more closely.

Consent: The exchange of promises, or consent, during the ceremony gives the couple the opportunity to say yes to each other publicly. Even though the couple have told each other of their love many times before this moment, the promises (vows) gain meaning because they are proclaimed in a formal, public setting. This consent is an essential part of the rite.

Blessing and exchange of rings: The words accompanying the blessing and exchange of rings refer to the rings as "signs of love and fidelity." Rings are an ancient symbol of wholeness and unity. Kings and queens wore rings as a sign of their office. Some fantasy tales center on losing or finding

8. Circles and rings are used symbolically in many cultures and religions and in the art, architecture, celebrations, and writings of those cultures and religions. Draw a picture or write a story or poem that incorporates circles or rings as symbols of wholeness and unity.

rings with magical powers attached to them. On a more practical level, wearing a ring given by another person keeps that person in our thoughts and reminds us of that person's love. In some cultures, however, the exchange of rings does not fit in with the people's customs, so it can be omitted.

Nuptial blessing: The nuptial blessing is a prayer for God's grace, peace, love, and strength to be with the couple through all of their life together, and for the gift of children.

Personalizing a Wedding

The bride and the groom can personalize their wedding by selecting from the many scriptural readings and various versions of the prayers and blessings those that seem most fitting to their experience and circumstances. The couple can compose petitions for the Prayer of the Faithful and select their music with the help of someone versed in liturgical music. There are two standard forms of the consent (vows) to choose from in the United States—the traditional and the revised—but many couples compose their own vows, finding that the writing itself is a clarifying and unifying process. The couple's friends and relatives can be invited to participate in special ways in the rite, as lectors, eucharistic ministers, musicians, and so on.

Some couples have added to their celebration a gift for the world's poor people, symbolized by bringing a basket of food to the altar. Other couples have given a certain percentage of their wedding's total cost to groups or organizations involved in helping poor people. This action is a reminder to themselves and the community that they want to foster, in their marriage, an openness and a reaching out to persons in need.

Cultural Variations

Different cultures have different symbols and rituals within the marriage ceremony. In the Eastern Catholic church, for example, crowning the bride and groom is a central ritual during a wedding. Many Hispanic weddings include customs such as the offering of the *Lazo,* a figure-eight band or "true-lovers' knot" (made, for instance, by putting two rosaries together) as a symbol of the union of the man and woman. Another Hispanic custom is the bride's offering of her bouquet to the Blessed Mother as a way of asking her protection over the marriage.

Parents or other guests might extend good wishes or blessings to the couple at some point in the ceremony. As mentioned earlier, the exchange of rings is not customary in some cultures and so can be omitted. Persons from cultures

A ring, an ancient symbol of wholeness and unity, is given in the marriage ritual as a sign of love and fidelity.

9. Of the various ways you could personalize your wedding or incorporate traditions from your own culture, which two ways would mean the most to you? For each one, explain in writing what you would do and why.

Couples celebrating the sacrament of marriage are encouraged to incorporate customs from their own culture into the ritual.
Photo: In a Hispanic wedding, the couple offer homage to Mary and ask for her blessing on their marriage.

that have long-standing wedding customs are encouraged to incorporate their customs into the church ceremony, provided the customs do not detract from the meaning of the celebration.

Customs from Pre-Christian Cultures

Interestingly, many wedding customs that people have assumed to be Christian are actually rooted in pre-Christian cultures. For instance, in Greek and Roman cultures just prior to the time of Christ, marriage consisted of three basic activities still sometimes observed today. First, the father of the bride hands over his daughter to the groom. Second, the bride, in a white gown and a veil with flowers, solemnly proceeds to her husband's house, where her husband picks her up and carries her over the threshold. Third, once in the house, the couple eat a special wedding cake.

When considering such customs for inclusion in their wedding, many modern-day couples find it helpful to look at why the customs were originally practiced. Consider one custom we still see today—the father walking his daughter down the aisle and "giving away the bride." This practice originally arose because the father *owned* his daughter. At the time of her wedding, he was simply transferring his "property" over to the husband, who would now *own* the young woman as his wife. Recognizing the traditional roots of this custom, many contemporary couples prefer other variations for their wedding procession, such as the bride's being accompanied by her mother and father, or the couple's being accompanied by both sets of parents.

For Review

- How is the sacrament of marriage different from the wedding ceremony?
- What are the primary symbols of marriage?
- What are the three possible rites for marriage in the Catholic church?
- Describe three things couples can do to personalize their own wedding.

Marriage's History

A Gradual Increase of Church Involvement

From its beginning, the church recognized the marriages of baptized persons as sacred undertakings with a covenantal meaning. The Christians' rejection of divorce and infidelity contrasted sharply with the practices of the non-Christian Romans of the time, who treated the bond of marriage rather lightly. However, during its early history, the church took no special role in the wedding ceremonies of its members. The early Christians married the same way everyone else did in their various cultures.

Eventually, the church got more involved because many couples presented themselves to their bishop after their wedding to receive the bishop's blessing, although the church did not require this. Also, priests or bishops often attended the weddings of Christians, adding a greater sense of church approval.

Not until the period from the seventh to the eleventh centuries, when the church was the most stable force in society, did it become actively involved in marriage laws and

Marriage in Words and Symbols

Liturgy of the Word

A reading from the first letter of John:

> Beloved, let us love one another, because love is from God; everyone who loves is born of God and knows God. Whoever does not love does not know God, for God is love. (4:7–8)

Consent

[The couple join hands.]
I, [Name], take you, [Name], to be my wife [or husband]. I promise to be true to you in good times and in bad, in sickness and in health. I will love you and honor you all the days of my life.

Consent

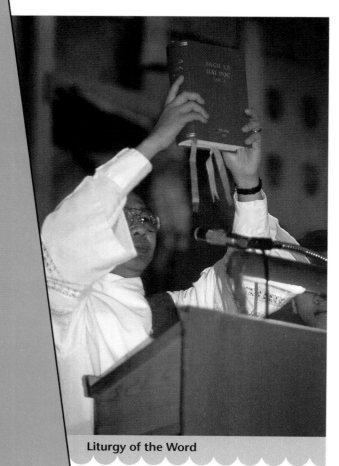

Liturgy of the Word

Blessing and Exchange of Rings

Blessing and Exchange of Rings

Lord, bless and consecrate [Name] and [Name] in their love for each other.
May these rings be a symbol
of true faith in each other,
and always remind them of their love. . . .

[Name], take this ring as a sign of my love and fidelity. In the name of the Father, and of the Son, and of the Holy Spirit.

Nuptial Blessing

Father, to reveal the plan of your love,
you made the union of husband and wife
an image of the covenant between you and
	your people.
In the fulfillment of this sacrament,
the marriage of Christian man and woman
is a sign of the marriage between Christ and the
	Church.
Father, stretch out your hand, and bless [Name]
	and [Name].

Lord, grant that as they begin to live this
	sacrament
they may share with each other the gifts of
	your love
and become one in heart and mind
as witnesses to your presence in their marriage.
Help them to create a home together
(and give them children to be formed by the
	gospel
and to have a place in your family).

Nuptial Blessing

Communion Meditation

Final Blessing

May almighty God, with his Word of blessing,
unite your hearts in the never-ending bond of
pure love. . . .

May your children bring you happiness, and
may your generous love for them be returned to
you, many times over. . . .

May you have true friends to stand by you,
both in joy and in sorrow.

May you be ready and willing to help and
comfort all who come to you in need. . . .

May daily problems never cause you undue
anxiety, nor the desire for earthly possessions
dominate your lives. . . .

May the Lord bless you with many happy
years together, so that you may enjoy the
rewards of a good life. . . .

rites. At the time, no other authority existed in Europe that could protect people from abuses of marriage laws, so the church began to fill that role.

By the twelfth century, the typical marriage ceremony took place in front of the church building, was presided over by a priest, and was followed by everyone's going into the church for Mass. Gradually, marriages took place more often in the actual church building and during Mass. By the thirteenth century, marriage was viewed as one of the seven official sacraments of the church.

A Tradition of Marriage's Permanence

Since its earliest times, the church has maintained that a valid marriage is permanent and cannot be dissolved—a sentiment based on Jesus' teachings in the Gospels. In practice, however, a man was sometimes allowed to divorce and remarry, if his first wife had been unfaithful to him. However, the reverse did not hold true. Even though a man might be adulterous, his wife was obligated to remain married to him. Clearly, such allowances were more rooted in a patriarchal culture than in any authentic interpretation of the Gospels.

An Unequivocal Teaching

Saint Ambrose, a fourth-century bishop, reiterated Jesus' teaching that marriage could not be dissolved under any circumstances. A few years later, one of his students, Saint Augustine, taught that divorce and remarriage for either a man or a woman was prohibited. This teaching has essentially been handed down through various official church statements over the centuries. At the time of the Protestant Reformation, Catholicism re-emphasized its clear teaching that the bond of marriage is permanent.

Annulment Versus Divorce

The Catholic church has always recognized that there are cases in which a marriage blessed by the church was never actually valid as a sacrament. This could be because, at the time of the marriage ceremony, either or both of the partners had not entered the marriage willingly, had been dishonest about their intent, or had been unable to make a permanent commitment. In such a case, after a thorough investigation of the situation, a local church marriage tribunal may determine that the marriage never existed sacramentally in the first place. A person whose marriage has been annulled is free to marry again.

10. People who marry today often face pressures that did not exist a century ago. Name and discuss in writing three changes in modern culture or in the way society operates that have added pressures to married life today.

11. Imagine yourself in your late forties, still married to your spouse of twenty-five years, whom you love dearly. Imagine too that your spouse, though healthy in body for the time being, suffers from Alzheimer's disease and no longer even recognizes you. Would you want to divorce your spouse because you are now strangers? Why or why not?

What does your response tell you about the value you place in a steadfast, personal relationship? Explain your response in writing.

An annulment is not the same as a divorce. A divorce dissolves a marriage that once existed, and a divorce is given by civil authorities. An annulment, on the other hand, declares that a marriage never did exist sacramentally, and an annulment is given only by the church. The Catholic church maintains that a valid sacramental marriage can never be dissolved or annulled.

For Review

- Why did the church first become actively involved in marriage laws and rites?
- What is the Catholic church's teaching on whether a valid marriage can be dissolved?
- What is the difference between an annulment and a divorce?

In a loving, enduring marriage, a joyful hope is created that becomes a light to the world.

A Light to the World

Marriage is a natural experience and a powerful symbol. As a sacrament, it depicts God's covenantal relationship with people in the very human "body language" of two persons becoming one flesh. On the human level, such a total gift of self through the whole of a life together is an ideal that can never be completely reached. Nonetheless, with the inspiration of Jesus and the support of the church community, couples continue to desire and strive for that ideal. They know, almost instinctively, that the rewards for such a relationship are great. When husbands can, in Saint Paul's words, "love their wives as they do their own bodies," and when wives can do likewise, a joyful hope is created that becomes light to the world.

Like the sacrament of marriage, the sacrament of holy orders gives Catholics a path to allow their whole lifestyle to reveal God's goodness and love to the world. We will turn to the sacrament of holy orders, the other sacrament of vocation, in chapter 13.

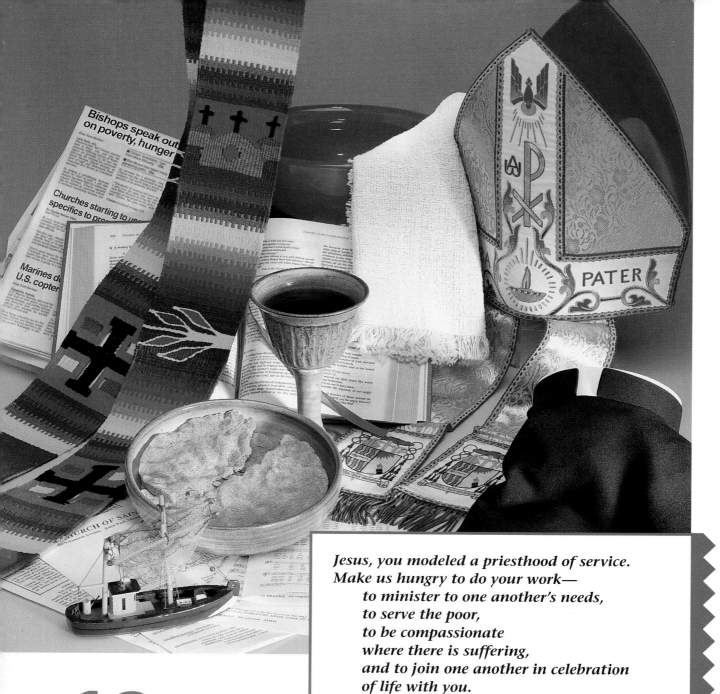

Jesus, you modeled a priesthood of service.
Make us hungry to do your work—
     to minister to one another's needs,
     to serve the poor,
     to be compassionate
     where there is suffering,
     and to join one another in celebration
     of life with you.
Amen.

13

Holy Orders:
Celebrating Ministry
in the Church

The sacrament of holy orders, along with the sacrament of marriage, is one of the sacraments of vocation. Holy orders consists of three officially designated orders of ministry in the Catholic church: bishop, priest, and deacon. Together with all members of the Christian community, persons ordained into the sacramental ministries act as sacraments in the church and the world. Specifically, ordained persons lead the community in worship, give witness to God's presence, and call the community to live out its mission. These persons, like Jesus, serve as spiritual guides to the Kingdom of God.

Before we examine the role of such spiritual guides, however, let's begin by following up on a story that is probably familiar to you, about another kingdom and the guide to that kingdom.

After her whirlwind visit to Oz, Dorothy continued to live in Kansas, first on the farm owned by her aunt and uncle, and later in the town nearby. Soon Dorothy became a cherished member of the farm community. In her life as a mother, then as a grandmother, and as the town's favorite "adopted aunt," Dorothy was someone to whom people both young and old could turn when they felt down or hurt.

Invariably, Dorothy would be asked to retell the story of Oz—no matter how many times her listeners had heard it before. The children were especially enthralled by Dorothy's tales about the magical land over the rainbow—a land of witches, Munchkins, talking lions, and tin woodsmen with real hearts. They found these images startling but irresistibly alluring.

Dorothy captivated the adults with her special talent for painting a vivid picture of the courage of the lion, the wisdom of the scarecrow, the generosity of the tin man, and the goodness of Glinda the witch. People who heard her stories— really heard them—discovered deep truths in them and were often transformed by the rich messages they contained. In their enthusiasm, the people of the community could not help but share the stories they had been told with others.

Once, a small child who had been listening to Dorothy with spellbound attention very quietly whispered, "Can I go to Oz, too?" Dorothy responded with a gleam in her eye, "Why, Oz is all around you. Just look at the people you know—if you see courage, wisdom, and good-heartedness, then you've found Oz!"

1. If you could choose a spiritual guide either from history or from the world today, someone to be present and talk with you in your everyday life, whom would you choose—other than Jesus? Explain your choice of a spiritual guide in writing.

Catholic Tradition traces the ordained ministry back to Jesus' Apostles.
Photo: Thirteenth-century artist Duccio's "The Calling of the Apostles Peter and Andrew"

What Does Holy Orders Celebrate?

A Doorway to Sacred Mystery

Dorothy, the hero in Frank Baum's famous book *The Wizard of Oz,* may at first seem an unlikely character to compare with Jesus. However, some similarities do exist.

- Dorothy's firsthand experience of Oz left her uniquely qualified to pass on the truths she learned on her visit.

  Jesus' special relationship with the One he called Father enabled him to open people's eyes and hearts to a loving, compassionate God in a way no one else could.

- Dorothy spent her life sharing the stories of her trip to Oz with the people of her community. In the process, she lived out the truths of courage, good-heartedness, and wisdom that she had learned in Oz.

  Like Dorothy, Jesus did not keep his Good News to himself, but instead proclaimed it to others through the stories he told and through the ways he lived his life and treated other people.

- Dorothy's stories transformed people's lives and moved them to share what they had learned with others.

  Jesus, too, preached a life-transforming message and instructed his followers to spread that message to the ends of the earth.

2. In your community, where have you seen service to others most clearly evident? Describe in writing the people, organization, and activities involved.

In short, both Dorothy and Jesus served as doorways into the mystery of life. Ordained ministers, and in particular, priests, are examples of modern-day people who lead others to confront and experience the mystery of life.

As a priest, Jesus performed two important functions:

1. He led people to an encounter with God—the most profound mystery of life—and revealed God as ultimately loving and alive in their midst.

2. He linked God's love to service, to being a person of service for others.

The Heart of the Christian Life

Being a person for others is at the heart of Christian life. Jesus was a person for others; Christians are to do as Jesus did. This is the essential meaning of baptism in Christ: All Christians are part of the **priesthood of all believers** established by Jesus. From this insight about what it means to be a Christian, we can also learn about what it means to be an ordained minister in the Catholic church.

Holy Orders Flows from Jesus and His Church

Both the ministry and work of Jesus and the sacramental priesthood of all Christians form the basis out of which the sacrament of holy orders flows. To help us better understand the unique character of those charged to serve as ordained ministers within the Catholic community, let's first take a closer look at Jesus' own ministry, the ministry that the whole Christian community is called to continue in his name.

The Ministry and Work of Jesus

The Catholic sacrament of holy orders first and foremost celebrates the ministry and work of Jesus. In the Christian tradition, three terms portray the roles of that ministry: *priest*, *prophet*, and *servant-leader.* Let's look now at why Christians ascribe these three roles to Jesus and see how they have shaped the Catholic understanding of ordained ministry.

Jesus the High Priest: Different from the Rest

Although the Christian Testament refers to the priesthood of all believers, no reference is made to any particular group of persons being set apart from the rest of the church community for priestly functions. As a matter of fact, the general notion of a priestly class was looked down on by the early Christians. They associated it with pagan cults and superstition, with different groups of people who all claimed

3. Imagine yourself as a priest who has been asked to write a newspaper column responding to the following questions:

- What are your greatest joys as a priest?
- What are your greatest difficulties as a priest?
- If you could change anything about how people treat you as a priest, what would you change, if anything?

Write down your answers, and then ask a priest these same questions. Record his responses and compare your answers with his. Which response did you most closely agree on? differ on?

Presiding at eucharistic celebrations is the central priestly function of Catholic ordained ministry.

4. Think of a stereotype or a mistaken notion that many people believe about priests as a group. Draw a cartoon or a comic strip that illustrates one mistaken belief.

to possess special powers and "secret" knowledge of God. The early Christians saw Jesus as the one and *only* true priest.

The most thorough portrayal of Jesus as the one true priest comes to us from the Letter to the Hebrews, written to Jewish Christians after the Romans' destruction of the Temple in Jerusalem in the year 70 C.E. The author of the letter compares Jesus to the high priests of the Jewish faith. As part of their role, Jewish high priests regularly offered sacrifices at the Temple in order to bring the Jewish people back into a faithful relationship with God. However, as the author of the Letter to the Hebrews explains, Jesus' greater sacrifice of himself on the cross *permanently* restores people's relationship with God, which had been broken by sin. Unlike the sacrifices of the Jewish high priests, Jesus' sacrifice does not have to be repeated over and over again. Thus, the Temple is no longer needed: "We have been sanctified through the offering of the body of Jesus Christ once for all" (Hebrews 10:10).

This explanation of Jesus as the One High Priest offering himself in sacrifice on the cross was soon linked to Christians' celebration of the eucharistic meal. In the process, a lasting connection was forged between the notion of sacrifice, the Eucharist, and leadership in the church. Celebrating the Eucharist was the central expression of faith for Christians. Thus, presiding at eucharistic celebrations (which commemorate Jesus' life-giving sacrifice) would come to be seen as the central priestly function of Christian leaders.

Jesus as Prophet: A Living Reminder

A prophet is someone who unceasingly reminds people about God and God's ways. Jesus, and the message that he preached to the people of his native Palestine, was truly prophetic: God's word was revealed not only in spoken form but in the flesh-and-blood person of Jesus. Ordained ministers serve as living reminders of Christ's prophetic message. When they preside at the Eucharist, visit the sick, witness a couple's marriage, lead prayer at a funeral service, or preach the Gospels, they do so in Jesus' name. The words and actions of Jesus—as prophet—are part of the ideal of Christian life and official church ministry.

Jesus as Leader: One Who Serves

Jesus' disciples had a strong sense that he was the Messiah, the Anointed One sent by God to usher in God's Reign, even before the Resurrection. What confounded them was the *type* of leadership Jesus embodied.

Jesus flatly rejected the desire of many of his followers to make him a political or military ruler. He did not trick, coerce, terrorize, or manipulate people in any way to get them to follow him. Instead, he treated them with compassion and respect, forgave their sins, healed their wounds, and gave them nourishment for both their body and their soul. He was seldom seen with the "respected," powerful, and influential people in the community. In fact, he was ridiculed and viewed with suspicion for associating with poor or ill people, women, "obvious sinners" like tax collectors, and other marginalized people in his society.

Jesus literally turned the disciples' expectations of him as a leader upside-down. Perhaps no incident shows this better than the story of Jesus washing the feet of the disciples at the Last Supper:

> During supper Jesus . . . got up from the table, took off his outer robe, and tied a towel around himself. Then he poured water into a basin and began to wash the disciples' feet and to wipe them with the towel that was tied around him. He came to Simon Peter, who said to him, "Lord, are you going to wash my feet?" Jesus answered, "You do not know now what I am doing, but later you will understand." Peter said to him, "You will never wash my feet." Jesus answered, "Unless I wash you, you have no share with me." Simon Peter said to him, "Lord, not my feet only but also my hands and my head." . . .
>
> After he had washed their feet, had put on his robe, and had returned to the table, he said to them, "Do you know what I have done to you? You call me Teacher and Lord—and you are right, for that is what I am. So if I, your Lord and Teacher, have washed your feet, you also ought to wash one another's feet. For I have set you an

5. On paper, list four qualities that you think are necessary for any leader to possess. For each quality, write a sentence explaining its importance to you. Did the Apostle Peter ever fail in any of these qualities? After all, on three occasions he denied even knowing Jesus, and in some Gospel accounts he can seem unreliable and contradictory. What quality or qualities did Peter possess that so redeemed him as a leader?

example, that you also should do as I have done to you. Very truly, I tell you, servants are not greater than their master, nor are messengers greater than the one who sent them." (John 13:2–16)

Loving service to one another, Jesus teaches his followers, is to be the hallmark of Christian life and leadership. Ordained ministers are to lead in part by the example of loving service they set.

The Church: A Priestly People

The Christian Testament tells us that every person who has been baptized into the body of Christ is called to share in the threefold mission of Jesus as members of a holy and royal priesthood (see 1 Peter 2:5,9). This further confirms our earlier discussion, in chapter 5, about how the whole church is to be a sacrament of Jesus to the world. Every Christian is to make the God revealed by Jesus present to the world. All Christians are called to act as priest (reconciling people with God), prophet (proclaiming God's truth), and servant-leader.

You may be wondering: If the roles of priest, prophet, and servant-leader belong to the whole Christian community, why should there be ordained ministers? What specific roles do bishops, priests, and deacons have in the life of the church? And why is an ordained role considered a sacrament? With an understanding of the ministry and work of Jesus and the priesthood of all believers, we are ready to address these questions.

6. Prophets, even the most nonviolent of them, like Mohandas K. Gandhi, Martin Luther King, Jr., and Oscar Romero, usually face adversity and often die by violence. Servant-leaders, like Dorothy Day and Mother Teresa, go through life pretty much penniless. Yet none of the persons mentioned here would have chosen to live otherwise. Research the writings of one of these persons and record the reasons given for living as he or she did.

Today's priests have a variety of functions, including teaching and preaching the faith.

Ordained Ministers: Sacraments to the Church

Today's bishops, priests, and deacons continue the tradition of leadership in the church. On a practical level, ordained ministers coordinate the work of the church. On a symbolic level, ordained ministers are living sacraments, reminders to the community of its Jesus-inspired roles of priest, prophet, and servant to the world.

Models of Ministry

Perhaps a few examples from history will shed some light on the sacramental role of ordained persons in the church:

Laurence, prophetic deacon: Saint Laurence, a deacon, lived before Christianity was legal and therefore during a time when persecution of Christians still occurred. According to legend, the prefect (political leader) of Rome heard that the Christian church possessed great wealth. He ordered Laurence to hand over the church's riches to the emperor. Laurence agreed but told him that he would need a few days to gather them together. Laurence then set out to bring together homeless, poor, and crippled persons, persons afflicted with diseases like leprosy, and widows and orphans—all the needy of Rome who were then being supported by the church. When large groups of these people were gathered, he invited the Roman official to come and see the "wealth" of the church. For making his point so strikingly, Laurence was martyred by the angry prefect.

Nicholas, servant-leader: Probably the most famous bishop in all the world is Saint Nicholas, whom North Americans know as Santa Claus. During the fourth century, Nicholas served as bishop of Myra, in what is today the country of Turkey. Although he was born to wealthy parents, Nicholas grew up an orphan. Always concerned for poor and sick persons, especially children, he gave away his possessions to those in need before being elected bishop of Myra. One story about Nicholas recounts his walking by a house and overhearing young children inside talking about their lack of food and money. Instinctively, the kind bishop took out his purse of money and threw it into the window to the surprised and delighted children. During one of the early persecutions of Christians under the Roman Empire, Bishop Nicholas was chained in prison. Today, Saint Nicholas—whom we also know as Santa Claus—is recognized as the patron saint of children.

Saint Laurence

7. If you, like Saint Laurence, wanted to present the "wealth" of the Christian community in a symbolic way, how would you do it? As a challenge, try to think of a symbolic presentation that would touch the receiver's heart and possibly convert the receiver.

Priests and other ordained ministers in the church serve as living reminders to faith communities of Christ's presence among them.

Jean Vianney, reconciling priest: One famous model of a dedicated priest was Saint Jean Vianney (1786–1859). Vianney is not known for his great works; he wrote no books, lectured at no universities, and traveled to no distant lands. He is not known for great preaching. Sometimes he stumbled his way through his sermons or broke down in tears because he couldn't remember what he wanted to say. He simply served faithfully for most of his life as parish priest to the people of a little French village called Ars. At the time of Vianney's assignment to that parish, Ars was a town where no other priest wanted to go because the people there had a reputation for being crude and uncivilized.

During his service at Ars, Jean Vianney spent most of his time hearing confessions, leading many people to change their ways. People flocked to him because of his great yet humble holiness, and he inspired many townspeople and visitors from great distances to do good works. Jean Vianney stands out because he did so exceptionally well what priests do regularly—be present to a community and lead the people in prayer and in celebrating the sacraments. Jean Vianney is known today as the patron saint of priests.

The Sacrament of Holy Orders Today

A contemporary understanding of the sacrament of holy orders can be summed up in the functions performed by ordained ministers. Bishops, priests, and deacons all carry out the following six tasks:

1. to serve as living reminders of Jesus within the church by their priestly, prophetic, and leading actions
2. to gather the community together, calling upon it to remain true to its task
3. to give public witness to Christ's vision of justice and peace for the world
4. to represent the Catholic church as a public institution
5. to coordinate the moral, spiritual, and structural life of the faith community
6. to preside at official sacramental celebrations

In summary, bishops, priests, and deacons serve as sacraments within the church. They do this by giving witness to God's loving presence in the community, by calling the community to live out its mission to be a sacrament of Jesus to the world, and by leading the community in its worship of God.

For Review

- How was Dorothy, the hero from *The Wizard of Oz,* similar to Jesus in serving as a doorway into the mystery of life?
- What two important functions did Jesus perform as a priest?
- What does the Catholic sacrament of holy orders celebrate, first and foremost?
- What three terms, in the Christian tradition, portray the roles of Jesus' ministry? Briefly describe how Jesus carried out one of those roles and how modern-day ordained ministers serve in that role.
- According to the Christian Testament, who is called to share in the threefold mission of Jesus?
- What are the six tasks carried out by bishops, priests, and deacons in the Catholic church?

Bishop Maurice Dingman: A True Sacrament to the Church

Throughout the church's history, God has gifted the Christian community with individuals who stand out in their commitment to imitating Christ through their charity, dedication, and self-giving service to others. Bishop Maurice Dingman (1914–1992) was one such sacrament of Jesus to the church.

Known as a friend to the poor, a champion of justice, and a promoter of dialog among religions, Bishop Dingman served the church from 1968 to 1987 as the bishop of the Diocese of Des Moines, Iowa. He is remembered for his active, personal involvement in issues of social justice and peace as well as for his simplicity, gentleness, and concern for "the poor and hurting, those discouraged by the slow pace of change in society and the church." Admirers cite his many Christlike actions and accomplishments:

- He repeatedly cried out against government policies that destroyed family farms and put the nation's food system in the hands of a few "profit-driven, land-owning elite."
- His social concerns found him selling the luxurious bishop's residence and moving into a modest apartment; voluntarily spending a night in jail to show his support for the humane treatment of prisoners; marching with activists against the arms race; and touring Nicaragua and publicly criticizing the U.S. government's policy in Central America.
- He called the feminist movement in the church "the working of the Holy Spirit," encouraging those working for change to travel the long road ahead armed with a commitment to constant and patient dialog.
- His ecumenical (interreligious) concerns were symbolized by his joining members of other faiths in 1980 to commemorate the atomic bombing of Nagasaki, Japan; by his help in forming the Iowa Inter-Church Forum; and by the fact that he was almost as well-known and well-liked by non-Catholics in his diocese as by Catholics.

In 1985, Bishop Dingman explained the reason for his activism; several years later, a newspaper recounted that explanation: "'My problem is that I suffered a conversion about ten years ago,' he said. He came to the realization, he said, that bishops can sin as much by what they don't do as by what they do."

Bishop Dingman took his responsibilities as a bishop with utmost seriousness, preaching Jesus' message of hope and joy to all people and reflecting that message in his personal example. In Bishop Dingman's own words, "I can think of no better ministry than to be where there is life and death, struggles and dreams, the search for meaning, crowds of people and children, celebrations, and sometimes weeping." (Quoted material excerpted from *The Catholic Mirror*)

Holy Orders' Symbols and Rituals

The Whole Church Community

Just as it is with all the other sacraments, the church community as a whole is a primary symbol in holy orders. The community as a symbol is acknowledged in the rituals of holy orders in this way: Prior to consecration, those to be ordained as bishop, priest, or deacon are presented to the presiding bishop for approval in the name of the institutional church. At the same time, the ordaining bishop asks the people in the assembly for their approval of the candidates. This part of the ordination ritual emphasizes the fact that ordained ministry in the church flows out of the whole community's responsibility to carry on the ministry of Christ.

8. How well do you think the church community of a diocese really knows the persons who have been recently ordained in the diocese? List five suggestions for how the community could get to know new priests before ordination. Interview a recently ordained priest on what his first assignment was like. He may have some surprising (and funny) stories to tell you!

The Laying On of Hands

The laying on of hands is the other main symbol in the sacrament of holy orders. As in some other sacraments, such

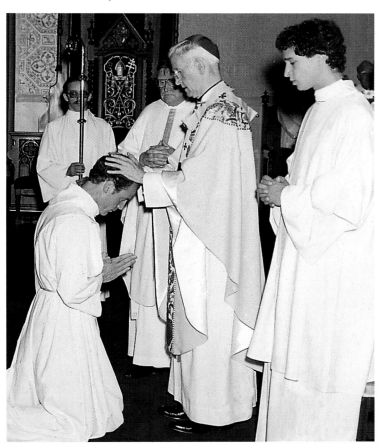

In the ordination ritual, the laying on of hands by the bishop symbolizes the empowerment of the newly ordained person with the Spirit.

as confirmation, reconciliation, and anointing, the church uses this ritual in holy orders to symbolize empowering persons with the Spirit.

In this sacrament, the laying on of hands also emphasizes that the power and responsibility of the office are shared:

- At the ordination of a bishop, the presiding bishop and all of the other bishops present (there must be at least two more) lay their hands on the head of the bishop-elect.
- At the ordination of a priest, all the other priests present lay their hands on the head of the one being ordained after the bishop has said the words of consecration.
- The laying on of hands at the ordination of a deacon is done only by the bishop, but the action still symbolizes the deacon's sharing in the ordained ministry of the church.
- All ordination rituals include a sign of peace among the bishops, priests, and deacons present.

Through these actions, the collegiality of ministry is emphasized; that is, new bishops, priests, and deacons become part of an order or "college" with shared or interrelated responsibilities.

Three Orders, Three Rituals

Each of the three orders of ordained ministers—bishop, priest, and deacon—has its own ceremony and its own specific functions of service, which are symbolized during the ceremony.

- **Bishops** hold the fullest expression of sacramental ordained ministry in the Catholic church. They can preside at all the sacraments, and they have the primary teaching and governing responsibilities in the church.

  Symbols and symbolic actions received by new bishops at their ordination include the book of the Gospels; the anointing of their head; a ring, which signifies marriage to the church; a miter (a type of hat symbolizing authority); and a shepherd's staff, a symbol of the leadership style of Jesus, the Good Shepherd.
- **Priests** receive their mission from the bishop whom they represent. Their responsibilities include preaching and teaching the Gospels, presiding at celebrations of the sacraments, and serving local Christian communities.

  The ritual of ordination for new priests includes vesting them in the official garb of the office, anointing their hands with oil, and presenting them with the bread and wine.

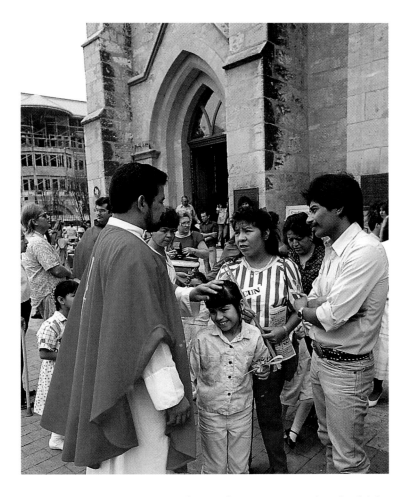

Priests are official leaders in the church, but their style of leadership is to be servants among the people, caring for them and building up the Christian community through love.

- **Deacons** are consecrated at ordination to assist the bishops and priests in serving the church through preaching, doing charitable work, distributing the Eucharist, and presiding at liturgies of baptism or marriage, at wakes, and at funerals.

    New deacons, like new priests, are also dressed in their official garb during their ordination ritual.

For Review

- What are the two primary symbols in the sacrament of holy orders, and what does each emphasize or symbolize?
- Name the three orders of ordained ministers and briefly describe their specific functions of service.

Holy Orders
in Words and Symbols

Presentation of the Book of the Gospels
(Ordination of a Deacon)

Receive the Gospel of Christ,
whose herald you now are.
Believe what you read,
teach what you believe,
and practice what you teach.

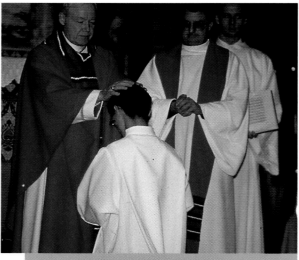

Laying On of Hands (by Bishop)

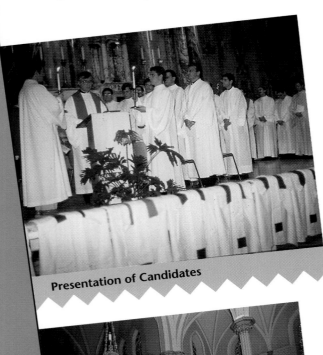

Presentation of Candidates

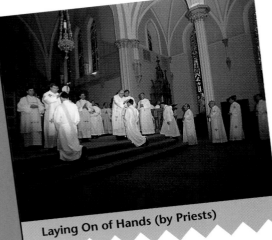

Laying On of Hands (by Priests)

Election by the Bishop
and Consent of the People
(Ordination of a Priest)

We rely on the help of the Lord God and our
Savior Jesus Christ, and we choose this man,
our brother, for priesthood in the presbyterial
order.

    Thanks be to God.

The Laying On of Hands
(Ordination of a Priest)

[This is done in silence first by the bishop, then
by the other priests present.]

Prayer of Consecration
(Ordination of a Priest)

Almighty Father,
grant to this servant of yours
the dignity of the priesthood.
Renew within him the Spirit of holiness.
As a co-worker with the order of bishops
may he be faithful to the ministry
that he receives from you, Lord God,
and be to others a model of right conduct.

Presentation
of the Gifts of Bread and Wine
(Ordination of a Priest)

Accept from the holy people of God the gifts to
  be offered to him.
Know what you are doing, and imitate the
  mystery you celebrate:
model your life on the mystery of the Lord's
  cross.

Examination of the Candidate
(Ordination of a Bishop)

Are you resolved to build up the Church as the
body of Christ and to remain united to it within the order of bishops under the authority of
the successor of the apostle Peter?
   I am.

Anointing the Head
(Ordination of a Bishop)

God has brought you to share the high
  priesthood of Christ,
May he pour out on you the oil of mystical
  anointing
and enrich you with spiritual blessings.

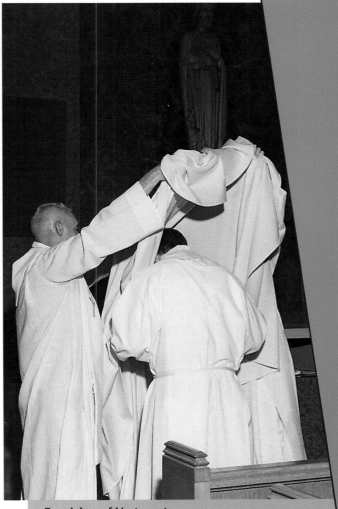

Receiving of Vestments

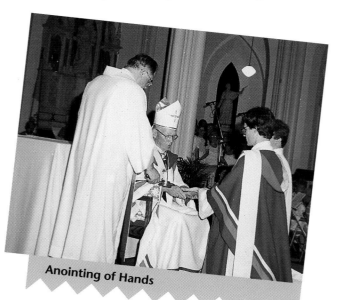

Anointing of Hands

Investiture with Ring, Miter,
and Pastoral Staff
(Ordination of a Bishop)

Take this ring, the seal of your fidelity.
With faith and love protect the bride of God,
  his holy Church.
Take this staff as a sign of your pastoral office:
keep watch over the whole flock
in which the Holy Spirit has appointed you
to shepherd the Church of God.

A person's charism—a special talent or gift for performing a certain ministry or service—is given by God to benefit and enlighten the whole community.

9. Name two people you know who exhibit a particular charism or talent for helping others. Describe the special talent each person shows, and list the approach, characteristics, and actions that make him or her so effective.

Holy Orders' History

The First Century: Charisms and Shared Leadership

Information about the first Christian communities indicates that many different types of ministry and leadership were present, several of which were performed by both men and women. Often, specific duties fell to people who exhibited a particular **charism** (that is, a talent or gift) for that role. Some people, for example, had a charism for taking care of widows, orphans, and others in need. Others had a charism for prophecy; still others, for leading prayer. The person at whose home the people gathered often led the community at the Eucharist.

Early on, it became common policy to appoint or elect either a person or a group to take the leadership role both in coordinating the various service activities of local communities and in presiding at the Eucharist and other liturgical services. Appointed or elected persons were known individually as *bishops* (meaning "overseers") or, if they were a group, as *presbyters* (literally, "elders"). *Deacons* ("servants") assisted the bishops in works of charity and in the celebration of the Eucharist. Thus, the three holy orders recognized by the Catholic church today had their roots in early Christian communities. Other ministries existed as well in the early church, and some of these came to be recognized as having official status.

At its beginning, leadership in the Christian movement was a shared ministry. Those who held leadership positions in one local community shared their authority with the individual or group leaders of other communities.

The Second to the Sixth Centuries

A Specialization of Roles

Over a period from the second to the sixth century, leadership roles became more specialized in the church. Ordination rites developed for each kind of ministry. Toward the end of this period, the orders of bishops and presbyters (later called "priests") gained more prominence.

By the sixth century, the role of deacon was by and large taken over by the presbyters. Rather than being an official order in and of itself, the diaconate was made part of the process of becoming a priest.

A Concentration of Power

Other significant changes occurred during the period between the second and the sixth century, including an increase in the power and leadership role of priests. Bishops needed more priests to minister to the growing number of church communities in Europe and elsewhere. As a result, more and more responsibility was delegated to priests. Also, priests—along with bishops—acted as judges and counselors in the Roman government. As a result, priestly ministry became associated more with power and authority than with service. Indeed, priests became regarded as "other Christs" with special power.

The Sixth Century Through the Reformation

A Separate Class

The major change in image that ordained ministry took from the sixth century up through the Protestant Reformation was toward the establishment of bishops and priests as

10. If you were a bishop today facing a serious shortage of priests for your diocese in the coming year, what options might be open to you? Could you close parishes? combine parishes? "borrow" priests from another diocese? List your options. Then write a letter to your bishop asking him how these organizational problems and assignments of priests are handled.

Some priests today are also monks, living a contemplative life in monasteries.

a group set apart from the rest of the church community. The influence of monastic life had a great deal to do with this distinction. Some early Christians felt drawn to living apart from society in caves, in the desert, or in isolated communities called monasteries. Through their solitude, they believed they could experience Christ in a more intimate way. These monks (men) and nuns (women) were regarded by other Christians as living a lifestyle that bred holiness and wisdom. Some monks were also priests, but the vast majority of priests were not monks.

All priests, however, soon began to mirror characteristics of these monastics. That is, they dressed differently from other people and said special prayers that monks and nuns said as part of their spiritual discipline. From about the middle of the twelfth century, priests in the Western church were also required to follow the monastic practice of celibacy, meaning that they did not marry.

The Church's Primary Ministers

By the end of the twelfth century, becoming a priest meant becoming a member of a separate class known collectively as the clergy. This group was exclusively charged with administering the sacraments. Over the centuries, priests had taken over the responsibilities of leading the community in all of its religious affairs, especially for worship and devotional ceremonies. Almost no role was left for laypeople in the church's ministry. This pattern of ministry changed very little during the Middle Ages and persisted well into our modern era.

The Reformation and Ordained Ministry

The increase in the power and status of ordained persons in the church during the Middle Ages was one of the conditions that spurred the Protestant Reformation, which was led by the monk and priest Martin Luther. Among the protests that Luther and other reformers voiced, regarding abuses within the church, were that many priests were not well trained and were careless in their duties; that bishops often abused their religious authority to gain political influence; and that a general condition of immorality pervaded the clergy.

Soon after these protests, in the mid-sixteenth century, the Council of Trent responded by setting out to establish a more pious and better-educated clergy than had existed during the Middle Ages. Seminaries were to be established in each diocese, and bishops were obliged to be residents of their own dioceses. Except for the work of non-clergy reli-

Women in Ministry in the Early Church

In Saint Paul's Letter to the Romans, we read:

> I commend to you our sister Phoebe, a deacon of the church at Cenchreae, so that you may welcome her in the Lord as is fitting for the saints, and help her in whatever she may require from you, for she has been a benefactor of many and of myself as well. (16:1–2)

Just who Phoebe was, and in what capacity she helped Paul, we do not know. But in the same letter, we find many more references to women who obviously played significant roles in the early church, among them a woman named Prisca:

> Greet Prisca and Aquila [Prisca's husband], who work with me in Christ Jesus, and who risked their necks for my life, to whom not only I give thanks, but all the churches of the Gentiles. Greet also the church in their house. (16:3–4)

As a matter of fact, information about the precise roles played by women in the early church is very sketchy, although the Christian Testament does indicate that a number of women like Phoebe and Prisca were influential leaders.

The most amazing stories about early church women are the accounts of martyrs such as Perpetua, mother of a newborn, and her pregnant servant Felicity, both of whom gave their lives rather than renounce their faith. (Listen for their names during the Canon of the Mass.) Women also served in forms of ministry—such as "prophecy"—that were important and widespread at the time but that later did not achieve status as official ministries.

gious orders, however, ministry and leadership within the church were still mainly in the hands of ordained persons until the Second Vatican Council.

Ministry in the Church Since Vatican Council II

A Return to Shared Ministry

As mentioned in chapter 6, the Second Vatican Council of the 1960s sought to get back to some of the root traditions of the early church. Included in these efforts were a number of changes in emphasis regarding the church's understanding of ordained ministry. Once again, service was stressed more than power and authority. Mutual decision-making, among the clergy and within the community, was now called for. Additionally, the Second Vatican Council renewed the church's recognition that many facets of Christ's priesthood are the shared responsibility of ordained persons *and* laypeople together. Bishops, priests, and deacons still had important, specific ministries, but they were encouraged more to work along with laypeople in helping to provide for

Saints Perpetua and Felicity

11. Women rabbis and women ordained as Protestant ministers have existed for a number of years. Interview a woman minister or rabbi about her personal experiences as a woman minister—why some people may be more comfortable, and others less comfortable, with her as a minister because she is a woman. Record her responses.

the spiritual needs of the community. The role of permanent deacon, which had disappeared after the sixth century, was restored, and the permanent diaconate was opened to married men.

Broadening the Ministries of the Church

The Second Vatican Council's call for involvement of laypeople in the Catholic church has given rise to lay participation in various ministries previously reserved for ordained persons. Now when Catholics walk into a church, they expect to see their friends and neighbors distributing Communion, reading the Scriptures from the pulpit, and even serving as ordained deacons. Catholics who are sick or hospitalized are not surprised to find a group of laypeople visiting to pray with them or to bring them Communion. Laywomen and laymen direct retreats, teach religion, serve as spiritual directors, and hold administrative positions in Catholic schools and parishes.

For Review

- How did leadership roles generally develop in early Christian communities?
- What significant changes occurred in the roles of deacon and priest over the period from the second to the sixth century?
- What major change in image did ordained ministry take from the sixth century up through the Protestant Reformation? How did this distinction come about?
- What were some of the protests voiced by Martin Luther and other reformers regarding abuses within the church? How did the Council of Trent respond to these protests?
- What changes in the church's understanding of ordained ministry came about from the Second Vatican Council?

Toward the Church of the Twenty-first Century

As the church continues to read and respond to the "signs of the times," encouraged in such efforts by Vatican Council II, it must continue to examine the role of ordained ministers and its understanding of Christian ministry in general.

Today, laypeople participate in various church ministries that were once reserved for ordained ministers; the distribution of Communion at Mass is now frequently performed by lay eucharistic ministers.

Many challenges face the church in its task of being a sacrament of Jesus to a hurting world:

- What exactly is the relationship between the pope, the clergy, and laypeople? How can these groups best function as a unified priestly people carrying on Jesus' work of service and worship?
- Would official recognition of different ministers—teachers, those who care for the sick, choir directors, eucharistic ministers, ministers of hospitality, social workers—boost participation of all baptized Christians in the practice of their common call to priesthood?
- Does the increased involvement of laypeople in ministries that were formerly performed only by priests blur the distinction between what is "priestly ministry" and what is "lay ministry"?
- What effect will the diminishing numbers of persons entering ordained ministry have on the leadership and priestly functions in the church?
- What forms of leadership will emerge as more Catholic Christians become involved in the study of the Scriptures and theology, or seek an active role in their church?

These are only a few of the questions about ministry now facing the church. Answers to questions such as these will determine the shape of the Catholic church moving into the next century. Of course, the question underlying all the others is, How can the people who make up the church today best serve as a priestly symbol of Jesus?

The sacrament of holy orders represents an important instrument of leadership and service in the Catholic Christian community. In the future, the church's understanding of ministry and leadership will continue to develop so that the church can be an effective sacrament of Christ's presence to the world.

Jesus, this course has come to an end,
    but our journey with you continues.
Help us to see and celebrate
    your sacramental presence
    throughout our lives.
May you continue to nourish your church
    through the seven sacraments.
And may we always serve as signs of your love.
Amen.

Conclusion:
The Sacrament of You

This section is more a commissioning than it is a conclusion. In other words, it asks you to see yourself as a sacrament and then to act on that recognition. Five areas of your life, it is suggested, are worth focusing on, celebrating, and developing. But first, let's consider one last story.

O*nce there was a couple who had long since given up any hope of having their own children. Then, to their joy and amazement, the wife indeed became pregnant. The couple called their soon-to-be-born baby "our little Sacrament," because to them, the child symbolized God's love filling their life together. Tragically, on the way to the hospital for the delivery, the couple were killed in a car accident. An emergency operation saved the child. The baby girl was christened with another name.*

The child was adopted by relatives who took very good care of her. She grew up like most people. As a young woman, she spent most of her time doing the things that everyone believed to be important. Occasionally, she lost herself in distractions and diversions.

One day at a bus stop, she happened to overhear an elderly couple talking to each other. They were talking about religion. One said to the other: "Wasn't there a time when sacraments meant something to us, when God's friendship for us was something we felt and believed? Whatever happened to that awareness?" The other merely agreed that something had been lost in their life.

That conversation touched off the young woman's curiosity: What was this awareness that led to God?

She asked a teacher at her school. The teacher knew quite a bit about the subject, so he told her about the long history of sacraments in every religious tradition and about the many ways that people came to know God.

The young woman was impressed. "How can I find this awareness of God in my life?" she asked.

The teacher thought for a moment and said: "That's something you have to discover for yourself. But I don't think you will have to look far."

The young woman was disappointed in the teacher's answer, but she remembered what he said.

The next day, she went to a great church in the city. As she walked up the center aisle, she admired the many statues of saints and the marvelous stained-glass windows. Near the front of the church, she met a priest. She told him what the teacher had said and spoke of her search.

The priest said: "What you have been told is true, but you are missing a vital ingredient if you are to realize an awareness of God in your own life. If you have walked through this magnificent church and you still question how God can be found, then your search is not complete. But don't worry, you are surrounded by ways of seeing God."

The young woman realized the truth in what the priest was saying. Surely a church as grand as this one should have made her aware of God. But the priest seemed to be referring to more than the church when he said she was "surrounded." What did he mean?

On her way home, she passed by a convent. "Perhaps this place will provide a clue," thought the young woman. She peeked into the chapel and saw rows of nuns praying silently. Watching their peaceful silence, she felt that they knew what she was trying to discover. Yet she also found their peace and silence somehow disturbing.

A few days later, the young woman visited her aunt, who was gardening in her backyard. "Aunt Mary, what are you doing?" she inquired.

"Just planting," replied her aunt.

The young woman examined the packets of seed lying on the grass. "How do you know the seeds will grow?" she asked.

"Being a gardener takes quite a bit of faith," answered her aunt. "Gardeners have to have faith in many things—the soil, the rain, the sun, and of course, the plant hidden in the seed. I have faith that each seed contains an entire plant wonderful to see or to eat."

A sudden thought startled the young woman. She said: "Aunt Mary, I have been searching for a way to find God. Maybe God is hidden in sacraments just like a plant is hidden in a seed."

"That's a good way of putting it," smiled her aunt.

"But if God is everywhere, then everything is a sacrament. I don't have the faith it takes to see God in everything."

"Where you are searching may be the problem," suggested her aunt. She thought for a while and then said, "You need to start by looking at what is in front of you. Look at yourself. What do you see?"

"I'm a girl just like any other girl, I suppose," replied the young woman.

"Ah, but perhaps you are more than that," her aunt said. "Perhaps you are like a seed, and within you there lies hidden something special that calls for seeing with the eyes of faith. Your parents certainly saw you that way. Did I ever tell you that before you were born your parents called you 'our little Sacrament'? To them, you were God's gift."

Suddenly, a lot of things the young woman had heard began to make sense. She understood what her teacher and the priest had been suggesting to her and what she had seen in the peaceful nuns. To her parents, she had been a sacrament. They had seen God hidden in her even before she was born. She felt that her search for a sacrament was over—she was a sacrament herself. Yet, curiously, she could also see that her search was just beginning, because now she wanted to know how to live as a sacrament for others.

The Story of Sacrament Is Your Story

You are a sacrament. People meet God through you. You make God visible in the world. Yet, just like Sacrament, the young woman in the preceding story, you might not be aware of when or how you reveal God.

This course has looked in detail at sacrament as a fundamental religious concept. It has also explored the meaning of sacrament as Christians understand it and as Catholics understand it in the seven sacraments.

Along the way, you have been invited to examine your own life in light of this course. This concluding section invites you to look at five specific areas of your existence and to try to see them sacramentally. These five areas are awareness, celebration, community, service, and life.

1. Think about someone who has been a role model for you. Then briefly describe in writing a moment when you noticed that person revealing God to others.

Each of us is a sacrament. We make God visible in the world even though we might not be aware of when or how we reveal God to others.

We celebrate God's gift of life by enjoying it to the fullest.

Sacramental Awareness

To see God, we must see with the eyes of faith. Underlying all sacraments is sacramental awareness. As sacraments, we view life with the loving eyes with which God sees us.

- We wonder about the mysteries of life and death.
- We intently listen to nature, silence, and other people.
- We look closely at the familiar until it appears fresh and new.
- We see God in a flower or in a friend or in a stranger—in all of creation.
- We say, "There is more to life than meets the eye."

Sacramental Celebration

Every sacrament is a celebration, filled with joy, peace, and love. As sacraments ourselves, we can also be a celebration.

- We celebrate God's gift of life by enjoying it to the fullest.
- We celebrate the sacredness of each moment.
- We glory in our body, mind, senses, and emotions.
- We celebrate our becoming fully human and tapping into our potential for love, goodness, truth, and beauty.
- We consider the value of things, not just their cost.
- We take time to play and pray.

Sacramental Community

People are not Christian all by themselves. Likewise, we cannot be sacraments by ourselves. The human face of God is a family portrait—including the kind grandmother as well as the brother who always manages to say the wrong thing. Sacramental community *includes* rather than *excludes* others. Sacraments exist within a community that strives to be the body of Christ.

- We peel away our protective armor of selfishness.
- We invite others into our circle and open the door to new friendships.
- We celebrate the body of Christ—its past, present, and future.
- We find God in shared meals and shared lives.
- We glory in the uniqueness of each person.

2. Without using the words *sacrament, God,* or *religion,* list five questions you would ask a community to determine whether or not sacraments existed in that community.

We live in community and strive to be the body of Christ by inviting others into our circle and opening the door to new friendships.

Sacramental Service

Jesus was a person for others. Being a sacrament, therefore, means living a life of service. Sacramental awareness challenges us to act on behalf of those in need. Being a sacrament through service translates God's word into human body language.

- We realize that "if one suffers, all suffer."
- We ask, "What more can I do?"
- We see poor, needy, and forgotten persons and call them brothers and sisters.
- We work to move the world along toward its goal of becoming God's Kingdom.
- We treat others with respect—looking at them as loved by God.

Sacramental Life

Life is growth and development. Each of the seven sacraments is a celebration of a passage from one kind of life to another. As sacraments, we seek the new life that comes from sharing our life with others.

Being a sacrament means sharing our life with others.

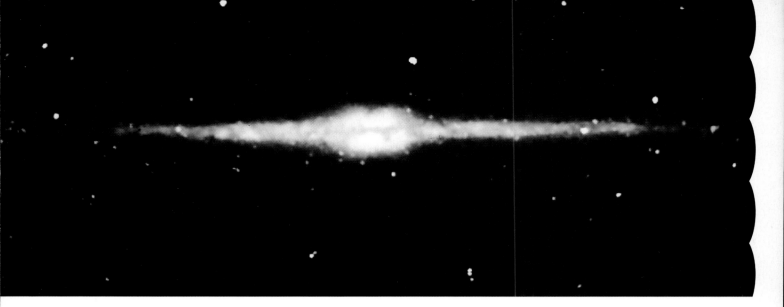

- We live with a spirit of zest and adventure.
- We welcome each new day.
- We celebrate a God who is always ahead of the crowd.
- We have faith that resurrection follows every cross.
- We say yes to life.

Sacramental awareness enables us to sense God's presence in our everyday life and in the wider world beyond us. We become aware that God's love fills the whole universe.

Photo: In this view of our galaxy, the Milky Way, our own sun lies in the thin part of the disk, about 28,000 light years from the center.

Celebrating God's Presence

Fishes, asking what water was, went to a wise fish. He told them that it was all around them, yet they still thought that they were thirsty. (Anonymous Sufi saying)

Then Jacob woke from his sleep and said, "Surely the LORD is in this place—and I did not know it!" (Genesis 28:16)

The Christian church is like a wise fish. It began with a group of people so convinced and so excited by Jesus' message that at every opportunity they celebrated the continuing, living presence of God in their life: The Lord is here! They celebrated meals, new members, individuals' talents, healings, weddings, and commitments. The Catholic church today continues to celebrate all these occasions.

When you hear the word *sacrament,* remember that it refers to those ways that God reaches out to us in friendship. When we see God in our life and respond through prayer, celebration, sharing, and service, we become living sacraments. When we celebrate the seven official sacraments of baptism, confirmation, the Eucharist, reconciliation, anointing, marriage, and holy orders, we are joining with the church past and present in making Christ alive and visible in the world. And by being a sacramental presence ourselves, we help make those around us more aware of God's love.

3. Imagine that sacraments—experiences of God's presence—came wrapped like candy and packaged in a large, plain, chock-full box. Create a label with instructions for using the contents.

Index

Italic numbers are references to photos or artwork.

E

early church: baptism in, 142, 146, 148–150; and Eucharist, 149, 185, 195–196; history of, 106–110; marriage in, 250–251, 261, 264; ministry and leadership in, 269–270, 282–283, 285; RCIA modeled after initiation in, 153; and reconciliation, 221–222; and Sunday worship, 196, 199; Vatican Council II sought roots of, 126–127

Eastern Catholic churches, 112, 151, 259

Eastern Orthodox churches, 112, 151

Easter Vigil, 148–149, 155–156

El Salvador, 76

Eucharist, sacrament of: and Christ's sacrifice, 270; in early church, 106–107, 108–109, 149, 185, 195–196, 221, 222, 282–283; and Eucharistic Prayer, 193; history of, 194–200; and hunger, 188; as lifetime endeavor, 256; meanings of, 179, 189; realities celebrated by, 177–187, 201; Rite of, 192–193; and Rite of Dismissal, 155; and sequence of initiation sacraments, 151; as source of strength, 175; symbols and rituals of, 188–194, 257; uniformity in celebration of, 122, 123. *See also* Christian initiation; Communion; Mass

Eucharistic Prayer, 193

examination of conscience, 209, 210

excommunication, 221–222

Extreme Unction, 242

F

faith, Christian: and prayer, 59; as response to God's presence, 22, 23; symbols used to express, 35–37; and teachings about God, 8, 9, 11

forgiveness. *See* reconciliation, sacrament of

Francis of Assisi, Saint, *225*

friendship: as communication of God's love, 12, 15–16, 246–247; depends on honest communication, 16, 17, 18; grace revealed in, 15–16; and healing, 203–205, 206; in marriage, 246–247; nurturing, 59; and presence of God, 17, 18, 23

"friendship meal," 106–107, 108–109, 196

G

"Gift of the Magi, The," 245–246

gifts of the Holy Spirit, 164–165

God: Christian beliefs about, 8, 9, 11, 103, 109, 121; church as sacrament of, 91, 92–93; communicates in many ways, 12, 13, 14–16; and creation, 8–9, 15, 16, 32, 112; encountered in the Scriptures, 68, 189–190; forgiveness of, 203, 208, 210, 224–225; and the Incarnation, 79, 80–85; invites us to divine life, 140; love of, 11, 13, 16, 23, 60, 178–179, 179–180, 231–232, 249; paths to intimacy with, 58–59, 60–62, 62–65, 66–77; presence of, celebrated in seven sacraments, 22, 37, 77, 127, 134, 140, 153, 199, 229, 230, 295; relationship of people with, 16, 17, 18, 205, 210, 229, 249–250, 265; revealed through Jesus, 268, 269, 270–271; revealed through people, 246–247, 291; rituals open people to Spirit of, 44; and sacramental awareness, 9, 18–20, 22–23; and sacramental blindness, 9–11. *See also* Jesus Christ; Spirit

godparents, 152. *See also* sponsors

Good News, 23, 147, 268

Gospels. *See* Bible

grace, 77; and Council of Trent, 121; definition of, 13, 15, 134; Jesus describes, 15; revealed in friendships, 15–16; and the sacraments, 22, 116, 122, 127, 136, 252–253

guided meditation. *See* meditation

H

hands: symbolism of, 168–169. *See also* laying on of hands

healing: and anointing, 227–236; communal aspects of, 229–236; in early church, 239; experienced in reconciliation, 208; and friendship, 203–205, 206

healing, sacraments of. *See* anointing, sacrament of; reconciliation, sacrament of

Hebrew Scriptures. *See* Bible

High Middle Ages: church and sacraments during, 113–119, 197–198, 284–285

high priests (Jewish), 270

Hinduism, 64, 72, *167*

Holy Communion. *See* Communion

holy ground, 73

Holy Land, 73

holy orders, sacrament of, 265; history of, 282–286; as instrument of leadership and service, 287; realities celebrated by, 267–275; Rite of, 280–281; symbols and rituals of, 277–281

Holy Spirit. *See* Spirit

Holy Thursday, 148

hunger, world, 186–187

I

Incarnation, 79, 80–85

initiation, Christian. *See* Christian initiation

inner space, 60–62

Israelites: and covenant with Yahweh, 249; experience God's body language, 14–15; and Passover, 82–83, 179, 194–195; and sacred places, 73; and sacrifice, 53; symbolic use of water in story of, 141–142

J

Jean Vianney, Saint, 274–275

Jesus Christ, 12, 127; actions of, as basis for Christian rituals, 53–54, 97–98; and baptism, 137, 138, 142; the church, and sacraments, 88, 89, 91, 92–93, 95–101, 127; as doorway to sacred mystery, 268–269; on grace, 15; as healer, 203, 220, 227, 231, 242, 243; Incarnation of, 79, 80–85; and the Last Supper, 179–181, 194–195, 201; as the light of the world, 146–147; on marriage, 247, 250–251, 264; meaning of term, 143, 169; ministry of, 203, 269–272; and paschal mystery, 82–85, 129; and Pentecost, 87–88; and prayer, 62–63; presence of, celebrated in the sacraments, 120, 177, 181–184, 187, 188, 189, 190, 199, 200, 295; promise of, 167; Resurrection of, 234–236; as sacrament, 79, 81, 82, 85; Sacred Heart of, 120; sharing in mission of, 138–139, 166–167; use of symbols by, 15, 35, 179–180. See also God; Spirit

Jewish Law, 249

Jewish ritual, 82–83, 194–196

John Paul II, Pope, *225*

John XXIII, Pope, 123, 126

journal writing, 68–69

K

Kingdom of God. *See* Reign of God

L

L'Arche communities, 60

Last Supper, 179–181, 194–195, 201, 271–272

Latin (language), 122, 197, 198

Laurence, Saint, 273

laying on of hands: and baptism, 170–171; and confirmation, 150, 168–169, 172; in early church, 54, 108; and holy orders, 277–278, 280; and sacrament of anointing, 238, 239, 242

laypeople: role of, in medieval church, 113, 197–198, 284; and shared ministry, 285–286; and Vatican Council II reforms, 198

Lazo, 259

lector, *190*, 198, 286

Lent, 155, 222

light, 28–29; symbolism of, in baptism, 146–147, 149

listening: gift of, 22; and healing, 205, 207, 221; and prayer, 61–62, 71–73; and sacramental awareness, 8, 18–19

literal thinking, 33–35, 117–118

Little Prince, The, 46

liturgy of the Eucharist, 189, 190–194

liturgy of the word, 189–190, 192

love:
—of Christians, 91–92
—and creativity in marriage, 252–255
—expressing, in symbolic terms, 33–34
—of God, 11, 13, 16, 23, 60, 246–247, 249; celebrated in baptism, 134; revealed by Jesus, 79, 81, 82, 83, 85, 231–232; symbolized by bread and meals, 178–179, 179–180
—God communicates through, 15–16
—as impetus to spiritual awakening, 12
—and sacramental awareness, 9, 22
—world created out of, 11

Luther, Martin, 119, 284

Lyons, Second Council of, 116

M

magical thinking: and anointing, 242; Council of Trent addresses problem of, 121; and magic as distinct from ritual actions, 53; regarding the sacraments, 117–119

Malcolm X, 75

marriage, sacrament of: history of, 109, 260–261, 264–265; realities celebrated by, 245–255; Rite of, 262–263; sacramental understanding of, 37, 113; and sexual intercourse, 248–249, 256–257; symbols and rituals of, 255–263, 265; and trap of consumerism, 247–248

Mary (mother of Jesus), 120, 259, *260*

Mass: and anointing, 236–237; definition of, 189; experience of, in 1950s, 124–125; experiencing deeper significance of, 43; lay involvement in, 113, 197–198, 286; and marriage, 257, 258, 264; and RCIA, 155; Sunday, 199; vocal prayer in, 63. *See also* Eucharist, sacrament of

maturity, 164–166, 174, 206, 208

Mead, Margaret, 44

meals: as rituals in early church, 53, 106–107, 108–109, 196; symbolism of, 179–180, 194–195

medieval church, 113–119; Eucharist in, 197–198; role of clergy in, 284–285

meditation: and contemplation, 65, 69–75; external, 74–75; and music, 72–73; as path to God, 63–64; and praying with our imagination, 66–67; using Scriptures for, 68

ministry. *See* shared ministry
Missionaries of Charity, 60
monasticism, 222–223, 284
mortal sin, 208, 219
Mount Sinai, 249
movements and gestures: as characteristic of rituals, 45–46
music: encouraged by Second Vatican Council, 198; as prayer form, 72, 73–75; in worship of early Christians, 107, 108–109
mystagogia, 150

N

Native Americans: and meditation, 64; revere earth, 9; and ritual, 52, 53; and story of Corn Mother, 178; and story of Jumping Mouse, 7–8
Nativity, 29, 72
natural world. *See* creation
Nero, Emperor, 108
Nicholas, Saint, 273
Nicodemus, 137
Notre Dame Cathedral, *115*

O

oil, anointing with: and baptism, 143; and confirmation, 150, 168, 169, 172, 173, 236; in early church, 149; and holy orders, 278, 281; and sacrament of anointing, 238, 239
Olympic Games, 40, 47
ordained ministers: church examines role of, 285–287; concentration of power of, 283–285; and holy orders, 267, 271, 272, 277–281; sacramental role of, 273–275, 276. *See also* bishops; deacons; holy orders, sacrament of; priests
ordination, 277–279, 280–281, 283
original sin, 135–136

P

parable of the lost sheep, 235
parable of the prodigal son, 208, 210
paschal mystery, 82–85, 129, 252; and anointing, 234–236; and baptism, 138; and Eucharist, 175, 181; in everyday life, 86, 211–212
Passover, 82–83, 179, 194–195
Paul, Saint: beliefs of, about Jesus, 83; beliefs of, on body of Christ, 89; epistles of, 108, 109, 196; on marriage, 250–251, 265; on prayer, 66; on sin, 205–206; on singing, 74
Paul VI, Pope, 25
penance. *See* reconciliation, sacrament of
Penitents, Order of, 222
Pentecost (Christian), 54, 87–88, 147, 161
people of God, 88–89, 91–93
persecution, 106, 108, 110, 148, 273
Peter, Saint, 147
pilgrimages, 73
popes, 25, 111, 123, 126, *225*
practical actions, 41–42
prayer: and anointing, 238, 239; can change us, 75–76; definition of, 59, 77; and healing, 242; from liturgy of the Eucharist, 193; and Order of Penitents, 222; and reconciliation, 219–220; and sacramentals, 120; and sacred time and place, 58–62; tradition of, in church, 64, 66; various forms of, 57–58, 62–75; and Vatican Council II reforms, 198
presbyters, 113, 283
priesthood of all believers, 269, 272

priests:
—central function of, 270
—gain prominence in church, 283–284
—and holy orders, 267, 273–275, 278
—Jesus, 269–270
—not sole reconcilers, 221
—role of: in anointing, 242; in Christian initiation, 150, 172, 173; in marriage, 257, 261, 264; in Mass, 190, 194, 270; in medieval church, 197; in reconciliation, 208, 210, 214, 218–219, 223
—Saint Jean Vianney, 274–275. *See also* ordained ministers
proclaiming the word of God, 189–190, 192
prophets, 269, 270–271
Protestant Reformation, 119, 284
psychosomatic illness, 230

R

RCIA, 153, 155–156, 163–164
real presence of Christ, 177, 181–184, 189, 197
reconciliation, sacrament of: and anointing, 238; celebrates the forgiveness of God, 203–208, 210–215, 224–225; community focus of, 213–214, 218–220, 221; definition of, 212; history of, 220–225; penance as another name for, 210; recalls healing ministry of Jesus, 203, 227; Rite of, 216–217; symbols and rituals of, 215–220; three forms of, 218–220
Reign of God: Eucharist anticipates future, 201; and Jesus, 82, 179–180, 271; people build, 91, 92–93, 94, 138–139, 255
relics, 117, 118

responding: as gift of grace, 22; as key to communication and sacramental awareness, 18–19; and personal quality of presence, 181–182

Resurrection: anointing and message of Jesus', 234–236; disciples' reaction to, 87, 147; as Jesus' sacrifice for humankind, 247; meaning of Last Supper made clearer by, 180; and paschal mystery, 82–85; and Sunday worship, 199

rings, 258–259, 262, 278

Rite of Christian Initiation of Adults (RCIA), 153, 155–156, 163–164

rituals: characteristics of, 45–47, 49–51; as distinct from routines, 42–43; in early church, 53–54, 106–107, 108; as expressions of what is important, 39–41; pagan, 109, 260–261; and play, 43–44; rooted in worship, 52–54, 55; seven sacraments as, 41, 55, 98–101; and symbols, 39, 77. *See also* individual names of sacraments; prayer; sacraments; seven sacraments

Roman Empire, 106, 108, 110, 111, 148

rosary, 120, 122

routines, 42–43

S

Sabbath (Christian), 199

Sabbath (Jewish), 195

sacramental awareness: definition of, 8–9, 77; lack of, 9–11; necessary skills in, 18–20, 22; prayer deepens, 75–76; underlies the sacraments, 292

sacramental blindness, 9–11, 19

sacramental celebration, 292

sacramental community, 293

sacramental life, 294–295

sacramental moments, 20–22

sacramentals, 120, 122

sacramental service, 294

sacraments: Augustine's view on, 111–112; definition of, 15, 101; history of, 53–54, 101, 103, 105, 106–119, 121–129, 147–153, 155–156, 173–175, 194–201, 220–225, 239, 242–243, 261, 264–265, 282–286; as rituals, 41, 55, 98–101; and symbolic thinking, 35, 36–37; two dimensions of, 23. *See also* individual names of sacraments; rituals; seven sacraments

sacred, the: being blind to, 9–11; encountering, 8–9, 73; symbolic thinking helps us recognize, 33, 35, 36–37

Sacred Heart Cathedral, *117*

Sacred Heart of Jesus, 120

sacred mystery, 99, 268–269

sacred time and space, 59–62

sacrifice, 53, 180–181, 270

Saint Peter's Basilica, *121*

Santa Maria Maggiore (basilica), *110*

Scholasticism, 122

Scriptures. *See* Bible

Second Coming of Jesus, 72

Second Council of Lyons, 116

Second Vatican Council. *See* Vatican Council II

servant-leader, 271–272

service: experiencing growth in, 166–167; healing linked to, 233–234; and Jesus, 269, 271–272; sacramental, 294

seven sacraments: celebrate crossings in our life, 129; and Council of Trent, 121–123; as lifetime endeavors, 256; made official at Second Council of Lyons, 116; paschal mystery a central reality in, 252; presence of God and Christ celebrated in, 22, 37, 77, 120, 127, 134, 140, 153, 177, 181–184, 187, 188, 189, 190, 199, 200, 229, 230, 295; role of, in Catholic church, 95–101; and sacramental awareness, 8, 19–20, 22, 77, 292; and symbolic thinking, 35, 36–37; and Vatican Council II, 127. *See also* individual names of sacraments; sacraments

shared ministry, 198, 282–283, 285–286

sharing the cup, 189, 190–194

signs, 27

silence, 60–62

sin: baptism's effect on, 136; as break in a relationship, 205, 211; burden of, 205–206; mortal, 208, 219; original, 135–136; and reconciliation, 208, 210, 211–212; ripple effects of, 213–214; venial, 208

Sinai covenant, 249, 250

song. *See* music

Spirit: confirmation celebrates growth in the, 159, 161, 163–167; and laying on of hands, 277–278; and Pentecost, 87–88, 147; and sacraments, 127; transforming power of, 137, 139. *See also* God; Jesus Christ

spirituality, 12, 17–18

sponsors, 148, 155, 156, 163, 164, 172

stations of the cross, 120

suffering: as cause of sacramental blindness, 10–11; Christians encounter, in identifying with Jesus' life purpose, 139; God present in, 229; and paschal mystery, 82–85, 86, 234–236; and wounded healers, 233–234. *See also* persecution

superstition. *See* magical thinking

symbolic actions: express complex meanings, 55; rituals as, 39, 40–41, 42–44, 45–47, 48–49, 49–51; versus practical actions, 41–42. *See also* rituals

symbolic thinking, 33–35

symbols: characteristics of,
27–29; communicating
through, 25–29, 30–32;
cultural, 30; definition of,
25–26; as doorways to the
sacred, 33, 35, 36–37; universal,
30, 31; use of, by Jesus in
Gospels, 15, 35, 179–180. *See
also under* individual names of
sacraments
synagogues, 195–196

T

Teresa, Mother, 60
Tertullian, 109
thinking, literal, 33–35, 117–118
thinking, magical. *See* magical
thinking
thinking, symbolic, 33–35
Thomas Aquinas, Saint, 116, 122
Torah, 195
Trent, Council of, 120, 121–123,
126–127, 198, 284–285

V

Vanier, Jean, 60
Vatican Council II, 122, 123,
126–127; and changes in
celebration of sacraments,
152–156, 198, 200, 218, 219,
223, 224, 243, 257–258; and
people of God, 88–89; and
return to shared ministry,
285–286
Velveteen Rabbit, The, 253
venial sin, 208
viaticum, 237
Vietnam war memorial, *34*
vocal prayer, 62–63, 68–69
vocation, sacraments of. *See*
holy orders, sacrament of;
marriage, sacrament of

W

water, 53–54, 140–143, 147–148,
148–149
white garment, 143, 146, 149
wine, 191, 194, 197, 200
Wizard of Oz, The, 267–268

Acknowledgments

The scriptural quotation on page 15 is from the Good News Bible, in Today's English Version. Copyright © 1966, 1971, 1976 by the American Bible Society.

The scriptural quotations on pages 16, 66, 68, 73, 74, 81, 84, 87, 89, 137, 167, 179, 185, 188, 199, 206, 208, 239, 240, 246, 250, 250–251, 251, 261, 270, 271–272, and 285 are from the New Revised Standard Version of the Bible. Copyright © 1989 by the Division of Christian Education of the National Council of the Churches of Christ in the United States. Used by permission. All rights reserved.

The scriptural quotations on page 192 are from the New American Bible with Revised New Testament, copyright © 1986 by the Confraternity of Christian Doctrine, Washington, D.C.; and the New American Bible, copyright © 1970 by the Confraternity of Christian Doctrine.

The quote on page 15 is from *Sacraments and Sacramentality,* by Bernard Cooke (Mystic, CT: Twenty-Third Publications, 1983), pages 81–82. Copyright © 1983 by Bernard Cooke.

The excerpts on pages 21, 213, and 233–234 are from *The Sower's Seeds: One Hundred Inspiring Stories for Preaching, Teaching, and Public Speaking,* by Brian Cavanaugh, TOR (New York: Paulist Press, 1990), pages 8–9, 11, and 5, respectively. Copyright © 1990 by Brian Cavanaugh, TOR. Used by permission of the publisher.

The excerpt on page 46 is from *The Little Prince,* by Antoine de Saint Exupéry (New York: Harcourt, Brace & World, 1943), pages 83–86. Copyright © 1944 and renewed 1971 by Harcourt Brace Jovanovich. Reprinted by permission of Reed Book Services and Harcourt Brace Jovanovich.

The story on pages 48–49 is by Chris Nagel.

The quotation by Barbara Hixon on page 51 is from *RCIA Ministry: An Adventure into Mayhem and Ministry* (San Jose, CA: Resource Publications, 1989), page 35. Copyright © 1989 by Resource Publications.

The quotation on page 60 is from *Community and Growth: Our Pilgrimage Together,* by Jean Vanier (New York: Paulist Press, 1979), page 104. Copyright © 1979 by Jean Vanier.

The excerpt on page 63 is from *Sadhana: A Way to God,* by Anthony de Mello, SJ (New York: Doubleday, 1984), page 78. Copyright © 1978 by Anthony de Mello, SJ, Poona, India. Used by permission of the publisher.

The excerpts on pages 65 and 71–72 are from *Taking Flight: A Book of Story Meditations,* by Anthony de Mello, SJ (New York: Doubleday, 1988), pages 29 and 17, respectively. Copyright © 1988 by the Center for Spiritual Exchange. Used by permission of the publisher.

The quotations on page 70 are from "Contemplation: A Long Loving Look at the Real," by Walter J. Burghardt, *Church* (Winter 1989), page 15. Copyright © 1989 by the National Pastoral Life Center.

The excerpt on page 75 is from *The Autobiography of Malcolm X* (New York: Grove Press, 1964), page 170. Copyright © 1964 by Alex Haley and Malcolm X; 1965 by Alex Haley and Betty Shabazz.

The excerpt on page 76 is from *Salvador Witness: The Life and Calling of Jean Donovan,* by Ana Carrigan (New York: Simon and Schuster, 1984), page 218. Copyright © 1984 by Ana Carrigan.

The poem by Ruth Kulas on page 90 is from *Womenpsalms,* compiled and edited by Julia Ahlers, Rosemary Broughton, and Carl Koch (Winona, MN: Saint Mary's Press, 1992), pages 51–52. Used by permission of Ruth Kulas.

The quotation on page 91 is from "Understanding Sacraments," by William J. O'Malley, SJ, *America* (7 March 1992), page 190. Copyright © 1990 by America Press.

The excerpt on pages 91–92 is from *The Eucharist and Human Liberation,* by Tissa Balasuriya (Maryknoll, NY: Orbis Books, 1979), page 26. Copyright © 1977 by the Centre for Society and Religion, Colombo, Sri Lanka. Used by permission.

The quotation on page 92 is from *The Documents of Vatican II,* edited by Walter M. Abbott (New York: America Press, 1966), page 15. Copyright © 1966 by America Press.

The story on page 94 is adapted from "Water in the Slums," by Maria Teresa Porcile, in *New Eyes for Reading,* edited by John S. Pobee and Bärbel Von Wartenberg-Potter (Bloomington, IN: Meyer Stone Books, 1987), pages 35–36. Copyright © 1987 by Meyer Stone Books. Reprinted by permission of the Crossroad Publishing Company.

The rites excerpts on pages 144–145, 170–171, 192–193, 216–217, 240–241, 262–263, and 280–281 are from, respectively, the English translation of *Rite of Christian Initiation of Adults,* copyright © 1985, International Committee on English in the Liturgy, Inc. (ICEL); the English translation of *Rite of Confirmation,* second edition, copyright © 1975, ICEL; the English translation of *The Roman Missal,* copyright © 1973, ICEL; the English translation of *Rite of Penance,* copyright © 1974, ICEL; the English translation of *Pastoral Care of the Sick: Rites of Anointing and Viaticum,* copyright © 1982, ICEL; the English translation of *Rite of Marriage,* copyright © 1969, ICEL; and the English translation of *Ordination of Deacons, Priests, and Bishops,* copyright © 1975, ICEL. All rights reserved. Used by permission of ICEL.

The story on pages 177–178 is adapted from "Send Me," by Joseph J. Juknialis, *Modern Liturgy* 5, no. 4: 26–27. Copyright © 1978 by Resource Publications. Reprinted with permission from *Modern Liturgy,* 160 East Virginia Street, No. 290, San Jose, CA 95112.

The second story on page 178 is from "Native Americans and the Land: 'The End of Living, and the Beginning of Survival,'" by George E. Tinker, *Word and World* (6 June 1986): 143. Copyright © 1986 by Luther-Northwestern Theological Seminaries.

The story on page 181 is an old Hasidic tale retold by Martin Buber and cited by Rabbi Laurence Kushner in *Context,* 15 December 1991, page 1. Reprinted with permission of *Context,* published by Claretian Publications, 205 West Monroe Street, Chicago, IL 60606.

The excerpt on page 188 is from "Why Is the World Hungry?" by Wendy Bauers Northup, *Youth Update* (June 1988). Used by permission of the publisher.

The excerpt on page 214 is from "Bless me, Father, I'm not sure I want to be here!" by Kathleen M. Paiva, *Youth Update* (October 1982). Used by permission of the publisher.

The quotation on page 230 is from *Doors to the Sacred,* by Joseph Martos (Tarrytown, NY: Triumph Books, 1991), page 339. Copyright © 1981, 1982, 1991 by Joseph Martos.

The story on pages 245–246 is adapted from "The Gift of the Magi," by O. Henry [William Sydney Porter], in *The Complete Works of O. Henry* (Garden City, NY: Doubleday & Company, 1953), pages 7–11. Copyright © 1953 by Doubleday & Company.

The excerpt on pages 247–248 is from *Christian Families in the Real World: Reflections on a Spirituality for the Domestic Church,* by Mitch and Kathy Finley (Chicago: Thomas More Press, 1984), pages 52–54. Copyright © 1984 by Mitch and Kathy Finley. Used by permission of the publisher.

The 1978 church document quotation on marriage on page 249 is used as quoted in "Revising Church Legislation on Marriage," by Francis Morrisey, *Origins* (20 September 1979), page 211.

The excerpt on page 253 is from *The Velveteen Rabbit,* by Margery Williams (New York: Avon Books, 1975), pages 16–17.

The quoted material about Bishop Maurice Dingman on page 276 is from the *Catholic Mirror,* the newspaper of the Des Moines (Iowa) Diocese, 6 February 1992 and 20 February 1992.

Photo Credits
Cover: Bob Roloff, McHugh and Associates
Sam Abell, National Geographic: page 201
American Library Slide Company: pages 110, 112, 113
Bill Bachmann, ProFiles West: pages 99, 235, 254
Patricia Barry-Levy, ProFiles West: page 10
The Bettmann Archive: page 119
Vic Bider, ProFiles West: page 107
The photo on page 128 is reproduced from *The Faces of Jesus,* by Frederick Buechner, with photographs by Lee Boltin, published by Harper & Row, with permisson from Stearn Publishers. Copyright © 1989.
V. Cassaro, ProFiles West: page 141
Catholic News Service: page 123
Cleo Freelance Photography: pages 34, 60, 63, 67, 83, 100, 181, 221
Gail Denham: pages 9, 16, 18, 27, 206, 246, 259
Diocese of Des Moines: page 276
Duccio (di Buoninsegna), "The Calling of the Apostles Peter and Andrew," from the Samuel H. Kress Collection, copyright © 1992, National Gallery of Art, Washington, D.C.: page 268
Duccio (di Buoninsegna), "Jesus Healing the Blind Man," reproduced by courtesy of the National Gallery, London: page 231
Editorial Development Associates: pages 144 (left), 145 (bottom left), 146, 157, 170 (top and bottom), 171 (top and middle), 189, 190, 192 (top), 217 (top), 237, 240 (left and right), 241 (middle), 242, 250, 262 (left, top right, and bottom right), 263 (left), 280 (top and middle), 281 (bottom)
Jack Hamilton: pages 41, 55, 58, 68, 70, 89, 135, 144 (right), 145 (right), 151, 192 (bottom), 291
Tim Haske, ProFiles West: page 43
Jack Hoehn, ProFiles West: page 32 (left)
Michael J. Howell, ProFiles West: pages 117, 121, 248

KNA, Catholic News Service: page 225
K-Six, ProFiles West: page 235
Copyright © J. P. Laffont, Sygma: page 256 (bottom)
Phil Lauro, ProFiles West: page 149
Jean-Claude Lejeune: pages 48, 50, 64, 104, 209
Bob Lienemann, ProFiles West: page 136
Mary E. Messenger: page 161
H. Corat Moran, ProFiles West: page 31
National Aeronautics and Space Administration (NASA): page 295
Paul Pavlik: pages 20, 153
Gene Plaisted, Catholic News Service: page 287
Nicolas Poussin, "The Baptism of Christ," from the Samuel H. Kress Collection, copyright © 1992, National Gallery of Art, Washington, D.C.: page 81
Raghu Rai, Magnum: page 167
Cyril A. Reilly: pages 93, 108, 187, 282
Bob Roloff, McHugh and Associates: pages 6, 24, 38, 56, 78, 102, 130, 158, 176, 202, 226, 244, 266, 288
Allen Russell, ProFiles West: pages 72, 94, 142
James Shaffer: pages 126, 139, 145 (top left), 154, 171 (bottom), 173, 182, 185, 193 (top, middle, and bottom), 195, 197, 199, 207, 213, 214, 216 (top, middle, and bottom), 217 (bottom), 219, 223, 233, 238, 241 (top and bottom), 260, 263 (right), 270, 272, 274, 277, 279, 280 (bottom), 281 (right), 284, 292
Steve and Mary Beran Skjold: pages 12, 14, 23, 90, 95, 97, 163, 210, 228, 265, 293, 294
Ellen Skye, ProFiles West: page 45
Paul Spinelli, ProFiles West: page 115
Frank Staub, ProFiles West: pages 76, 129
G. B. Steinmetz, ProFiles West: page 32 (right)
Denis Stock, Magnum: page 256 (top)
Bob Taylor: pages 52, 74, 84, 132, 164, 174
Kent Vinyard, ProFiles West: page 253
Cheryl Walsh-Bellville: page 192 (middle)
Nancy Wiechec, Catholic News Service: page 169
Wiley and Wales, ProFiles West: page 86
Bob Winsett, ProFiles West: pages 29, 36